HIDDEN VICTIMS

Hidden Victims

The Other Side of Murder

by
Violet M. Franck

NEW HORIZON PRESS
Far Hills, New Jersey

Library of Congress Catalog Card Number: 92-060569

Hidden Victims
  Violet M. Franck

ISBN 0-88282-117-2
New Horizon Press
1997   1996   1995   1994   1993 / 5   4   3   2   1

"Hatred stirreth up strife,
But love–
Covereth all sins."

Bible
Proverbs

Author's Note

These are my actual experiences. The personalities, events, actions, and conversations portrayed within the story have been reconstructed from interviews and research, utilizing letters, personal papers, and the memories of participants. In an effort to safeguard the privacy of certain individuals, I have changed their names and, in some cases, altered otherwise identifying characteristics and chronology. Events involving the characters happened as described; only minor details have been altered.

Contents

To my parents who taught me
about unconditional love

Prologue

It could have been your brother, not mine, and then it would have been your family. I realize that now . . . years after the blood coated my soul.

Then, when it first happened, it was as if it had never happened to anyone but me.

He was my big brother, you see. Big brothers tease you with jokes and tricks. They hide in the bushes and growl like Alaskan bears and make you feel scared. Yet with time the fear goes away.

But on March 4, 1980, what my brother did changed my life forever. His actions produced the kind of fear that horror movies thrive on. This horror, however, was real.

Nightmares kept me from sleep; terror charged my emotions. My values, goals, and personal relationships disintegrated. The hearts of my parents crumbled.

I hope it never happens to you—that your brother, or son, or husband, or friend never kills anyone.

But they might.

Chapter One

Ken's cold, calloused hand reached behind the television carcass and pulled out the .30-06 Browning propped in the corner of the dark attic. A large man, a logger by trade, he checked the cartridges in the chamber and again stared out the window across his yard. It was dark except for the light from his kitchen, and he vaguely made out the outline of a house a good hundred and fifty feet away.

Reaching into the pocket of his wool-lined denim jacket, he fingered the four extra shells clustered on top of the red handkerchief, a gift from his parents a couple of Christmases back. Quietly he descended the stairs and crossed the dark living room. Hesitating momentarily he stepped out into the steady Oregon rain. With the gun tucked under his arm Ken strode along the driveway beside the old farmhouse. It had been his home for eight years now. With each step water splattered onto the sides of his oiled boots and legs of his shortened jeans.

His strides were long and deliberate. His clothes were damp from a day of working in brush and mud. He noticed none of this.

He did notice, when he passed the window, Lee, his gray-haired father, huddled close to the gas wall furnace, and his mother, Betty, wearing a quilted coat, standing at the sink peeling potatoes. He dismissed them. They were not included in his plans.

Rain dripped off a patch of dark matted curls onto his lashes and down his scraggly beard. He left the driveway and entered the one-lane graveled road that skirted his property. A few feet more and he was in front of the house.

The deep blue drapes on the large living room window were open. Beyond them Rich, a tall blond man in his thirties, reclined in an easy chair. Close by, his wife, Doris, and their ten-year-old son Jacob sat on the couch. The three of them focused on the television and evangelist Billy Graham.

Jacob was close to her, too close for Ken's liking. His quarrel was not with children.

The trespasser, not visible to those inside, switched off the safety, shouldered the gun as he had so many times, and took aim. The peep site lined up over Rich's left eyebrow. With the steadiness of a marksman Ken slipped his index finger in front of the trigger and slowly squeezed it back.

An explosion ruptured the night, its voice caustic and deafening. Glass cracked, shattered, and the impact launched fragments into the room. In a millisecond the bullet crossed the room and parted Rich's eyebrow, ripping into his brain. It pulverized the gray matter. Rich's left eye bulged forward and down. Propelled onward the slug burst out the back of his skull and into the chair, taking with it blood, curdled tissue, and a chunk of scalp.

Down the hall toward the back of the house Doris and Jacob fled, their eyes filled with terror.

In one step Ken was at the door, twisting on the knob. It refused to turn. Again he aimed and shot, this time at the knob. Still the door would not open. Holding the barrel with a logger's grip he bashed the stock of the rifle into the window, spewing glass inward. Slivers crunched beneath his boots as he climbed over the sill and into the living room.

One dead eye stared at him. The second eye gazed at the floor.

Trembling all over, Jacob ran into his parents' bedroom and hid behind the clothes hamper. Pursuing Doris, the woman who had invited him to dinner the night before, Ken raised the rifle.

The phone, she must get to it, the one in the family room at the end of the hall. It was all Doris could think of.

Ken reached her as she dialed the operator. With the shell already in place he thrust the gun to her head. A scream—he heard it somewhere in his mind—and then the explosion.

Brain tissue, hair, and blood splattered onto plasterboard walls. Phone fragments and bone embedded in the strips of molding.

Ken heard no human sound in the house as he descended the stairs to the basement. He exited through the side door. The boys were of no concern to him, not the first boy, who fled with his mother, nor the second boy, who hid in a wall of water inside the shower stall. He was fixated on his next target.

Replacing the expended shells, Ken again released the bolt and drove a shell into the chamber. The rain, heavier now, drenched him completely. Hiking up the road, he neared his driveway and saw shadowed figures running toward him, first his father, then his mother.

"Son, son," Lee called, his voice sounding worried yet gentle, as it always did no matter what the catastrophe. "What are you doing, son?"

"Get out of my way, Dad," yelled Ken, his eyes narrowed. He turned from them, headed up the lane, around the corner, and toward the McCalls.

A few minutes later, a pickup rumbled down the

road beside Ken's house. A man jumped from the vehicle and grabbed the two children, Jacob and his brother, Shawn, who had run out of their home.

"Ken is out there with a gun. I am sorry, I am sorry," Betty cried. She stumbled and tried not to fall, hurrying over the bumpy road toward the man.

The man did not stop to talk. He did not think. He pushed the children into his truck and lurched up the road away from the scene. At home he had a revolver and a wife who was alone.

Betty ran back to the house and through the doorway, Lee behind her. By the time she reached the phone she was shaking and gasping hard, as if she would never regain her breath. The police . . . she had to reach the police. Someone had to stop him. Gulping sobs convulsed her body as her finger spun the dial. Dear Lord, someone had to stop her firstborn, her only son.

Alder limbs and fir bows slapped Ken's face as he climbed the canopied road called Happiness Lane. In a few moments he reached Kathy and Maurice McCall's house. Ken hurried over the spongy lawn and stood outside. Through the window he spotted Kathy over the kitchen sink.

He blond hair and glasses spanned the rifle's rear site. Back and forth she moved beyond the window. The front site followed her until the shot was sure. For the fourth time Ken pulled the trigger, ejected the cartridge, and advanced another shell into the chamber.

With a moan Kathy dropped behind the counter, dead before her knees even buckled.

Ken's eyes focused on the dining room window and saw Maurice run into the room, followed closely by Christy and Cal, both teenagers, the only McCall children who still lived at home. A finger growing numb from cold launched a bullet one more time, blasting a hole into Maurice's chest. Maurice fell to the carpet.

"Go on, get out of here. Turn out the lights. Go hide

under the bed," Maurice gasped out to his children. They fled.

Turning from the window into gale winds, Ken walked to the road and thrust his rifle into the bushes. It was a good tool and had served him well for many years. Now he no longer needed it. He could head back and wait for the police. Now he could wait to die.

Into the hovering nighttime, raindrops, large and plentiful, fell upon the forest of fir and cedar above the creek-side cabin. Gray squirrels and striped chipmunks withdrew into their dens. Beside the back door of the cabin a tulip bloomed and a watchdog waited.

I wrestled my car down the steep bumpy driveway and parked to the left of Dave's Toyota pickup, which sat next to a detached garage. Inside, his '68 Camaro, 129,021 miles strong, sat in protective retirement alongside the Coleman canoe and chest freezer.

I stepped from the car into a large puddle, soaking my foot all the way up to my ankle.

Wind blasts from around the corner of the house blew my hair into my mouth and in front of my eyes. The trees groaned against the force of the coastal storm. Glancing up toward the woods and thick underbrush, I shivered and tried not to think of who might be hiding there. The dreariness of the March night surrounded me as I crossed the concrete slab and opened the wooden door onto the cork-tiled floor.

The living room was black. So I rounded the leaded-glass partition that separated the dining room from the hall and found Dave staring out the window at the darkness. The house was quiet, very quiet. For a few moments he did not say anything, just stood there.

Then he spoke. "Think you better sit down, Violet."

The man I had lived with for four years turned from the rain-splattered glass. Seeing he was serious, deadly

serious, I sank onto a hard-backed chair, one we re-
stored a couple years before.

"Well, he did it," he said. He straddled a dining
room chair and sat down facing me, the expression in his
sloping blue eyes unreadable. Darkness shadowed in
from the corners, the fire in the fireplace long since
dead.

"Who did what?" I asked, trembling.

"Ken, he killed Kathy and Maurice McCall and a
couple of other people." He ran his large muscular hand
through rumpled blond curls and stared directly into my
eyes. "With his hunting rifle."

"No," I cried out.

Sighing long and deep he settled wearily against the
uncomfortable chair.

The rain, pounding now, as it had been most of the
day, hit the shake roof overhead. Strong wind struck the
community of Lakes End, a hamlet where resort dwell-
ers met red-necked loggers.

I leaned back in the chair and gripped its wooden
frame; the edge cut into my fingers. My voice, not normally timid, reduced to a hoarse whisper. "When did it
happen?"

"Tonight about six. Your dad called about a half an
hour ago right after I got home. Your folks were at Ken's
when he did it. He just went across the street, up the
road, and shot them, all four of them."

"Didn't think he'd do it. Just didn't think he'd do
it," I repeated in a voice that floated in space. The floor
shimmered, rising up to me. The walls and draped windows seemed to come closer, grasping me, choking my
small body.

How was I supposed to deal with this? There was no
appropriate response. My brother . . . a killer. A killer.
Dear God.

Disjointed thought jumped into my deadened brain,
jarring me into motion. I stumbled into the kitchen, try-

ing to locate our pastor's phone number. Muttering to myself I dialed his number.

The soft female voice at the other end of the receiver startled me; I had expected a man. "Is Pastor Young home?"

"No. He's downtown at a meeting. This is his wife, Sharon. Can I help you?"

I did not want to talk to her. Could not handle it. Could not think fast enough.

Squelching my panic, I said, "I guess, I don't know . . . uh . . . this is Betty Andre's daughter, Violet. I'd like your husband to call my momma. My brother shot some people tonight," I heard myself say, my voice distant as if I were someone else.

"Your mom called about an hour ago and we talked for quite a while. I'll have Bob call her when he gets in," she said, her voice almost a sedative. A picture of Sharon's long brown hair and heavily lashed eyes tumbled into my mind, and I could see the kindness, the sympathy in those eyes even over the phone. It did not help.

"How did Momma seem when you talked to her?" I said gasping as if I were being choked.

"She was crying."

"I guess she would be . . ."

A silent scream at the stupidity of the question thundered through my brain. I felt the muscles in my body jump and quiver out of control. The receiver crashed to the floor, leaving me suspended in a haunted spinning room. A voice, which I only faintly perceived, shouted, "Vi? Violet, are you all right?"

With my consciousness still swirling I slowly reclaimed the receiver and in a disconnected voice said, "I've got to go. Please pray for us, for Momma and Daddy." I hung up.

Trying to clear my brain I finally managed to refocus. Dave had not budged; his face had gone pale. I turned back to the phone and dialed again. "Daddy. Dave and I will be right over."

"Okay, Violet," came the soft, strained voice of the most gentle man I had ever known. "Thank God you're coming."

I hung up, tugged on a heavy parka, and told Dave I was ready to go.

"Okay, hon. Want to leave any light on?"

"I guess," I said, my voice childlike, masking my surging emotions.

We headed out onto Highway 101, which followed the coast, passing mountains of sand and sparse, wind-twisted trees. They were blackened now, the night and the storm obliterating the stark beauty.

Generations of lumbermen, my brother, father, and grandfather included, had carved away the thick ever-greens that layered the steep slopes of the Coast Range, leaving mostly alder and younger trees. The headlights reflected off of thick sheets of water. An occasional car splashed past.

The town of Dayton, a half hour away, with its lumber mills and port activities was largely blue collar. The addition of a college twenty years before provided a source of enlightenment. The town, however, remained mostly the same, a community of folks who disvalued education.

Liquor and religion kept the town alive, or so it seemed to me. Ideas and beliefs, unexplored and unex-amined, passed down through generations. That's why I left after high school, and why on returning years later I did not fit in.

Turning to Dave, I studied his rugged profile in the light from the dash. Thankfully he remained quiet. I did not want to talk about it; talking made it seem too real.

New gusts of rain pelted the windshield and made it almost impossible to see. The walls of the car trapped us on a small stage that move slowly toward a frightening reality.

We could see lights from the kitchen window as we drew closer and pulled down the long graveled driveway to my parents' house. Water from the many puddles whished against the underside of the car. Dave eased in close to the old stationwagon and stopped on the edge of the carport. In the semidarkness he reached across the seat and grasped my hand. "If you want to spend the night, we can."

"Thanks," I managed to croak. Mist needled my hot cheeks as I trudged up onto the back porch.

I took a deep breath, entered the cold kitchen, thinking absently the fire in the wood furnace must be out, and nodded to Billie, my sister's teenage daughter. She was seated at the dining room table. I had forgotten she was staying with my folks. The double doors to the living room creaked open enough for Daddy to squeeze through. He stood uncertainly on the edge of the darkness, his eyes shaded with pain.

Crossing the distance I pulled him to me, feeling his thin body tremble against mine.

"Where's Momma?" I asked.

"In the bedroom resting."

Tentatively extracting myself I asked, "How is she?"

"Pretty upset." He eased onto a chair at the edge of the warm-yellow Formica table, and lowered his head onto folded hands. The pull-down lamp shimmered above his wavy silver hair, and he hunched against a world of sudden disaster.

My daddy suddenly owned so much pain . . . yet he used to bounce me on his knee, his blue eyes reflecting such fun, used to stroke my long hair and hug me. I remembered the cookies he waved under my nose, teasing me as he always did. He and grandma Andre were so poor after grandpa died he never had store-bought cookies; so he wanted to make sure Ken, Denise, and I did.

Dear Daddy, we watched sad movies together as I grew up. He reclined in the easy chair next to the bookcase Ken made in wood shop; he pretended not to cry. Tender man, always. Soft hearted, but strong. I was never afraid with him around. It hurt me to see him now, his eyes closed against Ken's nightmare.

A door cracked open at the other end of the house, followed by feet padding down a tiled hall. For a moment Momma stood in the doorway to the dining room, then moved into my arms and covered her face with my shoulder. Taking the chair that Billie had vacated for her, she sat down at the table. Momma looked young for sixty-one, even now with her face red and puffy from too many tears.

I took a seat, grasped her large hand in my own small one, and allowed my long brown hair to fall before my eyes, hiding the beginnings of tears. I would not fall apart, I had decided, not in front of Momma and Daddy, not when they needed me.

Daddy carefully watched his wife of forty-two years. Worry wrinkled his forehead. He began to speak.

"Momma and I were in the kitchen at Ken's," he said. "We went up to be with him after he got home from work so he wouldn't be alone. He called Teresa at her folks in California to beg her to come back, but she and the kids would not come home.

"Momma was fixing dinner and we were waiting for Ken to come back in and eat. We thought he was out feeding the dog. That's when we heard the first three shots."

"Oh, God!" Dave said.

Momma sagged against the table; tears surged from her dark eyes. "We didn't know what had happened. At first I thought he shot himself and the dog." She paused and looked away, then she spoke again. "I should have warned them after what he said yesterday. I just never thought he'd shoot anyone," she said, lowering her gray-brown curls onto clenched hands and sobbing.

In two steps I was behind her, massaging her shoulders, but she did not respond. The pain, grief, and guilt were too deep.

"How'd he get the gun out of the house without you seeing it?" Dave asked and leaned against the kitchen stove that divided the two rooms.

Oh, God! I thought, putting my hands up to cover my ears, I wanted to know everything that had happened, yet I did not want to hear it. Could not tolerate hearing it. I heard anyway.

"I don't know," Daddy said. "It must have been hidden someplace."

The numbness wrapped around my heart was beginning to thaw. My skin felt prickly as though covered with ants. I ached to escape the whole mess, tear out of the house and never return. Instead I sat down again and tried to control my desperation.

"What did you do when you heard the shots?" Dave asked.

"We ran out onto the porch, Daddy first, then me. He about stumbled down the stairs over the cats and hurried across the street in the direction of the shots. By the time I got there Ken was gone . . . to the McCalls.

"I saw two little blond kids come running from the house. They didn't cry. They just stood there like scared little rabbits," she said. Her face crumpled and she sobbed into a twisted tissue.

"They just stood there in the porch light," Daddy said, "the wind blowing rain against their poor little bodies. They couldn't have been more than ten years old. The next thing I heard was a truck crunching down the road alongside Ken's house. Momma yelled something to the guy in the truck. He picked up a kid under each arm, put them into his truck, and tore off up the road backwards."

"Who was he?" I asked in a quiet voice.

"Some neighbor, probably. I never saw him before that," Daddy said.

"I ran back into the house and dialed the operator," Momma said. "When I got the police I told them our son had gone berserk and was shooting people. I begged them to come in a hurry. I was bawling so I can't remember what I said, but they asked me a lot of questions."

Her tears stopped and she stared at the pile of shredded tissue beneath her fingers.

"What did you do then?" I hoarsely whispered, trying to block out the horror.

"Ken came back and said he'd be down by the road waiting for the police. Momma and I sat there waiting, didn't know what else to do . . . just waited for the police to show up." Daddy took a breath as if about to say something else. Instead he checked his pulse, something he had done repeatedly since his heart attack.

"How's your heart, Daddy?" I asked, afraid of the answer.

"Don't worry, Violet," he said.

I could not help but worry. There was nothing to do except be there, and that was not enough. None of the counseling skills I learned in college prepared me for this. All those theories on crisis counseling were garbage, just garbage. The two people I loved most were in more pain than they knew how to handle, and nothing would change that.

Where was God? Why wasn't He helping? If ever I needed Him it was now. Maybe there was no God. I had suspected that for years.

Billie, who had been leaning against the papered wall behind Momma, wrapped her slender arms about Momma's shoulders, her long dark hair falling around Momma's face.

"Ah, Grandma, don't cry."

Momma did not respond, but after several moments she said, "I'm going up to bed."

"Do you want us to spend the night?" I asked.

"No. Denise and Ted will be here sometime tonight, and Billie is here," she said.

"I thought maybe it would help if we were here too," I said.

"No . . . I just need some time."

When Momma left I turned to Daddy, feeling the need to insist. "Are you sure you don't want us to stay?"

"No, Vi. Your mother . . . we just need some time."

I sighed heavily with relief. Now I could go home and hide.

I grabbed my purse and prepared to leave. "Daddy, I think we should get Ken an attorney."

"Guess you're right," he said, looking old and exhausted, as if he had aged ten years since he, Momma, and I met for lunch at the mall a few hours before.

"I'll be out first thing in the morning and we can go to town to see one."

He nodded. "Thanks for coming, Vi, Dave," Daddy said so softly I could hardly hear him. He grasped Dave's outstretched hand and then turned to me.

I held my father for a long time, feeling a chill penetrate us both. I had so many unanswerable questions, like why this had to happen to them . . . to Daddy. His life had been so difficult.

Grandpa Andre, his father, died when Daddy was sixteen, the year the stock market crashed. Daddy quit school to support Grandma and returned to graduate a couple of years later. It took determination to do that during the Depression.

Daddy had worked as a logger and later in a sawmill. Most days he came home exhausted. Lord knows, we were not always grateful either, only expected more, as kids do; but I had never heard him complain.

Finally Dave and I left, stepping out into the cold and headed for the car; my legs nearly buckled. He slipped an arm around me and helped me onto the bench seat.

A feeling of desolation passed through me as we drove the forty-five minutes home. I tried to pray, tried to gain comfort from the God I believed in as a child, the God who had been so elusive for years. Finally I mouthed the words, "Please help me, help us all."

Back home I waited in the rain for Dave to unlock the door; we trudged inside.

"Want a drink?" he asked, pulling a bottle of Hiram Walker from under the counter.

"No, thanks," I said numbly. "Think I'll take a shower and go to bed." I stepped into the wet needles and tried to remove the chill that now seemed a permanent part of me.

Climbing in between the cold sheets I buried my face. Minutes later Dave slipped in beside me and tried to snuggle close, but I found no comfort in his body and pulled away. Tension stiffened my limbs. It was hours before I slept.

Then guns and murder dominated my dreams. Shocked awake I bolted upright. As I sat staring at the darkened drapes, thoughts of the shootings, the dead people, and the children in the rain accosted me.

Those poor little blond babies. How could they ever feel safe again? My brother had done that to them. It was too horrible to be real . . . but it was.

Shadows lurked through the drapes, and bushes scraped the outside of the house beneath the window. Wind, so often present in the coastal community, echoed down the chimney at the far end of the house.

Shivering, I huddled deeper into Aunt Ida's quilt and old wool blankets and clamped my eyes shut.

I felt so alone. My brother had killed four people. If he could do it, anybody could. My sense of safety had perished with the murders.

I was not safe now. I would never be.

Chapter Two

Heavy clouds descended onto alder tops and halfway down the old fir above the house. Across the valley, beyond the reclaimed marshlands, the slough cut its way through dark, sucking mud. A quiet settled on the farmland and over the inhabitants, of whom I was one. The valley had been my home while I was growing up and always before had seemed friendly.

Inside the small country house, I positioned my feet in front of the electric heater and shivered. I hated waiting.

A green and white pickup pulled down the canopied driveway and under the huge alder I had spent so many hours climbing as a child. The truck stopped behind my car.

Wondering who it could be I glanced at Billie, but she offered no help. Sprawled on the couch with a book inches from her face, she seemed totally absorbed, as if Ken's crime did not bother her. How could she concentrate on a book now?

Pulling aside the flimsy curtain I peered through the window in the old wooden door and stared out as three intruders climbed from the truck. Not caring if I appeared rude, not even thinking about it, I studied them.

Sighing in recognition I saw that it was my father's three nephews, each retirement age. They slowly climbed the back steps. It had been a while since I had seen them, especially George. He was Daddy's favorite.

Opening the back door I greeted them. "How nice of you to come. Come on in," I said quietly. My voice always softened when I was upset. Otherwise, I was too likely to lose control.

"Thanks," Art said. He switched the Bible he was carrying to his left hand and extended the right one in greeting, as did his two brothers. They followed me to the dining room and sat down.

"Momma, Daddy, and Denise are in town trying to find Ken an attorney," I said. "According to Billie, they should be back any time. Can I get you some coffee?"

"No . . . thanks," Art said. I could see his mind scrambling.

It was Walt who found the words. "We heard about Ken on the news last night." Leaning forward he grasped his knees and stared at the window behind me, where small birds ate on the window-ledge feeder. His eyes were clear and faintly blue behind dark-rimmed bifocals.

"Knowing your folks," George said, shifting uncomfortably and rubbing a hand across his wavy gray hair, "we knew how hard this must be for them, so we thought we'd stop by.

"You know, I remember your dad when we were kids. . . . Lee was such a soft-spoken boy, thoughtful and considerate. The rest of us got into trouble turning over outhouses, drinking, and the likes, but not your dad. I never saw him get into mischief. Never even saw him get angry.

"He was so good to Grandma after Grandpa died . . . took care of her. Around here in those days there wasn't much for a woman to do to support herself.

There's no finer man—" Tears choked George's voice; he blew his nose and dabbed his eyes.

"This whole mess with Ken, it just doesn't figure. Both your folks are good, decent people. Who would have thought Ken could do something like this. Your folks never had much problem with him while he was growing up. Mostly he just liked to go hunting and fishing," George said, unsure where to direct his eyes. "Then again he stayed away from most of us, never came to family things and such, even when he was a teenager."

The house echoed silence and the living room clock seemed to tick louder than normal, as clocks do during awkward moments. In the eerie quiet, renewed horror shivered over me.

I bit at tissues inside my mouth. In our family we did not cry in front of other people.

"Teresa and Ken had been fighting quite a bit lately," I said. "She called me Saturday and said she was leaving Monday morning as soon as Ken left for work. That's what she did, day before yesterday, taking the kids with her. And then Ken . . ."

I could not say it, could not even think the word *murder*.

Art placed his hand on the Bible, his eyes glowing. "Just remember, the Lord is here to help you through this. Trust him."

I sighed. "Thanks so much for coming. I don't know what happened to the folks," I said, nervously glancing at my watch. "They should have been back by now." As if by plan the phone rang, and after talking a few minutes I hung up.

"I'm to meet them in town; we'd like you to join us for lunch. We have an appointment with an attorney at one."

"We'll join you long enough to say a few words to your folks. We're on our way to see Hazel," Walt said.

Hazel—her sister had been killed by Ken—I had forgotten about her. I tried to picture her: faded blond hair, metal-rimmed glasses, pastel-colored dresses. I hadn't seen her since I was a little girl. In my mind she still sat in the pew beside Kathy McCall and her family toward the back of the big white church, the white elephant we called it.

All those years Hazel served as a nurse and a missionary in Thailand, and for what? To come back and have her sister killed by my brother?

Now that I thought about it, Hazel and Kathy had other siblings as well. Three brothers, maybe. The only one I remembered was Joel. He had gone off to Bible college when I was four or five.

Of course, there were also Kathy and Maurice's other two children, Jered, the oldest, and Greg, the second son. All of them must be devastated.

After lunch we headed to the attorney's office. I pushed open the glass door and the four of us—Momma, Daddy, Denise, and I—entered the plush, leather-clad outer office. We waited in the little alcove next to the window and glanced through copies of *Business Week* and *National Geographic.*

"Mr. Thompson can see you now," the blond, sweet-looking receptionist said within a few minutes of our arrival. She ushered us down the dark mahogany hallway to his office.

"Please be seated." Clyde Thompson rose from behind his carved walnut desk and grasped Daddy's hand. "Now, what can I do for you?" His voice had a Harvard sophistication, out of place in a mill town like Dayton.

Silence.

Awkwardly I waited, hoping someone would say something. Finally I fabricated some courage, knowing I must take care of my parents.

"We're here to ask you to represent my brother, Kenneth Andre," I blurted out. Hesitating, I clamped my fingers around the arms of the wooden chair and straightened myself on the burgundy cushioned seat.

"If you heard the news," I said, "you know of the shootings last night up the river. My brother, Ken, is charged with those crimes. My parents were across the road when it happened. They need legal counsel as well."

Suddenly, I turned on the professionalism I learned dealing with the authorities on my last job, and stared resolutely at the attorney's nose.

"I see. Has your brother to your knowledge seen an attorney?" he responded in a detached, impersonal voice. I ignored it.

"No. Is it possible for you to see him this afternoon?" I asked.

Clyde buzzed his secretary. "Kathy, could you check to see when Kenneth Andre is to be arraigned and get back to me as soon as possible?" He hung up and checked his calendar. "I'm not a criminal attorney, but I'll see what I can do for the time being."

After we endured several minutes of stiff conversation, the phone rang. "I see. Thanks, Kathy." He returned his attention to us and said, "Ken is to be arraigned this afternoon at two. If you hurry you can still make it. In the meantime I'll do some checking and meet you here at five. I'll see Ken this evening." He extended his hand first to me and then my father.

"You can't make it to the arraignment?" I asked.

"No, my schedule is full."

I sighed.

"We need to know your hourly fee," I said and headed out into the hallway.

"Sixty dollars an hour."

Momma gasped and caught Daddy's eyes. When Daddy retired from the mill four years before, he earned six dollars an hour.

"I'm afraid, Mrs. Andre," Clyde said, "that's about as cheap as you'll find. We'll discuss it when you return."

The four of us hurried to my car. Momma said, "Lee, we can't afford that kind of money."

"I know, Momma," Daddy said, worry in his voice. "We'll think about that after we talk to Mr. Thompson this evening. Maybe he'll give us some idea as to how much all this will cost."

"Whatever it is, it'll be more than we can afford," Momma said, her voice trembling and her eyes, which I could see in the rearview mirror, reflecting desperation.

Heading inland over coastal hills toward the county courthouse, I tried to concentrate on driving, but couldn't. Panic percolated inside me. The veneer of control I had laminated around my feelings was close to cracking.

When we arrived, I parked the car in front of the old concrete building and the four of us hurried inside.

"Can you tell me where Kenneth Andre is to be arraigned this afternoon?" I asked the grayish-brown-haired clerk at the information desk. I worried what she thought of us, whether or not she guessed who we were, if she hated us.

Within me the panic still surged, but I tried not to show it. I needed to project strength.

"In Judge Jones's courtroom," she said with a bland expression, the one she probably reserved for strangers. "Turn left at the top of the stairs, head down the hallway, make a jog to the right and you're there."

We followed her directions and took seats in the fourth row of the busy room. Glancing about I noted that almost every row was filled, mostly with people in business suits. Facing front again I searched for my brother.

"I wonder where he is?" Denise whispered, her voice tense. She tugged her ruffled blouse down over the stomach of her doubleknit pants and pushed her curly hair back from her face. Her eyes, browner than mine, revealed the grief we all felt. The fingernails at the ends of her short, chubby hand were chewed back to raw skin.

"Probably still up in the jail," I said, not knowing what to expect in this strange environment with its unfamiliar rules.

Being there was important to me. I needed to know if they treated Ken fairly. Somehow I felt I had to show him I still loved him even though he had done such a terrible thing to Kathy and Maurice and the Bennetts.

Swallowing the terror I felt, I glanced down the row past Denise to study Momma and Daddy. They sat rigid and still, staring straight ahead.

They must be so ashamed. Their son has committed murder.

Everyone in the room seemed to be staring at us.

In the front of the room Judge Jones said something to a male defendant dressed in green khaki coveralls. The young man nodded, then the guards guided him to a seat in the first row. The judge proceeded with another case.

The doors opened and two guards entered with a tall, thin man. His curly black hair lay in clumps on his head. His skin was deathly pale, his beard long and course. The green coveralls that all the prisoners wore hung on his body.

A prickling chill shot up my back.

"That's Ken!" Denise whispered. "My God, I can't believe that's Ken!"

Nodding, I blinked involuntary tears; my arms and legs started shaking. To stop myself I clamped my jaw shut and dug my fingers into my palms until knives of pain shot through my hands.

Ken glanced about the room, and when he saw us, surprised recognition clicked momentarily in his eyes. He and the guards seated themselves in the first row. I stared at the back of Ken's head. My throat constricted.

Jumbled thoughts shot through my brain. He had

always been frightened of strange people and unfamiliar places. Was he now, or had he killed those fears when he killed the people?

An avalanche of feelings festered beneath my outwardly calm façade. Clamping teeth against teeth, I pictured an emotional switch and turned it off. Instantly I regained some semblance of control and looked again at my parents.

Daddy's arm lay on Momma's shoulder as they huddled together in the hostile room, waiting for the intolerable to happen. The stark eyes of the other occupants stared at us. We waited.

After several minutes Ken moved forward accompanied by the two guards. Judge Jones began speaking, but even straining I could not hear him.

"What's he saying?" I whispered.

"I can't hear either," Denise said.

Court recessed. Other members of the audience moved out the double doorway into the hall. My big brother and the guards waited next to the jury box.

With hesitant steps, I walked up the aisle. My legs shook inside thin woolen pants and my feet all but tripped on the even floor on my way to him.

I wrapped my arms about Ken. He remained stiff, his shoulders hunched against all invasions. The coveralls were all I could feel. His flesh beneath the thick fabric seemed unreachable. There was no sense of a living individual within the body, nor did he respond to me at all. Still, I held him.

After a couple of seconds one of the guards said, "No contact with the prisoners, please."

Frightened I backed away. My stomach ached with surging tension.

A few minutes later the guards handcuffed Ken, led him from the courtroom and down the faded green hallway. My family and I followed a few feet behind.

"I guess they'll all know who we are before this is over," Denise whispered as she stared at the reporters snapping pictures of Ken.

"I guess it can't be helped," I said.

When Ken and the guards disappeared behind the elevator doors, I leaned against the cold wall, my whole body shaking. Everything seemed impossible. Months, maybe years, of hearings hovered ahead.

A heavy Oregon fog settled around us as we hurried silently out the front doors of the courthouse; the chill exacerbated my loneliness and fear. Momma hesitated uncertainly on the top step and began to shake, crying. I switched off my emotions again, pulled her to the side of the gray slabs, and held her. I would deal with my feelings later. Helping her was more important than anything else.

At five we met Clyde Thompson back at his office.

"I just talked with the public defender's office," he said. "They believe an attorney will be appointed for Ken, but it's not definite. In the meantime I'll visit him this evening. I'll try to keep the cost down. I understand the family can't afford much. Is that correct?" Mr. Thompson said. He joined his fists behind his head. Light glistened on his coarse silver hair; he seemed young to be so gray.

"Yes," I said. "Do you have any idea how long it'll be before the court appoints the attorney?"

The legal office and all the tin gods it represented no longer intimidated me. Things could not get much worse. My brother was lost one way or the other.

Thompson scratched his head. "More than likely within the week, but he might have to furnish his own. From what I understand the court may require him to sell his home to pay legal costs. However, since he owns it jointly with his wife that may be a problem."

"You've done some work," I said.

"I've given it considerable thought. As I told you

this afternoon I'm not knowledgeable enough in this area of law to follow through. However, I have talked to my colleagues and decided on a temporary course of action. I'll meet with Ken until another attorney takes over."

"Good," I said. "Now should we—"

"You know he did it!" Momma blurted out.

"This is confidential, isn't it?" Daddy asked. He leaned toward the attorney. His eyes were earnest and worried. His hair had been slicked back, and a wave had popped out of place.

"Yes, but the records of our conversation can be subpoenaed; so I'll record only the essentials. Now tell me all you can about the incident, where you were, what Ken did, and anything you think might be helpful."

I listened to ensure the attorney correctly understood my parents, ready to bridge the educational and cultural gaps.

Momma and Daddy looked so frightened and out of place. They were more at home in overalls and knee-high rubber boots, driving a herd of cows across a bumpy field than they were in an attorney's office being led across the mine field of legal procedures.

Denise, leaning forward, paid careful attention. Her fingers clutched the chair and her forehead puckered in a way that created terrible lines. At thirty-eight those lines were likely to stay with her. Her skin had always possessed the dry look of a redhead, although her hair was auburn. Freckles dotted her face and arms. Problems with her weight had plagued her for years, but even so she looked good in the pantsuit. Never in the thirty years we had been sisters could I guess what she was thinking. Like Daddy she kept her worries to herself.

After nearly an hour we rose to go.

"I'll give you a call after I talk to Ken and a few members of the court," Clyde said. "At that time I may have a better idea how to advise you. You'll need to come in again in a few days. The police will probably be out to question you and you'll have to testify."

Momma gasped, "But my husband has a bad heart."

"We can try to get the police to accept a deposition. That's a written statement as to the events as you know them, but we may not be able to facilitate that. We'll see what we can do, Mrs. Andre," he said in a tone used to soothe a child.

"Oh, no. No," Momma muttered, once we were out of the office.

I bit and tore at my fingernails as we walked in silence to the Dairy Queen at the edge of the shopping mall. Pain arched through the top of my head. My need to scream grew.

We ordered, then retreated to the corner of the restaurant. I stared blankly at the wall, glad the place was mostly empty. I wanted to withdraw, to see and talk to no one.

"Where'd we go wrong, Momma?" Daddy asked in a quiet, jerky voice, fatigue and grief in his eyes.

"I don't know," Momma said.

"It's not your fault," I whispered, my voice shaking and intense. "A lot of things have happened since Ken left home, things that you had nothing to do with. You've been good parents to us. You did the best you could, and no one can ask more than that."

The words tormented me after we parted. Rain pelted the windshield, and my mind flicked back to a time I squeezed in beside my mother's love in the big chair in the living room. I listened carefully while she read me stories, the same ones each day, the ones I loved by heart.

And Daddy . . . I must have been about six and Ken sixteen. It was the only time I could ever remember Daddy losing his temper. Ken had been teasing me, as big brothers do. The memory was somewhat faded in the corners, but I could still feel Ken's strong hands pinning me to the dining room wall. I tried to twist away, but his fingers dug into my arms. I started to cry, first because he was hurting me and second from frustration born of helplessness.

Suddenly Daddy burst from his chair, ordering my brother to leave me alone. Ken was shocked, as we all were, by the anger. My father was a man who normally lived in quiet peace. Even then Daddy did not swear. In fact, I never heard him say one negative word about anyone.

Now Momma and Daddy wondered what they had done wrong. Nothing, I wanted to shout to the world, absolutely nothing!

Before leaving town I picked up a local paper. The shootings of March 4 had made the headlines. A picture of the murder scene was on the front page. The next page featured a photograph of Ken in handcuffs. It was an image of a bedraggled woodsman, one that branded itself on my brain.

An image of my brother.

Chapter Three

The light on the boathouse cast a yellow-white glow over the twisting current, which carried Dave's fishing line beyond sight. "You're a little late and I was getting worried. Did you see an attorney?" he said.

I scooted down beside him near the end of the dock and filled him in on the day's events. Afterward I leaned against the side of the boathouse and picked up the half gallon of wine he had placed there.

"Want any?" I asked.

"No thanks." He murmured.

Tipping the container to my mouth, I chugged as much as possible in one gulp and shuddered at the bittersweet taste. Huddled against the cold corrugated aluminum, I lifted the bottle once again, paused briefly, and chugged a third time.

Dave glanced back at me and nodded, a gesture that said whatever I needed to do was alright. His boyish face was silhouetted against the darkness. He resumed staring at the end of the pole, waiting for fish that mostly eluded him.

It was finally okay to cry. For a little while I did not have to pretend to be strong. Yet I could not release my feelings. I closed my eyes and sighed, trying to find refuge within my heavy jacket; but the stiff polyester hood rustled against my ears and amplified my restlessness.

Over the years I had recognized no warnings, no clues that anything was wrong with Ken. He seemed only shy and distant, staying away from gatherings of even the closest family members, including Christmas dinners with Momma and Daddy. In the infrequent times I had seen him during the past twenty years, our encounters had been brief, with no conversations lasting more than a few minutes.

I thought of Teresa and her Saturday phone call returned to me. In spite of all she had told me, I never thought something like this would happen, even though from the beginning there had been that awful feeling of doom.

Now I recalled Teresa's voice from that Saturday call:

"He threatened to kill us, Violet. I've got no choice but to take the kids and leave," she said.

"My God!"

"He threatened to cut my guts out with a butcher knife and lay them out for the kids to see. I'm not kidding, Vi. His eyes blazed crazy like and he threw me up against the dining room wall . . . uh . . . and kind of pinned me there. I was really scared. That's when Russ stepped in. You should have seen the way he stood up to his father . . . knocked Ken out of the way and everything. Took Ken by surprise, I guess. He stood there shaking in the doorway next to the refrigerator, as if he was about to explode."

"Ken?" Shivers shot across my body as horror penetrated the recesses of my spirit.

"Yeah. That's when he said the kids would

get it too . . . if we didn't stop ganging up on him and siding with the neighbors. He said he'd kill us all," she said. In my mind I could see her fleshy face contorted with fear, and an index finger twisting a strand of long brown hair.

"He threatened the kids too?"

"Yeah, and I was afraid he'd really do it. He even threatened the McCalls, said something about them trying to steal our property. He said he wanted to get rid of the whole bunch."

"The McCalls don't live next to you anymore."

"I know, they live down the road. The Bennetts do, though. We've had an ongoing dispute with both families over the property line. And he's upset because they've taken the kids to church."

"Yeah?"

"You know Ken's hated church ever since he was a kid, hates everything connected with it . . . says religious folks are a bunch of hypocrites. He thinks the McCalls have been turning the kids against him."

"That's not true—"

"No, but Ken thinks they are. Anyway, there was something different about him. . . . We all sensed it."

"Both kids were home?"

"Yeah, Russ was waiting for the McCalls to pick him up and take him to the beach. Kathy and Maurice are leaders of the church youth group. Guess you knew that. Anyway, Ken started yelling at us to leave him alone. I didn't know what to do. So I just stood there staring at him."

"Good grief. The whole thing doesn't make sense."

"He twists everything we say. I think he's gone nuts. Absolutely nuts! So, we're leaving Monday."

"Do you need money?"

"No, we'll be alright. We'll stay with my folks until I get a job," Teresa said, more resolve in her voice than I had ever heard.

"Where's Ken now?"

"Mowing the lawn. He acts as though nothing's happened, but I talked to the kids this morning and they're scared too. So, we're leaving Monday morning after he goes to work . . ."

The cold night air wrenched me from my thoughts. I shivered and stared into the gloom. Dave reeled in and cast out again, his voice silenced. A yard light at a house across the creek was the only light in the row of creekfront houses around the corner from the lake.

It had been a nice place to live, here by the water . . . a place to let my troubles be carried away by the current. This time, however, the healing powers of the water failed to work. There was no way to make peace with a murder.

Tugging the cork from the bottle I jerked the container to my mouth and took a long swig. The liquid gulped down my throat. With a moan, our dog Brutus flopped down beside me and placed his head on my legs, his eyes intent on my face.

Oh, God, I thought, why? My thoughts contained so many contradictions. That warranted another drink. Quickly I gulped the wine down.

"The phone's ringing. Do you want me to get it?" Dave asked, nodding toward the wine bottle.

"No, I'm fine." I hurried to the end of the dock.

With long, shaky strides I crossed the slippery ramp, then staggered up the vine-covered stairway and entered the house just in time for the phone to stop ringing.

"Damn," I muttered and dialed the number. "Hello, Momma, . . . uh . . . did you just call?" I asked, trying not to slur my words, not wanting her to realize I was drunk. It would hurt her. She must not think she had failed with me too.

"Yes, Clyde Thompson called a few minutes ago. Seems he just got back from the jail," Momma said. Her pain-flooded voice came through the line. "Talk to your dad."

"Momma's pretty upset," Daddy whispered. "She's been crying ever since we got home. Got to do something to help her."

He was taking care of Momma, as always. He had tried to protect us from the ugliness in life. It worked for me until I left home at eighteen.

I took a tissue from the box on top of the refrigerator and dabbed trickling tears. "What did Clyde say?"

"He visited Ken. Seems he confessed immediately on being picked up, even told the cops how he did it and where they'd find the bodies. . . . He said he wanted the death penalty," Daddy said, his voice a choked whisper.

"No." I grabbed the counter to steady myself.

Ken could be executed. I had avoided thinking of it. Death for death, it worked that way. But he was my big brother who taught me to whistle and bought me a doll during his time in Korea. Nobody must kill my brother.

"The police will be out tomorrow afternoon to take a statement," Daddy said.

"I think you'd better call Clyde Thompson."

"Could I ask you to do that first thing in the morning, Vi? Momma wants to make sure you'll be here. She's afraid she'll say something wrong. She says you know how to handle the authorities."

I took a deep breath.

"Sure, Daddy, I'll handle it."

The next afternoon Momma, Denise, and I gathered around a thick display book at a florist shop situated in tall fir on a ridge above Dayton. Slowly I thumbed through the pictures of wreaths and plants, the plastic pages sticking to my fingers. It was weird to be buying flowers for people my brother killed. I wondered if anyone would think it strange that we sent them. Maybe they hated us because of Ken.

Momma scanned the pictures and tried to concentrate. "I just don't know what to send," she said, tearfully.

"I think this small wreath will do. We could send one to both funerals," I said and glanced absently at the baskets of potpourri nestled amongst stuffed animals and tastefully potted plants.

"I agree," Denise said.

The clerk filled out the receipt with the names of the deceased. "Now, you need to sign the cards," she said, and handed Momma the pen.

"When are the funerals?" I asked, staring at the back wall to avoid the clerk's eyes.

"The McCall funeral is to be held tomorrow here in town at the Church of Christ. The one for the Bennetts will be held near Sweet Home on Monday."

A "this can't be happening to me" feeling came over me again, as it had so many times during the last couple of days. It seemed impossible . . . a few days before both couples had been making plans and raising their children.

Broken hearted, I thought of those kids, the ones who had watched Ken kill their parents. Would they ever be alright? And the brothers, sisters, and parents of those killed, what about them?

The three of us stepped from the shop into the cold wind. Each step toward the car was slow and deliberate.

My legs were almost too heavy to lift. Once inside the stationwagon Momma collapsed against the seat.

"I should go to Kathy and Maurice's funeral, should pay my respects, let them know how sorry I am," she said. She began to cry into a tissue. For two days her eyelids had been swollen; they were now angry and red. She huddled alone on her side of the car shaking with grief.

Daddy patted her leg but said nothing.

"No one expects you to go," I said, leaning forward and gripping her shoulder. "I couldn't sit through it either."

Denise sat across from me next to the door. Her head rested heavily against the window and her eyes closed. Daddy wiped tears from his eyes with a large blue handkerchief, started the car, and headed for home to wait for the detectives.

Since Clyde had told my parents to reveal nothing without an attorney present, the meeting with the detectives was short. After they left, Momma went into the bedroom to rest and Daddy began pacing the living room.

The phone rang and Denise moaned. "Not again. It's your turn to answer it, Vi."

"Violet, this is Sarah. Can I talk to your mother? I'm so sorry—"

"Momma is resting now. She's not up to talking, but we really do appreciate your concern," I said. I hung up and slumped against the papered wall.

"I'm going to walk up to the pond. Does anyone want to come?" Denise said.

"No thanks, Neecy," Daddy said. "I'll stay here and keep an eye on your mother."

The two of us headed out the driveway through the tunnel of alder trees and up onto the paved country road.

"I feel like I'm going to explode," Denise said. "Watching Mom and Dad . . . I can hardly stand it."

"I know. At least I can go home at night and get away. Maybe you should go home for a few days."

"I could use a little time with Ted, but I'll wait until after I see Ken this weekend."

We continued in silence down the paved road and then cut up the graveled drive that led to the neighbor's pond. I stepped over the barbed-wire gate and held it for Denise; we climbed the steep hill to the clearing.

"I always figured that the No Trespassing sign didn't apply to me," I said, trying to smile.

"Me too."

The land on which we stood had belonged to the neighbor, Clara Smith's family, for several generations. As children Ken, Denise, and I used to play in the clearing next to the pond with the Smith children. In the years since, it had changed little with the exception of an additional cattle fence.

We circled the pond, walking along the partially overgrown dirt road, mud squishing beneath our shoes. I took a breath and felt the cool air. The air was so clean on the coast. Moisture freshened my face, and the quiet of the meadow made it easy to slip back twenty years . . . Ken was about fifteen and I was five:

It was a cold winter and a group of us neighborhood kids assembled at the pond to skate. We didn't wear bladed skates because the ice never got thick enough. Each of us donned our slickest soled boots and slid out onto the ice. Ken, being the oldest, dared the farthest out toward the center. Suddenly the ice cracked and an astonished Ken fell through. The pond was only three feet deep and Ken nearly six foot. He came sloshing out of the water with mischief in his eyes. I sped home, knowing he meant to throw me in, both frightened and excited by the attention.

The two of us continued through the quiet forest as I pondered the relationship between Ken and Denise. It was so different than his and mine. I had always known he loved me. Maybe it was easy to love a baby sister.

With Denise it was different. Because they were born only two years apart, the sibling rivalry between them remained strong. They disagreed on nearly everything and made the fact known in ways that grated on each other. Ken had grown more unfriendly to Denise over the years. In fact, if he saw her in town or at the beach he would pass her without speaking.

"There was only one time I can remember Ken doing anything for me," she said as though our minds were following the same course. "We were in grade school. The bus used to let us off at the bridge up by the old Henry place, you know, about a mile and a half up the road. We walked the rest of the way home. Ken always walked on ahead of me.

"One day he'd disappeared around the bend by the log dump. Cliff, the dark Indian boy who lived up around the corner, had been following a ways behind. All at once he was upon me. He tried to pull off my panties . . . tried to rape me." She shuddered. "I screamed and screamed. Ken came back and pulled him off of me. I was so scared and so glad he was there."

"How old were you?"

"About eight. What will we do if Dad has another heart attack over this?" she said. Her voice was heavy, and she stared at her shoes as we trudged into twilight.

"I don't know."

When I returned home that night, I entered the blackened hallway cautiously. With Brutus preceding me I turned on the lights in each room, checked each closet and under the bed. Finally convinced that no one was in the house, I heated water for tea.

It was then I noticed it . . . the dark window over the kitchen sink. The ruffled curtain provided no privacy.

Immobilized I stared beyond the glass. A menacing face stared back at me from the edge of the light. Shadowed arms raised a rifle and pointed it at my head. Seized by terror I began to shake. A shot exploded and shattered the glass. The bullet penetrated my skull. Losing my balance I staggered back . . .

Brutus placed his furry head under my stiff hand and nuzzled it, breaking the illusion.

I shook my head and stared once again at the window. No one. Still disoriented I headed to the linen closet with Brutus behind me. I grabbed a few things. Back in the kitchen I tacked the long towel over the window above the sink. Next I doubled an old tablecloth and tacked it over the window in the back door.

Chapter Four

My mind spun backward. It was spring 1956, warm and rainy, a typical day on the coast. Momma, who was always too warm, opened the kitchen door and fanned herself with her apron as dinner finished cooking on the old range. Flies crawled across the dog food on the porch.

When dinner was ready, Ken, Denise, Momma, Daddy, I, aunts, uncles, and cousins sat down to prayer and good food . . . to hot biscuits with butter melting into the centers, steaming mashed potatoes with Momma's special gravy, venison roast, and a crisp shrimp salad . . . Sunday dinner. There was plenty. Daddy saw to that.

When he could not avoid it, Ken ate with the family but quickly departed. He took to the woods, his black cocker Tippy running on ahead. Tippy was the dog Daddy brought home for me, the dog Kenny turned into a hunter. I wished he hadn't; I never liked hunting, never wanted to kill anything.

Momma, Daddy, and the relatives hunched back in their chairs around the table. The men talked hunting and fishing; the women discussed children and family gossip. I listened for a while, then retreated with my cousins to my room full of dolls, the room I shared with

Denise. Denise waited for Ted to pick her up for an afternoon romp. That was Sunday after church, the kind of
Sunday we grew up with.

Now, nearly twenty-five years after those comfortable afternoons the four of us—Denise, Momma, Daddy,
and I—trudged up the steps of the country courthouse
and stepped into the cramped waiting area. I read the
sign on the wall and pushed the button below as directed.

"May I help you?" a bored male voice said through
the scratchy speaker.

"My family and I are here to see Kenneth Andre."

"Your relationship, please."

"His two sisters and parents."

"You'll have about a half-hour wait."

More visitors, very normal looking people, arrived
and were told to wait. Everyone huddled close together,
without touching.

A guard dressed in military beige stepped from the
elevator and unlocked the inner glass door, allowing the
people who accompanied him to leave.

"Will the family here to see Ken Andre please follow
me?" he said.

The elevator stopped on the third floor and the door
opened, revealing another door of black iron bars; the
guard unlocked it. Uncertainly we moved into a small
room that was divided by a black chain-link fence ex-
tending from the floor to the ceiling. The guard let himself through the chain-link door and disappeared down
the hallway. We sat down. The red vinyl couch, shoved in
the corner of the room, resembled an old car seat. The
walls and tile were a dreary institution green.

Ken rounded the corner at the end of the hall and
headed toward us, his steps shaky and unsure. He was
dressed in green coveralls like the ones he had worn to
court. His bare feet covered a pair of throngs and his
dirty black hair lay jumbled on the top of his head. Stop-

ping in front of us he grabbed the wire to steady himself, gazed timidly through the mesh, and then quickly looked away.

Even slouched over he looked tall. His sturdy logger build rose to six foot three inches, and he weighed about 225 pounds. Heavy eyebrows from the German side of the family capped eyes of Fudgesicle brown. His hands were stubby like mine, although considerably larger.

A sense of unreality pervaded the emotional atmosphere. I stood up and moved closer; the family closed in behind me. "We were wondering if we could get you anything? Do they provide a tooth brush and shampoo?" I said, keeping my voice low.

With a hand partially hiding his face, like a shy little kid, Ken stared at the floor and said, "Uh, well, I could use some underwear. They don't provide that here, and maybe some socks. They won't let me wear my shoes. I'm so cold. The heat seems to have been turned off," he said. "And I'd like to see Teresa. I just can't understand why she left. Things had been so good lately." He seemed close to crying. "I just can't face it. Everything is gone . . . since Teresa and the kids walked out on Monday."

So good? You threatened to kill her. Then you go after someone else. Why did you kill them? Why?

"I'd like you to find a home for my dog, Cristin," Ken said. He stared directly into my eyes, touching a place only a big brother could reach. "I mean a really good home. I don't want anyone abusing her. She loves to run on the beach. Give her to someone who will take her to the beach."

"I'll do the best I can," I said.

Momma and Daddy stood quietly beside me, their gazes directed at nothing. This place housed their son, the little boy who caught fish on a diaper pin when they lived in a lumber camp next to the gravel-speckled creek. He had always been a good fisherman, agile in crossing slippery stream beds—an ability that served him well as a logger—a man in love with trees and deer and little wild flowers, a man who loved the freedom of the forest. That freedom was forever gone to him, to a man now locked in a cubicle because he was dangerous.

Nothing in their experience prepared our parents for this, nothing could.

"Violet, don't just try, do it," Ken said, and scanned the hallway like a bird watching for a cat. Beyond the edge of the wall, beyond where we could see, guards watched Ken as he watched them.

"We'll try, Son," Daddy said.

"Get Teresa in here. We've got to talk about what's to be done with the house. There's no reason for her to live in California. I didn't work all those years so strangers could live in that house. And the kids, what kind of a fool thing to move them to a place where they don't know anybody? California is full of drug addicts and crazy people. You've got to convince her to come back. You've got to!" he said. His voice was tight. The muscles in his neck stood out.

"I've got to go," he said abruptly and hurried away, his thongs thug-thugging against the freshly buffed floor.

We did not speak, did not know what to do, and so we waited, forlorn and helpless, until the guard reappeared and took us back to the front of the building.

Outside again, the wind struck our faces. I drew the crisp air into my lungs, and as I did so the feeling of entrapment slipped away.

Each day since the murders Momma and Daddy appeared to be more broken, slower and more unsure. Now they clung to each other and stumbled through the crowded parking lot, their eyes reflecting the absence of hope.

Shoving my hands into the pockets of my winter coat, I fingered the frayed lining. Above me on the third floor were the barred windows of the jail. Ken was behind one of them. Was he looking out at us? Was he sorry?

The town of Kenton was Sunday quiet, church families long since returned home. Only an occasional car eased passed onto the uneven slabs of concrete. Nothing much ever happened in Kenton except for church socials and a random brawl at one of the dozen or so taverns.

Denise said goodbye and headed for her home in Eugene.

"Let's have something to eat at the A and W, Vi," Daddy said, and patted my shoulder with touches of love. "Momma, why don't you ride over with Sis."

Momma and I climbed into my Toyota and pulled away from the courthouse, the largest structure in town. Once out onto the main street I took a sideways glance at my mother, who was perched tensely against the back of the seat. She twisted and pulled at her farm-worn hands in unspoken desperation.

"Momma?"

"It's just that your dad won't talk about it," she said, tearfully. "I mean, every time I try to tell him how I feel, he changes the subject or tries to kid me out of it. I don't know how much more I can stand."

"Guess he doesn't know what else to do. Probably hurts him more if he talks about it," I said.

"How could we have gone so wrong? How could he do it?" she said. "I tried to teach Ken right . . . cuddled and loved him when he was little, like I did all you kids."

"It's not your fault. Did you notice the way he acted today? Looked like he was coming off drugs or something. Maybe he's mentally ill. I don't know. I mean, something caused this, something not related to any of us."

Expressing more of her own feelings and thoughts seemed to help my mother; when we rejoined Daddy at the drive-in, she seemed less tense.

It was mid-afternoon by the time I returned home

and headed for the beach with Dave and Brutus. We parked about a half mile from the jetty and climbed from the car. Brutus unfolded himself from the back seat and stepped onto the blowing sand. Then he bounded out before us, nosing under logs and marking clumps of grass.

The three of us hiked toward the dunes and skirted a small pond at the base. Wind lifted and whipped my hair. The sun warmed the back of my head as we crossed the top of the first dune, sand slipping beneath our feet. Glancing up I saw Brutus at the crest, his black coat glistening against the sand. He looked so magnificent and strong with his tail erect and head high, sniffing the wind.

Dave and I stood together overlooking the ocean. It was calm and foaming at the edge of the grass tufted-beach. In silence we dropped to the sand. Cold wet granules soaked the knees and seat of my jeans.

Finally Dave said, "I still can't believe it. I just can't believe your brother killed those people."

"I know. Do you think your family knows by now?" I said.

"No, and I'd just as soon keep it that way," he said in a tone that meant further discussion would be pointless. His eyes looked angry and his body turned rigid. He hunched away from me, retreating into a private space I could never penetrate.

Another time he had used that tone. A few years before, we returned to his hometown. His parents no longer lived there, but Effie, his nanny, did. She had raised him and his five brothers. At eighty-seven she was delightful and spunky, a person I loved at once.

He loved her as much as a grandmother. So I suggested we take her out to dinner. Instantly he became angry and aloof. I sensed a problem with social class, perhaps he considered her the maid and therefore felt taking her to dinner was inappropriate. His response shocked me.

We visited his parents once or twice a year. They lived in an expensive part of the desert in southern California. I had no idea what Dave or his father were worth, but I knew their holdings were substantial. When family business was discussed and financial decisions were made, the women who married into the family were excluded.

Now he excluded me again, from the inner part of himself I needed to connect with, needed support from. For the first few days after the murders he had seemed supportive. Then he withdrew. The only time he mentioned the subject was to ask about the most current events related to Ken.

Of course, he never had been one to talk things out. Still, he had been my teddy bear only a week before, cuddly and playful. Maybe I was the teddy bear, one he would abandon when I proved inconvenient.

I always hated conflict, any bit of it. I had learned the consequences of showing anger when I was nine.

"Violet, are you going to climb on?" my friend Cathy said as she plopped onto the wooden seat of the merry-go-round at the edge of the school yard.

"Yeah," I said, grabbed one of the vertical bars on the edge, and ran along the outside. When it was going well, I hopped on. Eddy, Darrel, and Butch joined us.

"Violet, are you going to help push?" Cathy said, disgust in her voice.

I grinned, jumped off, and pushed, then hopped back on again. The wind felt good blowing my hair from my face.

The boys climbed into the middle of the

merry-go-round themselves on the crossbars, the way we were forbidden to do.

"Violet, you want to go over and get some apples off of the trees?" Eddy yelled.

"No," I said and grinned impishly at him. It was nice to have so many boys after me all the time, even if some of them were too young. Eddy was only in the second grade after all.

Eddy jumped off and waited until I came around to him. "I love you," he screamed as I whipped by.

Shocked and angry I leaped from the spinning horizontal wheel. How dare he say it so loud that everyone could hear? Things like that were private. Without another thought I walked over and kicked him hard in the butt.

When my anger with Eddy subsided, I was embarrassed and humiliated at my behavior. Eddy never forgave me. Even in high school he would not talk to me and I was too stubborn to apologize. Over the years each time I became angry I recalled this event and remembered the words of our minister. He said anger was related to evil and sin.

Seated with my husband on the edge of the dunes, I considered his words of a few minutes before and knew I would not force a discussion. My emotions were too raw to tolerate any negative input. Better to face everything alone than risk further rejection.

A chill crept up my spine, and the ache called loneliness grew.

Chapter Five

"It says here that he killed 301 slugs in one day," I said, examining the note pad on the wooden table in the center of Ken's bedroom.

Dennis Conway, a bearded investigator from the public defender's office, joined me in the center of the attic of the old farmhouse. "That's a strange thing to write down. Is there a date?"

"March first, three days before he killed those people."

"Look, here are more notes," he said, picking up another pad. "This one states that he sent for a book on abnormal psychology. Just a week before the killings."

"He asked me for the name of it. It's a later edition of the one I read in college."

Scanning the room I saw several book cases and counted nearly twenty psychology books.

Numerous times since I started college six years before, Ken had requested information on the names of psychology books I studied. His interest seemed to match my own, and I was glad. I hoped to use that interest as a bridge to get closer to him. That hope failed. After reading the texts he became convinced that a person's personality was determined by body shape.

"Exactly what are we looking for?" I said.

"I'm not sure . . . anything that would hint as to your brother's state of mind," he said, seating himself at the table and examining a stack of notes.

A king-sized bed with no headboard was shoved up against the wall in one corner. Along another wall stood two bookcases with their contents neatly aligned. Several dozen record albums leaned against the wall in an alcove at the other end of the room next to the stereo. The albums included a large selection of classical music and one of whales singing that he played for me a few months before. Fishing poles, guns and shells, disassembled radios, and boxes of tubes and circuitry filled the spaces under the sloping roof.

Pausing in front of the dresser Ken made in high school, I fumbled through the contents of the drawers. "I think I've found something. Looks like a journal," I said and handed Dennis a green binder.

"He says here that some of the people he worked with were out to get him," Dennis said. Slipping the newest find into his briefcase with the other notes, he continued the search.

"Maurice, one of the men Ken killed, worked for the same company," I said.

I've got to get out of here. The place is choking me. I've got to get out of here.

Walking down the stairs, my panic mostly undercover, I found Daddy in the dining room rummaging through an old buffet. "Have you found anything?"

"No," he said in almost a whisper. "I just don't feel right looking through Ken's things."

"Me either, but we may find something that will help. Where's Momma?"

"She got too upset and went to the car. Being here brings back the awful memories . . ." Tears coated his eyes.

"Why don't you go home now, Daddy," I said and

squeezed his thin arm. "Dennis and I will manage. If we need anything we'll call."

"Alright, if you're sure it's okay. I think . . . we will, Vi," he said, gently touching my shoulder with calloused fingers, then heading out the doorway.

"I'll be over after I finish here."

The wind slipped through my loose-knit sweater. Shivering, I stood on the wooden porch and watched them drive up the graveled road. Involuntarily my eyes focused on the house across the street; a carpet-cleaning truck was parked in front.

Blood's splattered all over that house. All over it. I can't stand to be here any longer.

Slamming the door after me I met Dennis at the base of the stairs. He handed me his latest discovery. "This note says that the McCalls were destroying his family."

We searched for several more hours, my mind and emotions at war. At five Dennis stopped, and we agreed to meet back at the house the following morning at nine. After he had gone, I closed the gate, glancing again at the house across the street. A piece of plywood now covered the window, the window through which Ken killed them.

The house stood raped and forsaken.

I thought of our coming meeting with Dennis's boss, Kevin McDonald, on Friday, a few days away.

Kevin was the husband of a woman I had worked with at Children's Services Division, my last employer. When I first started working there he had defended a couple accused of murdering a little girl. The guy had gone to jail. I could not remember what happened to the woman.

Friday evening seemed darker than any Friday I could ever remember. The furnace blasted newly found heat in an attempt to warm the rooms. It was more efficient than the wood stove that used to sit in the kitchen.

Yellow-orange flames had been visible through the split seams on that old cast-iron thing.

Dave, Momma, Daddy, and I huddled at the dining room table waiting for Kevin McDonald, the public defender, to finish with small talk. Distinguished, yet friendly in his gabardine slacks and business shirt, he finally opened his briefcase and removed a blank pad.

"Can you tell me a little about Ken as a child, Mrs. Andre," he asked, thoughtfully scratching his beard, a kind, yet businesslike tone to his voice.

"Mostly he was quiet, kept to himself," Momma said as she braced her sturdy elbows on the table. "He liked to do things alone, like hunting and fishing. Of course he did boss Denise around and they got into fights, like most kids do."

"Did he have many friends?"

"A few, but he was shy, like me. I hurt for him and wanted to help him get over it. I just didn't know how," she said, her eyes sober. Momma pulled her white cardigan sweater down as far as she could over her knit slacks and self-consciously stared at the table.

"Did he ever outgrow the shyness?"

"No. In fact I think he got worse, don't you, Lee?" Daddy nodded.

"Of course, I don't know about the three years he spent in the army, especially the time in Korea," Momma said, gripping her hands as though they would get away if she did not.

"Mrs. Andre, I don't want you to think I'm interrogating you. I'm just trying to get at any information that might help explain Ken's behavior.

"Violet, can you tell me anything pertinent to your brother's mental state?"

"Did you talk to your investigator about what we found in the house the other day, all those weird notes, the journal, and the psychology books? I only glanced at them."

"Yes. I haven't had a chance to look at them, but I will in the next couple of days. Focus on other things you think might be unusual," McDonald said.

"One thing is his compulsion for cleanliness," I said. I read about it in psychology class in college. It was a symptom of schizophrenia, I remembered suddenly. "When we were kids if anyone touched his plate while he was eating, he'd take it over to the sink and wash the spot. I used to think it was dumb, as little sisters do. Anyway, he's still that way."

"Anything else?"

"He's a perfectionist and seems to think other people are stupid," I said. The inner feeling that I could not tolerate what was happening returned. I managed to suppress it.

Dave squeezed my fingers to reassure me.

"Mr. Andre, I'm interested in Ken's marksmanship. Did you teach him to shoot?"

"Yes. See, we're a hunting family. When Betty and I were first married and Denise and Ken were little shavers, I hunted to provide meat for the family. There would have been many hungry times if I hadn't brought in venison. Ken picked up my love for hunting, and when he was old enough I bought him a rifle. He took right to it," Daddy said. Then his face sagged and he stared out the window.

Over the next two hours Mom and Dad talked of Ken as a child, his hobbies, like collecting stamps, building model airplanes, photography, electronics, and the trapping of fur-bearing animals to make money when he was a teenager.

The meeting left us exhausted, and we were glad for the refuge of our beds that night.

The following morning after breakfast Dave peeked through the doorway to the kitchen. Water dripped from his curly wet hair; the towel wrapped around his waist almost did not meet. For a moment he watched me scrubbing berry stains from the kitchen counter.

"You aren't going to see Ken again today, are you?" he asked.

"Yes."

"He'll survive if you don't make it this one time."

"How'd you like to be stuck in that jail with no visitors?"

"He's only got himself to blame."

"Maybe, but I have to let him know I love him in spite of everything. He's my brother. You don't stop loving your brother."

"You going to visit him tomorrow too?"

"Yes, after I go to church with Momma. She wants to go and it's the least I can do for her. Denise is coming back down tonight so she can go too."

"Oh, for Pete's sake!" Dave said, as he stomped down the hallway to the bedroom and swore at the closet door that had come off its track again.

Through the streaked kitchen window I could see the barren alder trees along the creek below. There was no wind, no rain, no sunshine, only a stifling stillness.

The visit with Ken went much like the one on the previous Sunday. When it was over my parents and I ate lunch in town. They returned home. I stopped to see my friend Brenda. We had known each other for twenty-five years. Her brothers and sister had attended the grade school with mine when it was still a two-classroom structure. Brenda and I started school together in the new building.

She made us each a cup of tea, and we pushed back in the orange easy chairs next to the cold ashes in the painted brick fireplace. "I feel utterly lost," I said.

"I understand that kind of desperation." She stared at the house across the street, yet at nothing.

"Oh?"

"Remember when John left me for his eighteen-year-old cutesy-pie student?" she said and brushed her thick chestnut hair from her temples. Her hair had been cropped short even since I could remember. She colored it now to cover premature gray.

"Yeah."

"Well, I tried to kill myself. I figured there was nothing left. It was like I was in a trance or something."

"Brenda, how awful!"

She nodded, "I took Carla and Brandy over to my brother's house with enough clothes for the night, came back here, locked the doors, took the telephone off the hook, and got out the razor blade. Even iced the skin to numb it, then carved the blade across my wrist. The blade wasn't very sharp, but it was the only one I had; so I sawed back and forth."

"Didn't it hurt terribly?"

"I suppose. I really don't remember. Anyway, I finally broke the skin, cut the veins and the blood trickled down my arm. To hurry it up I held my wrist under the bathroom faucet. After a while I felt faint and wondered how long it was going to take to bleed to death.

"I took my arm out from under the faucet and examined the cut, and the blood began to clot. I was angry, really angry. I couldn't even kill myself right. But I was determined, so I picked up the blade to cut myself again.

"It was then that I heard the knocking on the door. I didn't answer it, just continued to saw at my wrist and hoped they would go away. Instead I heard a key turning in the lock, then two voices coming from the kitchen. My father and brother rushed in and grabbed the blade from me. They took me to the hospital and the doctors stitched up my arm."

"I had no idea."

"I'm only telling you now, so you'll realize I understand Ken. He was desperate and alone. All that mattered was gone. Somehow he believed those people were at fault, so he killed them. The difference between Ken and me is that I turned the desperation on myself. Women usually do."

"But you said you knew Doris Bennett. You don't hate Ken?"

"No. I'm sorry it had to be Doris. I'm sorry Ken couldn't reach out for help instead. But the fact remains that I do understand hopelessness," she said. Her voice sounded oddly detached and her eyes looked empty, dead.

Chapter Six

"'Does Jesus care, when my heart is pained too deeply for mirth and song . . .'"

The vestibule outside the auditorium resonated with tones of an organ and the semifervent voices of the congregation. Peeking though the small window in the heavy wooden door, I took a deep breath and surveyed the church.

Momma was not ready to talk to anyone, she said. It was still too difficult to face questioning eyes; so we arrived late. I eased open the door and walked directly in front of her. Denise protected her from the rear. We slipped in front of a pew close to the back and took out our hymnals.

" 'As the burdens press and the cares distress, and the way grows weary and long.'"

It was a song I had sung many times as a child. It meant little then, but of course life had been safe and full of love. Now it was different, now I was weary with no way to rest. Feeling ready to collapse, my legs close to buckling, I gripped the pew in front of me and listened, but I could not sing.

" 'Oh, yes, He cares. I know He cares. His heart is

touched with my grief. When the days are weary, the long nights dreary, I know my Savior cares.' "

The congregation rustled to stillness, I dared a glance at my mother and sister. They looked as miserable as I felt.

" 'We are pressed on every side by troubles, but not crushed and broken,' " Pastor Young began. " 'We are perplexed because we don't know why things happen as they do, but we don't give up and quit. We are hunted down, but God never abandons us. We get knocked down, but we get up again and keep on going."

"I chose this particular passage from the fourth chapter of II Corinthians because I know that some of us are experiencing pain beyond comprehension. We may wonder why, where God is in all this? Is He dead?"

The bearded minister kicked the microphone cord from beneath his feet, stepped from the stage, and started slowly down the isle. His demeanor was that of a friend giving a speech, rather than that of an authority figure dictating rules.

"I too have wondered these things during the crises of my life. I too have wondered where God was during my pain. What I want to say to you now is this: God is here. He is with each one of us right now. He is as real as you and I. He knows your pain and He will help you through it, if you give Him a chance."

I sighed heavily. It was difficult to have faith after all that had happened.

"When you think God is farthest from you, when your pain is so deep that it clouds your heart, remember this," the minister said, "that's when He's closest. All you need do is tear down the barriers and you will find Him standing there waiting to help you."

After a lengthy sermon the congregation rose to sing the final hymn. Abruptly Denise and Momma moved down

the aisle and out the door. Startled, I hurried behind
them.

"Thank you for coming with me, girls," Momma
whispered once we were safely inside the car. "It really
helped. I just wish your dad would come."

"He believes, Momma," I said. "He finds other
ways to worship. Church just isn't right for him."

I thought of when Ken and Teresa married. Momma
had invited Teresa to attend church with us. She came
only a few times. Of course Ken objected; he wanted her
at home with him. Teresa did not want to upset him.

Two days after the church service Ken's home
reeked of 409 cleaner and soaking dirt. Oozing droplets
of grease and cleaner hung from the turquoise ceiling.
Denise stood on the ladder in the corner of the kitchen
with a rag in one hand and the spray bottle in the other.

"I just can't believe all this grease," she said. "She
probably hasn't cleaned it since they moved here eight
years ago."

"It must have driven Ken nuts."

"That's probably why she did it."

I took a knife and scraped the ridge of grease and
dirt from the floor where the stove had been. Then I
squeezed a sponge mop against the linoleum and covered the hardened dirt with a large puddle of Lysol water. Bits of the yellow flooring crumbled off into the water as I started to scrub.

"If it weren't for Ken, and the fact that this is his
house too, I wouldn't be cleaning up someone else's
mess," my sister mumbled.

"I know, but you have to remember Teresa was
pretty upset when she was here."

"Think anyone will want to rent it after what Ken
did?"

"I suppose. Most people won't even know this is the
neighborhood where someone was killed," I said.

"Is Teresa planning to sell it?"

"Yes. This thing with Ken will have to be settled first, though. I talked with her brother, Rich. He's the one who came up with her sister and brother-in-law to help her move."

"Did you ask about Loni and Russ? I've been worried sick about those kids ever since this thing happened."

"Rich said they seem okay. Russ has started going to church. That's probably good. Maybe it'll give him some stability right now. Teresa sure can't give him any. She's been a mess, I guess. Loni's been really scared since it happened, has to sleep with the light on."

"I worry about her most," Denise said.

"It's been over two weeks and I still can't believe it," Denise said. We both began crying whenever we talked of it.

"I know. Even with visiting Ken in jail, seeing Teresa move out and the boards over the windows across the street. How's Ted taking it?"

"He just can't forgive him. He thinks I should write Ken off. I'm not sure how I feel, so we just don't talk about it. Otherwise we get into fights." Denise wiped her face with the back of her hand. She balanced herself precariously and stretched to scrub the corner.

"Dave won't talk either. He's coming up this afternoon after work to help us, though."

She and I continued to clean in silence. In the bedroom upstairs Momma, Daddy, and Denise's daughter, Billie, sorted through Ken's things.

"I guess Mom and Dad plan to take Ken's things over to the house with them today," Denise said finally.

"I hate the thought of the stuff sitting around their house," I said. "It'll remind them of the crime Ken committed, but I don't want to move it around with me. Dave has applied for jobs in other parts of the state, so as soon as he finds something we'll be moving."

"I sure can't keep it. Ted would have a fit."

Footsteps came down the stairs. Daddy stopped in the doorway and said, "Your momma is getting pretty upset; so I'm going to take her home. We've packed most of Ken's books and personal things. One of Teresa's friends is coming by tomorrow. He'll haul all the rest of it to the dump. We'll finish up tomorrow."

A look through the house told me we needed to come back another day to clean as well. I dreaded it. The house carried negative energy, like the ghost of murder. Tentacles reached out from every room, ripping at the fibers that held me together.

Afternoon passed, then evening. Home finally by eight, I dialed Kevin McDonald, the public defender, at home. I had left several messages at his office, but he had not called.

He and his wife lived in a small house not far from my parents. Dave and I had attended a party there a few Christmases before. It had been the cocktail kind. No one really knew anyone, nor could care what they thought about anything.

"I would like to know what's happening with my brother's case," I said, untwisting the telephone cord and raising myself to the kitchen counter.

"There's not much I can tell you. I'm sending Ken up to the state hospital for evaluation and to a couple of other psychologists. I can't give you a definite schedule," he said. His tone seemed antagonistic.

"All I'd really like to know is a little about the procedure in cases like this—"

"You and your family will just have to sit tight," he said, and the phone clicked dead.

Trapped within the legal structure, yet helpless to do anything to change the events that followed, my family and I did only the necessary things to get by day to day.

A short while later Dave received a letter from the Bureau of Land Management in Salem, the state's capital.

"Anything interesting?" I squeezed up behind him and peered around his shoulder at the letter. The kitchen light was dim; two of the three bulbs were out.

"I've been invited to interview for a job as a fisheries biologist. It's stream surveying—counting various populations of fish. Just my thing. It sounds terrific." For a moment his face reflected an excitement that had been missing for too long. Then his face fell. "But what do you think? With the mess your family is in and all, I can't see leaving them now."

He sat down at the dining room table and reread the letter and job description. I shuffled to the window and stared out at the paint peeling off the boards in the deck.

The job he currently held wasted his talents. He was a biologist. He might not have another opportunity. There were so few biology jobs available.

"Look, regardless of everything else, I think you should try for it. I'd like to live next to a larger city again, and I might be accepted into that graduate program at Portland State University anyway."

He twirled me around the living room nearly crushing my ribs. His eyes sparkled like a man in love. "Thanks."

I thought of my parents, of leaving them now, and wilted.

Early the next morning the phone shocked me out of the deadening mist of sleep. I groaned, and rolled over until my feet touched the floor.

"Who could be calling this early on a Sunday?" Dave asked. He twisted his face into the thick feather pillow and scrunched his eyelids shut. I stubbed my way into the kitchen and moments later wiggled back into the blankets.

"Who was it?"

"Momma. She wondered if I planned to visit Ken

today. I was going to write to him instead, but I guess I'll
go, since they'd want me to."

Dave turned over, plopped his arms on the outside
of the covers, and moaned. "That ruins the whole day."

"Did you have something planned?"

"No, but I thought we might go for a walk across
the dunes or something."

"We can go when I get back. If I make sure we are
in the first group of visitors I could be back by 1:30."

"You know that won't work. It would be dark before
we got back to the car," he said. "And I for one don't
want to wander around the dunes in the dark. Why don't
you just write Ken off? You can't do anything for him
anyway. He got himself into this mess. Let him get himself out!"

"What about Momma and Daddy? I suppose I
should write them off too." I jumped from bed and
headed for the shower.

"You can't shelter them forever," he said disgust-
edly.

My parents and I visited Ken, then headed to the
Dairy Queen for lunch. As I sat across from them in the
uncomfortable booth, my stomach was knotted and
grinding.

"Um . . . there's something I need to tell you," I
said.

"What is it, Vi?" Daddy said. His eyes were sad. He
stared beyond me and absently watched the traffic.

"It's Dave. He has a job possibility up north." I told
them about his interview the next day and watched their
eyes express new grief.

"Now, Violet, you must go where your husband
goes. Don't worry about us. We'll be alright," Momma
said. She stared down into a salad, dipped and twisted
her fork into the wilted lettuce.

"I'm really sorry." I pushed away the half-eaten
hamburger.

"It's okay, Vi," Daddy said, caressing my hair with a loving hand. "It's okay."

I've betrayed them. The kindest, most special people in the world, and I've betrayed them.

"You can come down when we need you," Momma said. Her face muscles sagged. She looked as if she would cry.

"Sure, Vi," Daddy said. "Don't worry about us. We'll manage."

Depression at my newest failure accompanied me home from lunch. Not only had I just broken my parents' hearts again, but now I had to face my husband and his anger.

Wind bent the trees, and bushes next to the house scraped the shake siding. Unlocking the door I pushed my way into the house with Brandy, the Lab puppy I had rescued from the pound a week before, prancing ahead of me.

There was no note from Dave . . . and no sign of Brutus. In search of them the pup and I headed outside into the sun and down the stairs to the dock. Water rippled by carrying twigs and reeds. I shivered and grabbed Brandy, made the loop through the orchard, up the path under the canopy of madrone and alder, and back to the house.

Seating myself on the rug in front of the cold fireplace I rolled Brandy over on his back and tickled him, lowered my head, and wiggled it on his tummy and tousled his little head. He rolled back over, wagged his tail, and barked.

The back door slammed open and tension shot through my muscles.

"Come on in, Brutus," Dave said.

Brandy ran to investigate and returned with Brutus close behind; the two dogs had become buddies already. Dave shuffled to the dining room and set a box on the table.

"Well, do you want any or do you want Brutus to eat it all?" he said, a little-boy grin on his face. He slipped the pizza from its container and poured two glasses of wine.

I smiled uncertainly and stood with my hands behind my back, like a child waiting for punishment.

"Come here."

Slowly I went toward him. He caught me and smacked a wet kiss on my lips. I could feel the rough wool of his plaid hunting jacket through my blouse.

"I'm sorry about this morning," he said, loosening his hold just enough to look at me with his large eyes, the eyes that I so adored. "I know this must be hard for you, trying to please all of us. Sometimes I just don't think. Forgive me?"

How could I not?

Monday morning came too soon, and I waited with apprehension as Dave packed for his trip to Salem. I walked him to the car and stiffened my limbs to stop shaking.

"Are you sure you'll be alright here by yourself?" he asked, leaning out the window of his Camaro.

"Yeah."

No tears . . . not 'til he's gone.

"Maybe you should spend the night with your folks."

"I'll make it by myself. Besides, I have Brutus. He'll let me know if anyone is around."

He pulled me halfway into the car and kissed me. "I love you," he said. Again the eyes . . . soft the way they were when we fell in love.

"Good luck with the interview," I said as he pulled away. Shivering, I watched the car vanish out the top of the driveway. Rain dripping from the trees echoed through the quiet and I hurried back inside. The house seemed haunted and empty.

I stripped and stepped into the shower, lathered and

scrubbed, and tried to rid myself of the fear. I spent the day with my parents.

When I returned home late, it was dark. I aimed the headlights at the door knob and unlocked the door. Before losing my nerve I hurried to the garage and rescued Brandy.

"Brutus? . . . Brutus?"

Shadows gathered and the fir on the hill behind the garage groaned in the wind. Shivering, I grabbed Brandy from the wet grass and entered the house, then checked the locks and closed the drapes.

Answering the scratch at the back door, I opened it to Brutus. "You big horse, where have you been?" I said and hugged him. "Thank God you're finally here."

Putting on the water for tea, I glanced out the window over the sink, at the blackness beyond the glass. Fear shot up my back. I grabbed the free end of the makeshift curtain and pushed the thumbtack through the fabric into the wooden frame. Next I hurried through the house and turned on all the lights.

Settling on the couch I wrapped my feet in the afghan and stared at the television. The back of the couch faced the hallway. I darted frantic glances behind me.

Hands could grasp my neck—large, brutal hands. I hurried from the couch to the corner rocking chair. Someone could see my shadow and shoot me through the windows just inches away.

Brutus slept in the corner of the room, Brandy on my feet. Suddenly Brutus charged to the window by the television, his toenails clicking on the tile along the edge of the rug. He began barking insistently.

He never barked at nothing. Someone had to be out there waiting to break through.

Brutus's barks became rumbling growls; he took his place beside me and fell asleep. Uneasily I watched the late movie and when it was over turned off the television.

"Brandy, Brutus, come here."

Brutus moaned but did not budge. I deposited Brandy in the yard and stood in the doorway waiting for him to relieve himself. Instead he scampered about, stopped several feet away, and stood staring up at me. I searched the perimeter of the light and swallowed hard; my legs were jelly.

"Hurry up, Brandy. I'm not going to wait all night."

We went back into the house, and after checking the locks again, I turned off all the lights except the one in the hall and climbed into bed.

Shadows shimmered beyond the drapes.

Chapter Seven

One last time I pulled the drapes aside and stared at the creek, swollen again by yesterday's rain. Thick, sagging clouds hid the tops of leafing alders.

"Well, what do you think?" Dave said and joined me in front of the plate of glass. "It's been a nice place to live, hasn't it?"

"Best place ever."

I would miss it, miss watching the storms whisk in from the ocean, miss the sometimes churning, sometimes quiet creek. Miss the gentle days when we first moved in when we wrestled, played, and loved in front of the fireplace. Batches of chocolate chip cookie batter, mixed up and eaten, but never cooked. The two of us and Brutus cuddled in front of the television.

Now the house was scrubbed and barren.

There was a knock. Dave rounded the partition and opened the door.

"Betty, Lee, come on in," he said, and the three of them joined me in the living room.

"We thought we'd see you off," Daddy said. His hair was neatly combed with only two rebellious waves popping up. His favorite burgundy windbreaker hung unfastened. Peeking from behind a Sunday shirt was the top of his long johns, which he wore even in warm weather.

Momma nudged up next to him. Her eyes looked pinched; her face was brightened only by the pink-flowered dress Daddy had given her for her last birthday.

"I'm so glad you came," I said. "It's been good living close to you. We'll miss the Friday night dinners. I'm sorry we have to leave," I said. I hugged my father, crooking my head against the curve of his neck.

"I'm sorry too," Momma said. Tears fell from her eyes as I hugged her.

"Ah, come on, you guys, let's not get mushy," Dave said. But I knew he would miss them too. Somehow he felt closer to my parents than his own. "We'll be back before you know it. Well, Violet, do you have everything?"

"I guess."

"Then let's get going. I hate to cut this visit short, but I think you understand. I start my new job tomorrow and we have a long drive."

The chilled air cut through my coat as I stepped out onto the concrete. I hugged my parents again and climbed into the car. Dave pulled ahead of me in the U-Haul truck.

In the rearview mirror I could see Momma and Daddy waving goodbye, forlorn and abandoned, silhouetted against the vacant house.

The drive was long and tiring. Finally we arrived at the house we'd rented. Moving always made me feel disrupted, as if everything was wrong. Each task was completed because it had to be, not for the joy in it. The following morning after Dave left for his new job, I scrubbed the floors and the bathroom fixtures, harder than I had to; the sting of disinfectant made my hands throb.

When finished I unpacked the sheets and towels, filling the linen closet. Moving from room to room unpacking and cleaning a house owned by a stranger, I felt a desolation creep in on me.

Lord, help me through this.

The clock on the bedroom dresser ticked loudly, and a car nearby ground to a start and faded off down the street. In the backyard Brandy and Brutus scuffled against the wooden fence. But I was alone. Waiting.

Sinking to the floor I lowered my head to my knees and tried to cry, but there were no tears, only hollowness. Minutes passed, long minutes. I glanced about the room searching for evidence of God.

In movies there was always a light shining in through the window or music in sacred tones. Here there was nothing, no sign, no special clues that God lived.

God was my last hope, and the way it looked He either did not exist or did not care. Making it through the events resulting from the murders and a move at an intolerable time appeared impossible without help. No help emanated from any source.

Ken had messed up everything. I wanted to help him, yet in some ways I no longer cared. There was no way to understand him. Besides, I did not want to understand; I was tired of understanding. I had spent my whole life trying to understand everybody and everything. I was sick of it.

For the first time in weeks I allowed myself to consider my own goals. I had been planning to go back to school. I decided to take some action on my plan.

The next day I rode my bicycle to the shopping mall on the east side of Salem and went to a group of phones not far from the entrance. Our phone had yet to be installed.

"Hello, this is Violet Andre. Could you tell me if the selections have been made for the Counselor Education Program."

"Uh, yes, here it is. . . . Your name is on the list."

"I've been accepted?" I said, excitedly.

"Yes," the secretary replied, a smile in her voice. "You should have been notified weeks ago. In fact, I remember the director stating how delighted she was to be adding a person with your academic excellence to the program. You need to talk to an advisor about your schedule. You start your master's program summer term."

"Fantastic!" I hung up, hugged myself, and twirled around in the center of the mall, not caring who saw me.

For the first time since Ken's crime my spirits lifted. Peddling back home I felt a breeze cascading across my back. April kissed the land. Fruit trees were in flower and the other deciduous trees were leafing out. The northern Willamette Valley with its freshly plowed fields was rich with beauty and fragrance of a reborn earth.

Unused to repetitious pumping, my legs cramped after only a few miles on flat land. With renewed determination I lowered my body and peddled on. A sudden wind gusted from the west and a thundercrash brought a deluge of rain. It felt cleansing, invigorating.

My excitement soon evaporated in daily reality, however. Graduate school was over two months away. In the meantime I had nothing to do but wait each day for Dave to get off work and to think of Ken and my poor family.

On a day in late April my family and I met in Eugene at the office of one professional woman, a psychologist.

"I wonder if it makes these business people feel important to keep us peons waiting," my sister whispered. She fidgeted in the straight-backed chair and crossed her arms on her large breasts. Irritation wrinkled her face.

"A forty-five-minute wait is ridiculous," I protested. Buttoning my blazer I strode to the receptionist's desk.

"Maybe we should reschedule when Dr. Hansen isn't so busy," I said.

"That won't be necessary," she answered, youth shining in her hazel eyes. She flipped her brown hair away from her face and beamed at me. "She assured me just a few minutes ago that she'll be right with you. There seems to have been complications with one of her cases."

After fifteen more minutes an attractive, somewhat pudgy woman in a blue-skirted suit opened the oak door. "Would you step this way, please?" she said.

We entered her office and sat down. The room was furnished with a love seat and a few easy chairs. A long, narrow window invited beams of light into the room.

I felt tense, and for several uncomfortable moments no one spoke. The psychologist appeared to ignore us.

Finally I said, "We're willing to answer whatever questions you have as openly as possible. We'd like you to know that—"

"Don't worry, Ms. Andre, I can handle this," Dr. Hansen announced. Her left eyebrow arched and sent wrinkles up her forehead. She leaned forward on her forearms and began tapping a pen. "I'll indicate the direction I want this interview to take . . . when I'm ready."

As if I was not there, she looked at Momma, who was seated beside Daddy on the love seat.

"Now, Mrs. Andre, I'll start with you. I want you to tell me about Ken as a child. I've compiled a list of questions, some for each of you. Many of them I developed following my interview with Ken yesterday."

"You saw Ken?" Momma asked. Her eyes brightened. She grasped a handkerchief, twisting at it.

"Yes, here in my office," the psychologist said. "Tell me about Ken as a baby, Mrs. Andre. Was he active?"

"I couldn't seem to keep him out of things. Once he

was walking I had to watch him all the time to make sure he stayed out of the creek."

"Was he aggressive? What I mean is, did he direct anger against other members of the family?"

"No more than seemed normal," Momma said.

"How about in school, was he rowdy or any problem?"

"No. In fact, his teachers commented how quiet and well-behaved he was," Momma said.

"Denise, do you remember Ken displaying hostility while you were growing up?"

"He and I fought some. Other than that, no. Of course there was that time that he and Ted got into a fight on the school bus. Ted smacked him in the face and knocked Ken backward over the seat. Both of them about got kicked off."

"Can you think of any events that may have had a significant impact on him as a child?"

"Herby, one of his friends, was hit and killed by a truck when Ken was in the sixth grade. It was a horrible accident. Ken was haunted by it," Momma said.

"Anything else," Dr. Hansen said in a tone almost human, "that may have affected Ken when he was little? Sometimes when traumatic events happen to us too young, we are unable to deal with them properly. So the reactions take other forms."

"There was one thing," Momma said. "Shortly after Herby died the school district sent the upper grades to town to school. The change was really hard on him. I remember when Ken returned home after the first day. He seemed to think all the kids in town were bad . . ."

Momma told the story with the softness of a mother. When she was finished she leaned on her husband.

"Do you think he stopped believing in God then?" the psychologist asked.

"I don't know," Momma said. "He continued to go to church with us for several more years. We never forced the kids to go. Mostly he just sat in church not saying much to anyone, although he did have one good friend there. In fact, he wants me to contact Larry's mother to see if Larry will write to him."

"Would you say that he was morally straight as a boy?"

"As far as I know," Daddy said, his voice quiet, as was his manner, leading one to believe he was at peace and in control. Only his haunted eyes gave him away.

"Do you think he accepted the rules presented in the Bible to guide his life?"

"I don't know," Daddy said.

"His grade school teacher, Mrs. Parker, told us that he always tried to be such a good boy," Momma said. "We went to this church that was really strict and the kids weren't allowed to dance. Mrs. Parker said that Kenny would not wind the maypole with the other kids. She said he thought it was wrong. Our involvement with that church was a twenty-year mistake."

"One time several years ago," I said, "he and I were talking about a person he worked with. The man was married and having an affair. Ken thought it was terrible. He said it was a sin to commit adultery."

"I just want to say on thing," Momma said. "He used to be such a good boy. He enjoyed the outdoors and would show me stories about the woods or the animals that lived there. He was such a joy. He had such beautiful thoughts."

"Mrs. Andre, your son is still a beautiful person, even with all that's happened. He shared some of that with me yesterday. Something went wrong to make him kill, but I don't know what it was. That's what I'm trying to discover."

"Do you think he could do it again?" I asked.

"I truly don't know. I have several more interviews scheduled, as well as some tests to give him. They may tell me more, but at this point I can't predict his future behavior."

I didn't know about my brother, but after we left I kept thinking of her words. My future behavior seemed permanently altered by Ken.

I parked in the structure across the street, met with my advisor, then made my way to the cafeteria in the student union building. Rochelle and I had agreed to meet there. I took a seat in a conspicuous spot.

The cushioned booth was comfortable, and I examined the outline for my master's program. Absorbed by the details, I missed Rochelle's approach.

"Have you been waiting long?" she said.

"About forty-five minutes."

"You won't believe what happened to me. I didn't realize the appointment with the attorney would take so long. Then I took the wrong turn on the freeway and ended up on the other side of town. I never learned my way around, even in all the years I've lived here."

"I figured I'd give you a few more minutes." She was prettier than I remembered. All those years ago she and her husband lived next door to me.

"I'm glad you're still here. It sure is good to see you." She smiled through blue-gray eyes; sun-blond curls encircled her shoulders. "I'd like you to attend the hearing with me," she said. Pain replaced the smile. "I think George is planning to try for custody of the kids. I'm really worried. Say you'll go."

"Unless something happens with Ken's case."

"You'll come, then?" she said.

How can I be strong for her as well as for my own family? I can barely make it now.

"Yes."

"It's been a nightmare ever since last fall. At least it's out in the open now," she said, staring down at the ice in her coke. Over a period of a half an hour she revealed the details of a disintegrating marriage, ending with an ugly scene that cemented the divorce. When finished she said, "It's helped so much to talk to you. Say, are you all right?"

"No," I said. "While you were talking I was thinking about my own marital problems. The loneliness and desolation I feel hurts, but they aren't half as bad as this thing with Ken. I've lost my trust in people and any illusion of good, and I'm frightened. It's destroyed my trust not just in one person but in everything."

"Oh gee, Vi, I've got to pick up the kids and I'm late already," Rochelle exclaimed as she eyed her watch. "We can talk another time. Oh, by the way, I've decided to apply to the graduate program you're in. Isn't that neat? Let's meet again real soon." I watched her hurry away.

The crystalline weather during the next few weeks did nothing to improve my mood. If anything the nice weather punctuated my misery.

The Oregon coast in June often brought anything but nice weather. After nine months of rain the locals grumbled at the gray days, and schoolchildren angrily looked out windows at drizzle on the first days of vacation.

June brought me back home to days and walls of gray, inside and out.

"You first, Violet. Ken hasn't seen you for a while," Momma said. She nodded me toward the seat in front of the window in the holding facility where Ken had been transferred.

I sat on the stool and picked up the receiver, trying to think of something to say.

"Do you hear them?" Ken asked.

"Hear what?"

"The voices," he said, and his eyes darted about the concrete cubicle. "Maybe you can't hear them out there. I heard them in my cell this morning. The guards are

trying to get to me, but they won't because I know where
the voices are coming from. The attorney working on my
case, my ex-boss, and the governor are all in cahoots
against me."

"What makes you say that?"

"It's pretty obvious," he said. "They all want to get
rid of me. That's why they had Maurice McCall bug me.
They thought I'd quit my job, but I wouldn't!" He leaned
closer and whispered, "The governor didn't like the way
I voted in the last election, so he wanted me out of the
way. Well, I may be in here now, but they can't get me. I
heard the district attorney and my lawyer plotting
against me over the radio. That's why I stay awake a lot
and listen to everything that goes on around here."

I looked at my brother sadly as he told me of imagined plots and fabricated intrigue. While I listened I examined my memories of him, trying to find something I
had missed, something that should have warned us his
mind had deteriorated this far. I found little.

Monday, the next day, arrived in a misty fog and
with it the dreaded meeting with the detectives. Momma
and I waited anxiously in the reception area outside
Clyde Thompson's office. Clyde, Daddy, and the two officers we talked with after the shootings had disappeared
down the hall forty-five minutes before.

Momma sat forward on the brown marshmallow
couch and twisted the handle on her purse. "What could
be taking them so long?" she said.

"I suppose they have to go over the details of the
incident several times to make sure they get it right."

"I hope your dad's alright."

"He'll be okay, Momma. Mr. Thompson will keep
things from getting out of hand."

"Thanks for coming down to be with us. I couldn't
stand sitting here alone without you, Vi," she said lovingly.

"Anytime, Momma. I'll help you any way I can."

For me it was a case of "if only." If only Dave, Rochelle, or someone who claimed to love me cared enough to be there for me. I had attended Rochelle's divorce court proceedings and supported her when she needed me. Now I needed her and she could not make it. Nor could Dave or anyone else. The support I needed so badly never came.

A long forty minutes later Daddy scuffled down the hallway toward us, followed by Clyde Thompson. Daddy's eyes were fixed on something unseen.

"Would you please step this way, Mrs. Andre?" Thompson asked.

Momma untwisted her dress and glanced at me.

"Want me to come in with you, Momma?"

"Please," she whispered.

I held her arm and we headed into the office.

"Mrs. Andre," Sergeant Green began. He leaned back in the wooden armchair and smiled kindly at my mother. "I understand this is difficult for you, but we're just trying to get at the facts. Tell us what happened as closely as you can remember. Take all the time you want."

"It was awful, just awful," Momma said in a strained voice. She told the story in jumpy, emotion-laced words. "We'd gone up to be with Ken when he got off work, you know . . ."

Again the details were no different than those she revealed the first night. As she talked the sergeant scribbled on a long pad. Recalling the events, she became increasingly upset. When she reached the shootings, tears charged her voice.

"I just can't believe he did it. I mean, we were right across the road. We didn't know he had the gun . . ." She seemed so alone and in pain, a mother's worst fear realized, a son gone so terribly wrong.

When she finished, the sergeant wrote for several

more minutes. Momma clutched herself, her eyes glistening with leftover tears.

Finally the sergeant handed the sheets of paper to Momma. "Please read this over. If I've recorded your testimony correctly, we'll have it typed up and you can sign it."

Momma scanned the pages and handed them to Mr. Thompson. "I'm having a hard time concentrating. Would you please check it for me?"

"Certainly."

When the interview was over and the officers left, Daddy joined us in Clyde Thompson's office.

"I think it went well," Thompson said.

"You do?" Momma said.

"You both did just fine. Do you have any questions?"

"Do you know when the trial will be?" Daddy asked, looking at the attorney through the eyes of a weary old man.

Clyde Thompson uncinched his tie and placed his reading glasses in the case. With the words of a kindly businessman, he addressed the three of us.

"As a matter of fact I don't. You should keep in mind, however, that the longer it is between the shooting and the trial, the better chance Ken will have for leniency. In time as the horror subsides people forget and judge less harshly."

Chapter Eight

Summer painted the foothills of the Cascades, and little mountain flowers bloomed in ditches along the road close to evergreens. Forty miles north Mount Hood peaked above a treed ridge.

We had found a farmhouse some thirty-five miles southeast of Portland. Property was cheaper that distance from the city, so a house, an aging orchard, and forty acres were affordable. At last I had clean skies, the mountain tops, and solitude.

Backed up to the three-car garage, the orange and silver moving truck was half empty. Dave and I uncovered our queen-sized mattress and lugged it to the brick steps inside the garage next to the kitchen. My muscles were tired. I tried not to think of the aches.

"A little higher. You're not going to clear the steps," he said and readjusted his grip on the edge of the mattress.

"I'm trying," I retorted, heaved my shoulder into the awkward piece of furniture, and tried again.

"Well, it's not enough." He turned his blond head and glared at me.

"I'm doing my best."

"I don't think you're trying very hard."

I dug my fingers further into it and lifted again.

"Oh, good grief! let's trade ends. I know you can do it, if you really try. Now, do you think you can pick up the back so it won't drag on the steps?" he snapped. His eyes were hard and cold, like those of a stranger.

"I'll try." Anger did not color my voice, but then it never did. The angrier I got, the more polite I became.

Again I wrestled the mattress, this time placing one hand on the bottom and the other on the end. With a groan and an umph I managed to lift it just enough to clear the door jam. "See, once you try you can do quite a lot, can't you?"

"Did it ever occur to you that I'm just not as strong as you? That you weigh twice what I do and you're much stronger? I'm trying my best. How can you expect more?"

I followed him to the bedroom, dropped my end of the mattress inside the metal frame, and marched out. Back at the truck I carted box after box to the appropriate rooms. When the truck was unloaded, we drove to Salem and dropped it off at the rental agency. Tensely Dave climbed into my car.

Traffic lights and crossing pedestrians—I attended to them carefully and did not look at Dave. As we headed toward the country, we passed a young farmer wielding a rusty John Deere tractor down the side of the road, the plow raised so it would not scrape the uneven pavement.

Beside me Dave fidgeted. We had driven about a half a mile when he cleared his throat and hesitantly touched my shoulder.

"Uh, look, I'm sorry. I didn't mean that. I know you try hard. It's just that I think you can do better. And it's this terrible temper of mine. Will you forgive me?"

I angled over to the side of the road and noted the sorry-little-boy look on his face. I felt nothing, but I took his hands and kissed them. "It's okay," I said sighing.

Sometimes I thought acting should be a prerequisite for marriage.

The summer term at Portland State University started the next day, the day after moving day. I donned my jeans, tee shirt, and a jacket, because it was cloudy, and made my way into Portland, a drive that took about an hour. The campus was less crowded than fall term. I found a six-hour parking meter and hiked the seven blocks to Lincoln Hall.

Stopping at the vending machines, I picked up a diet coke, located the classroom, and settled into a desk next to the window.

Other students meandered in. I worried what they would think of me when I told them about Ken, or if I would tell them.

Rochelle arrived a couple of minutes before class began and claimed the seat I had saved. The professor thumbed through his notes. More students hurried in, looking dazed, or confused . . . or perhaps like me they were thinking, what am I doing here?

I leaned across the isle and whispered to Rochelle, "Not bad, huh?"

She smiled and followed my gaze to the professor. "Look at that body," she sighed. "Looks like he works out, a lot." I looked at him more closely: he was about six-foot-two with thick black hair and green eyes. Indeed he was good-looking. I hadn't noticed.

"It's a warm day," the professor began, "and I know many of you would rather be out playing golf or sailing. But since you're here, I'm afraid you're stuck with me. My name is Aaron Roland. I'm the instructor for Fundamentals of Therapeutic Confrontation. If you're in the wrong room, now is your chance to escape.

"Please call me Aaron, as I believe we're all adults . . . well, maybe some of us anyway." He grinned and twinkles broke across his face, starting with his green eyes.

"Since this is only a four-week class, we need to get started on the material as soon as possible. First I'll outline the requirements, then begin an open lecture–discussion. I want as much input from you as possible, since I'm sure you have a great deal of cumulative experience."

Poised ready to take rapid notes, I tried to concentrate on the lecture.

After nearly an hour and a half he dismissed us, stating we could use the extra half hour to get supplies and finish registration.

"Well, what did you think?" Rochelle asked, when we headed down the dim hallway toward the doors next to the stairs.

"I've never been much interested in theory classes, but the professor's nice to look at," I said, smiling.

"Did you see the way his arms and chest muscles stretched out that shirt. He probably knows he looks like a god. Do you know where the next class is?

"Right upstairs."

"Good. I never have time to check those things out."

"You don't have to worry this term. I can take care of you," I smiled again.

After a cup of tea in the lounge the two of us found the next class.

"It's the same professor," Rochelle whispered when we entered the room.

"Just think, we can stare at him for four hours a day, four times a week," I retorted, mischievously. I placed my shoes flat on the floor, felt the boards of the desk pressing against my aching muscles, and listened carefully for two more hours.

"I think the second class is really going to be interesting," Rochelle commented as we left.

"Yeah. A class on intimacy is just what I need right now. I've been feeling so isolated. I'm so glad we have this time together, Roch. I really need to talk about what's been happening to me. Moving into an area where I don't know anyone is awful. I feel desperate."

"I really don't have time to talk today," she said. "I have several errands to do and I told the baby-sitter I wouldn't be late."

Over the next few days the situation changed little. Occasionally Rochelle and I spent a few minutes discussing my brother and my feelings, but she never seemed to have much time or interest in my problems.

At the beginning of the second week I arrived a few hours before class, searched the library for information for the two term papers, then made my way to the cafeteria.

The terraced room that housed the eating place was empty except for a half dozen Middle Eastern students seated next to the exit and a few others tucked in back corners. Light from the portholelike fixtures in the tiled ceiling dotted puddles of yellow in selected areas.

Ignoring an unexpected feeling of shyness I weaved passed numerous tables to a man seated on the far side next to the window.

"May I join you?" I hesitated at the edge of the table and smiled into his deep-brown eyes. He grinned and patted the seat next to him.

"Please do. I always like talking to a pretty lady."

"I enjoy being in class with you," I said and sat down.

"You add an element of fun."

"Why thank you, little lady," he said, John Wayne style, inflating his chest; his brown skin came alive with mock pride. "I'm so pleased that you consider me a desirable element."

I laughed.

"Your name is Violet, isn't it?"

"You even have a good memory."

"I make it my business to learn the names of the attractive ladies wherever I am."

"So tell me, Jim—see, I remember your name too— what brings you to school this summer. Are you a late bloomer?"

"It's a requirement. I'm a teacher turned principal, in charge of the junior high school in Mill City. Know where that is?"

"It's on the Santiam River out from Salem."

"I'm here for refresher courses. How about you?"

"Just started my master's program and I need—"

"I'll tell you about my need, if you'll tell me about yours," he said, his eyes mischievous.

"It's a deal."

"First you have to tell me why you seem so depressed in class sometimes, or is that none of my business?" His playful expression changed to one of concern.

"It's not very pleasant. In fact, it's quite shocking. Still want to hear about it?"

"Yes, and don't worry, at almost fifty I passed the point of being shocked years ago."

"You see—" I grimaced and stopped. How could I tell this man? What would he think of me? Did I care? Yes, I needed a friend, one who would be there to listen. . . . I had to take the chance.

"My brother killed some people."

"How did it happen?" he said. His voice expressed the quality of tenderness I had known only in my father.

"He shot them, four of his neighbors. My God, my brother did that . . ."

Renewed horror and visions of the murder scene as I imagined it recurred whenever I talked of it to anybody. An overwhelming shudder crept into where my soul lived. It was as though I had been catapulted into the pit and there was no way out.

"Do you mind telling me some of the details and who the people were?" He leaned forward.

When the story was complete, I deflated against the plastic chair, and I was cold and disconnected.

"It really hurts, doesn't it?" Bridging the gap of isolation and despair, his huge hands reached for mine and held them. "Your folks?"

"They're not well, and my being away doesn't help."

"Don't feel bad about that. If you were with them all the time the situation would constantly drain you. This is the best way, believe me," he said gently.

"You said the shooting took place outside of Dayton and one of the couples he shot was named Bennett?"

"Yes. Why?"

"I know Mr. Bennett's brother. He's a minister at Sweet Home. The kids from my school play basketball with kids from his youth group. I talked to him right after it happened. He was pretty shook up about it.

"Oh, Lord." My throat constricted.

"The world is getting smaller, isn't it?" he said. His voice had the quality of a sage steeped in all that was real.

"It's so hard, Jim. Sometimes I think the pain is interminable. I feel so bad for those people . . . so bad. If only there was something I could do."

"Remember, Violet, it was not your fault."

"I know, but I still wish there was some way I could make it easier for the victims' families. I've thought about visiting them to tell them how sorry I am, but I'm afraid I would make it worse."

"You said your parents are gentle people?"

I nodded, "It just shouldn't have happened to them. They say you reap what you sow, but they sowed nothing bad. They didn't deserve this. Daddy never mistreated us. He never even yelled at Momma. Ken couldn't have learned violence from him. And Momma stayed at home with us kids. Read us stories. Made us pancakes shaped like animals. We were well cared for. We didn't have much money, but love's the only thing that's important and we got plenty of that."

Jim focused on the ice in his cup and watched it twirl as he stirred it with a straw. Slowly he looked at me.

"I'm glad I met you," he said. "I'm glad to hear the story from the other side. It helps me understand. Thanks . . . for risking.

"Have you considered counseling? There's a counseling department here on campus."

"Yes," I said. "I went for one session. But the counselor was a student, like me. She wanted to tape the session. It made me freeze up. I felt like I was a laboratory rat."

"Have you thought of requesting someone else?"

"I don't have the strength for it. You know what I mean?"

"Yes. When my wife died I felt the same way. It's been five years now. She got sick with cancer. Within six months she was dead. Six months! Sometimes I still can't believe she's gone. We shared so many good things. She was such a gentle woman—" He choked on the words, pulled a handkerchief from his hip pocket and dabbed tears.

"How did you make it through it?"

"My kids really helped, especially the two older ones. They were nine and eleven, going on thirty. I would have been lost if they hadn't been there. I've never really gotten over her . . . so, I do understand."

For a special moment we were silent and I squeezed his hands.

The trip home was mellow. The peace of the afternoon quieted my turmoil. A stranger had reached out to me and offered the compassion no one else had.

When Dave got home he was angry.

"You're home more than I am," he snapped, looking

around. "The least you can do is to clean up around the place."

"What do you think I've been trying to do for the past two weeks?"

"Not much, as I see it." He flopped onto the bar stool on the other side of the counter and glared at me. Clenching my jaw, I fumbled with a package of hamburger and began forming the squishy meat into patties.

"Not much?" I mumbled, beginning to get angry. A small explosion began in my heart and I stared at the stranger before me.

"You could be doing more. You don't have to spend you time talking to strangers about things you ought not to."

Finally I erupted, "Oh, is that right! Look, I've gone to class. I've tried to do a little studying, but with all that needed to be done around here it's been difficult. I happened to be talking to someone who's suffered as much as I have. Even so I got home before you did."

"I don't see why you need to go to school anyway. It's not going to do you much good."

I shook my head. "I told you when we got married that I wanted to get my master's degree, and that's exactly what I am doing."

"You certainly don't need to waste time fooling around."

"I wasn't fooling around. And it was not a waste of time. I needed to talk and was fortunate to have made a friend who understood about Ken."

"I still don't know why you worry about him."

"When are you going to learn that I can't write off my brother just because he does something terrible. Ken's family. My memories include him. Somewhere along the way he got lost. I don't know why he ended up in this mess, but I plan to stick by him."

I forced my body to head for the door. As I entered the garage, Brandy and Brutus bounded toward me. The three of us crossed the lawn and climbed the hill to the pasture, where the tall grass of July touched my knees. I glanced back at the house. Dave was not following.

Slowing my steps I tromped across the uneven ground into the little valley and up the hill. Carefully selecting a dry spot, I seated myself under the larger of two maple trees that shaded the knoll. The evening sky was a delicious summer blue. Trees and small flowers were brightened by the fading sun.

The dogs flopped on either side and nuzzled me. I gathered them to me, stroked the tops of their heads, and tried not to think. Brandy wiggled closer and half climbed into my lap. He licked my hand; I hugged him to the ache inside my chest.

In the early summer days to follow I remained enmeshed in restless apathy. In spite of my difficulty with concentration and studying, the classes went well. Aaron was an entertaining teacher with an excellent ability to prod his students into an interactive learning process.

The third week of classes began with Aaron's lecture on various types of relationships and how they affect our lives. Seated before him in my favorite tee shirt and jeans, I pushed out the negative thoughts and listened. The metal tabs on my desk squeaked against the floor.

When it was time for the discussion period, he said, "I'm going to ask a bunch of questions and I want you to write down the first thing that comes to mind."

The class moaned, and seasoned students wiggled uncomfortably on the old seats.

"This is not a test," he said and grinned at us. "After you record the answers to the twenty questions, you'll break into small groups and I'll hand out the list of questions so you can discuss your answers."

Obediently I recorded each answer; once the questions were completed, the class divided and Aaron left the room. My group consisted of Rochelle and four others. I could hear Jim's laughter from the other side of the room. It made me feel safe.

"The first question was about love. We all know what that is, right?" said the petite Hispanic woman who assumed leadership. "What is the color of love?"

No one spoke, and the silence was uncomfortable.

"Ah come on, you guys. We can't be as bad as the kids we teach," she said.

"It's blue," said the slender fellow with intense gray eyes who was seated on the far side of the circle. "You know, like the song, 'Love is blue.' And I should know, I've been through enough marriages."

"How many?" I asked. "And what's your name?"

"Maurice. I've been married four times and in love more times than I can count. It's been painful, but fun." Twinkles lighted his face, and his eyes glistened with the vibrance of a survivor.

We laughed and relaxed, each of us slouching like old friends.

"Love is red, white, and blue. Like fireworks," Rochelle offered next. She removed her glasses and smiled at Maurice with the light of first attraction.

"I like your version better than mine. Maybe you and I could try it," Maurice said. Again he laughed. This time there was sincerity and interest in his artistic voice. Rochelle blushed.

"I've never really thought of love that way," said the group leader. "To me love is softer, more gentle, like a spring day. So I wrote love is yellow, like daffodils. My name is Tanya."

"A nice thought," I said. "I guess it depends on the experiences you're drawing from. Are you happily married?"

"Yes."

"Maybe that explains it," Maurice said. "I bet you've never been divorced either?"

"That's right."

"For me love is burgundy," I explained, "like the wine. If love is good, it grows fuller and deeper with the years. It caresses you and provides comfort like the warm rich glow of wine."

"And if it's bad?" Maurice asked.

"It turns to vinegar, bitter and repulsive. It becomes something you want to get rid of or as in the case of the wine, destroy. Sometimes its bitterness can cause a person to commit acts of violence, even murder . . ."

Again horror imprisoned me; I could not escape its tentacled grip. At the end of class Aaron approached me, his face concerned. "Stop by my office in about a week or so, when I'm less swamped. There are some things I'd like to discuss with you."

The rest of the summer, except for meeting with Aaron a few times, I discussed very little with anyone. Deciding against attending school for the second summer session, I stayed at home.

In the mountains where we lived the sun was just warm enough. I spent my days trying to relax. I allowed my skin to absorb the warmth. One day as I lay there the phone rang. Still blinded by sun spots I raced into the house, scraping my big toe on a brick step at the back door.

"Hi, Momma, what's up?"

"There's some kind of hearing scheduled for Ken tomorrow morning and we were hoping you could come."

"Of course. I'll wait until Dave gets home though, so I'll probably get in quite late."

I was standing in the doorway when Dave pulled onto the asphalt driveway and climbed down from his Toyota pickup. I met him with a kiss.

"Have a good day?" he asked.

"I guess. I have to head to Momma's and Daddy's tonight. There's a hearing tomorrow and they want me to come."

"That's short notice, isn't it?" He walked into the kitchen and slammed his lunch pail down next to the sink.

"That's all the notice they had. They learned about it this afternoon."

"What's it about?"

"I don't know. Anyway, that's not the point. They want me to be there, and I'll be giving Ken moral support."

"Like I've said before, just forget him."

Exasperated I looked into his angry eyes, not the eyes I loved at all.

"Dave, I wanted to tell you myself rather than having you come home to an empty house and a note."

"Doesn't make much difference. You're going anyway. When will you be back?" He followed me out to the car and leaned up against the quince tree next to the edge of the driveway.

"Sunday. I want to stay down long enough to see Ken."

"See you later," he curtly observed and went back into the house. No kiss, nothing. No love to help me through the events to come.

Those events, all the court visits that awaited us, hovered near each time we entered the courthouse.

The long hallway on the second floor was empty when Momma, Daddy, and I made our way to the courtroom the next day to await the hearing. The only noise was that of a typewriter in an office down the hall.

The place seemed eerie. Ghosts of people who waited for impossible verdicts lingered.

The courtroom was vacant. We waited outside.

"Did you ever discover what this hearing is about?" I asked.

"I'm afraid not, Vi," Daddy said. "We called Kevin and left messages, but he never returned our calls."

I slumped into one of the chairs beside Momma and chewed my fingernails, tearing the edges raw.

"Wonder where Ken is?" Momma said worriedly, and she watched the hallway as if doing so would make him appear. "I haven't seen them bring him down yet, have you?"

"No," I said.

"The hearing was supposed to start a half hour ago," Daddy said.

It was an impossible set of circumstances. Each delay seemed to spread gangrene deeper into the wound.

I walked out to the larger section of the hallway. The elevator did not open and no one appeared with my brother. A half an hour later the courtroom doors opened and a grandmotherly woman in a pink sweater-knit dress walked through.

"Are you folks waiting for the Andre hearing?"

"Yes," I replied.

"I'm afraid it's been postponed," she said.

"You mean I came all the way from Portland for nothing?" I said dejectedly.

"I'm afraid so."

"Do you know what happened?" I asked.

"I'm afraid not," the woman replied and disappeared.

"Well," I said, "we might as well get going. I guess I should have expected this, but somehow I didn't."

"Me neither, Vi," Daddy sighed.

The following morning I dragged myself from the bed nestled in the corner of the small wallpapered room. It was the same home that had been mine as a child. Slipping my robe over my Garfield nightshirt, I walked barefooted into the living room and found my mother seated in the easy chair, trying to knit.

"Where's Daddy?" Tucking my toes behind the edge of the cushion I folded myself onto the couch.

"He's gone down to the pasture to see how the grass is holding up," Momma said, her voice quivering. She did not look at me, just stared at the French windows at the end of the room, the windows I had always loved.

"Are you okay, Momma?" The skin around her eyes was puffy and red as it had been the first days after the murders.

"I don't want to burden you—"

"You won't."

"Well, it's just that, uh, I've said all this before."

"That's alright."

"Whenever I try to talk to your dad about Ken, he changes the subject. He seems to think that if we don't talk about it, it will go away, but it won't."

"I'll listen."

"Every morning when I wake up I still see those little children standing on the porch in the rain. Poor little things. Why did Ken do it? Maybe I didn't help him enough when he was growing up. He was so shy. Every time I tried to get close he pulled away. Somehow I failed. If I'd been able to do something, maybe he wouldn't have ended up like this," she said crying.

I wanted to hold her, wanted to cling to her and erase her pain. Yet I couldn't stop the pain; it was unchangeable. If I held her, I was afraid it would stop the tears she needed to cry.

"There's nothing you could have done. Lord knows, all of us have tried to get close to him. You can't get close to a person who doesn't want you to."

"I don't know what I'd do without you and Denise," she said in a shaky voice, her body tense against the cushioned vinyl. "You've been such a help, both of you. You even took time out from your husband to be with us. It means so much."

"Momma, I love you," I said softly.

Night found me back in my old bedroom. With mounds of covers pulled up around me I stared at the ceiling. The old house creaked, the same way it had when I was little.

I was so lonely. What had happened to my old friends like Brenda? We were once so close. And my cousin Tammy? So many nights we spent giggling and sharing secrets in my bedroom. Neither one of them had called since the murders. I was too broken to make the calls. I needed to know someone cared enough to make the effort. Apparently no one did.

Saturday, two days after the canceled hearing, the three of us entered the concrete holding facility where Ken had been transferred; we signed in and trudged to the back room.

The facility was located in a wing of a building that used to be the hospital—the hospital in which I was born.

In my first memory of it Momma and I had entered through the glass-plated doorway and stepped up the wide steps. Clutching her hand I followed her into a room just off the stairs. A lady in white shoes administered a shot. I tried not to cry, tried to be the big girl my momma asked me to be. I learned the lesson too well. I could no longer cry.

Ken was already waiting.

"They're spying on me, Violet," he whispered from behind the glass. "There are microphones hidden in my mattress and I know there's a camera somewhere in the cell. You may think I'm crazy, but I know it's true.

"The guy in the cell next to me is a plant. They put him there so I'll talk. That way they can find out what I'm thinking and can use that information against me in court. They censor my letters, you know. Whatever information I write can be used against me too. That's why I haven't answered any of yours. I hope you understand."

I nodded.

"I'm so glad you came. I needed to see you. It's nice

to have Mom and Dad visit me, but they aren't exactly intellectual. I need to talk to someone on my level . . ."

I could not trust myself to speak. Looking into his fevered eyes, I nodded slowly.

Chapter Nine

Dear Vi,

I'm really worried about how I'll be treated while Mom and Dad are gone hunting for a week and a half in October. I know the people here at the jail are just looking for excuses to harass me. I try not to let them get to me, but sometimes they read my thoughts and broadcast them over the loudspeaker. I didn't know other people had that kind of power.

Please continue to write. It helps me keep my sanity. The trial, as you know, is scheduled for the third week in October. Please sit in on the jury selection and the trial. Your presence could be crucial, since you are the only one in the family who could determine if they're screwing me over or not. You're the only one in the family besides myself with any brains . . .

Ken's words, recorded on prison paper, lingered in my mind and imprinted my thoughts. Hope was something that other people possessed. In me it had been dead for what seemed like eons.

Through the dusty windows of the remodeled house I could see heat shimmering up from the brown lawn. It was way too hot for September, way too uncomfortable to think about anything. I tried Ken's lawyer's number again.

"I'm sorry, Mr. McDonald still is not in. Can I take a message?" the secretary said.

"Please tell him to call Violet Andre."

The afternoon passed. At eight I tried him at home and counted each ring impatiently. Nothing.

"I just can't believe that guy," I said, and plopped beside Dave on the pillow in front of the television. "You'd think he'd have the courtesy to return my calls. I've been trying to reach him for days."

"Sounds like he's avoiding you. Maybe he's incompetent and trying to cover it up."

"I don't know. . . . I wish we could afford an experienced attorney. Kevin's just out of law school. It isn't fair."

"Ken deserves whatever he gets."

"He deserves to pay for the deaths, but he should have the same access to justice as the rich."

"I guess you're right."

A little later I dialed once more.

"Oh, yes, Violet," McDonald said, "sorry I haven't gotten back to you. What do you want to know?"

"I'd like some information about the trial. We need to know what to expect."

"Some of that isn't nailed down yet and I really don't have time to go into it. I'm taking the best possible course for your brother. His confession didn't help things much, but we do the best we can."

"Do you think he'll get the death penalty?"

"That's something I can't tell you. You'll just have to wait and see. If there's nothing else, I'll let you go," he said and hung up.

"He cut me off," I said to Dave. "He cut me off. It's

my brother's life here. Even if he did kill those people
he's important to me. I have a right to more information,
and McDonald didn't give it to me. He could have said
something about confidentiality, or not wanting to reveal
his strategy. If we were paying him, he'd tell us what's
going on."

Dave said nothing. He stared at the television and
ignored me.

The two of us coexisted until the last weekend of
September. It always brought deer-hunting season and
the annual family exodus to central Oregon, the land of
sagebrush and pine. Campers, motorhomes, and travel
trailers were loaded with enough provisions to last for
several weeks in case the group became stranded in
snow. Guns were sighted in to ensure their accuracy.
Bright red and orange clothes were donned by even the
smallest hunters to distinguish them from the deer. One
year I even made a red cape for Brutus. This year, however, he was staying home with me.

"Are you sure you're going to be allright here by
yourself?" Dave asked and loaded the last of the camping gear into the back of the pickup.

"I guess."

"Well, I'm ready to go." He leaned against the
pickup, gave me a hug, then climbed in and drove away.

"Have a safe trip," I hollered after him. The lights
from his truck disappeared into the descending night.

Shuddering I hurried into the house, bolted the
door, and fixed myself a strong drink to deaden the fear.

Cars and trucks passed the house, and lights
whisked across the closed drapes, sometimes hesitating
at the stop sign on the corner. The neighbor's peacock
screamed into the charcoal night, and a dog a half mile
up the road howled with the coyotes who lived in the
draw on the other side of the road. The wilderness was
close, and we were the intruders, though the house had
been there for seventy years.

Stillness haunted the empty house, and the grand-mother clock moaned its lonely song enroute to the hour. Shadows from the hanging lamp in the corner of the large living room fell across plastered walls. A log cabin–style couch, love seat, and a stately leather chair hugged the room on two sides. Other pieces of unmatched furniture filled the spaces. The stone fireplace was devoid of warmth.

The drapes, those tattered old things that I had come to hate, were too thin. From the outside even in early darkness one could see a clear outline of all that went on within. I huddled on the floor pillow feeling no safety at all.

Cop shows dominated television. Flicking the remote unit to avoid programs too similar to what Ken had done, I finally found a boring sitcom to fill the time. Brandy and Brutus cuddled on either side of me, but in spite of them fear crept up my limbs.

Finally it turned ten o'clock, soon enough to try to sleep, or at least hide in the darkness of the bedroom.

I dragged myself into the kitchen to turn off the lights, passing another set of shabby drapes in the dining room. Just as I was about to switch off the kitchen light, I saw him beyond the window over the sink . . .

The face with the gun. He's waiting out there.

My heart beats resounded; his form was clear, large and darkened by the night, and his face, that I could almost see, looked too familiar.

The paneled hallway leading to the back was illuminated by two covered bulbs. I turned them off. Once in the bedroom I slipped on one of Dave's tee shirts and climbed into bed. But there was no security midst the blankets. The sounds of the old house enveloped me. My ears strained to hear intruding footsteps.

Stumbling to a hallway light I turned it on and returned to bed. Sliding again into the blankets I saw them —the two gun cabinets—leering at me from the corners of the room. Twenty champions of death lined up in single file behind glass doors.

Ken had killed four people with one of those horrible things. I hated them. They stood in the corner of the place I was supposed to rest, a constant reminder. Dave insisted on keeping them in our room. The house had four bedrooms, enough to put them elsewhere.

I could not sleep. All night I waited for the man with the gun to kill me.

By Monday, the first day of classes for fall term, I was exhausted from lack of sleep. No one had called to see how I was doing. No one.

The valley between the foothills and freeway was dotted with small communities, dozens of houses and people locked in them. On the way into town I felt distant from them, as if they were withdrawn from me.

My first class, Intergovernmental Relations, was located in Cramer Hall, the building with a disjointed numbering system. Pushing fatigue aside in a room stuffed with desks I opened my notebook and watched a curly haired professor copy notes onto the blackboard.

"The list of required reading is in the bookstore. For the first part of this period I'd like to talk a little about each book," he said.

When the class was over I felt panicked. There were eight books to read and a five-page report to be written on each one, in addition to a twenty-page term paper synthesizing the data from all of them. How could I do it all and still be at the trial?

I went to my second class. Easing myself into the stale room with no windows I studied the students seated around two large tables. Most of the students were dressed in business suits, dark blue, brown and boring, a stark contrast to my jeans and bright shirt.

"The field of personnel management," the professor said, "has become clouded with forms, regulations, and other bureaucratic nonsense. If you're planning to focus in this area, I want you to realize right now that you will not become a substitute counselor. You'll spend most of your time dealing with legislation and regulations regarding discrimination and the like."

I listened for a few hours, but none of what he said seemed important. Again the assignments overwhelmed me, as did those from my class the following day. How could I do them in the midst of all the hearings?

After my last class I trudged to the Cheerful Tortoise and ordered a coke. I stared at my textbooks and tried to decide what to do. I thought of my family. They were only four and a half hours away. . . . I needed them.

Weaving back and forth through the pine trees, my little car plodded down the dusty road toward camp. On the seat beside me Brandy stared out the window at the low branches that slapped the side of the car, his eyes eager and excited. Acres of evergreens interrupted by meadows and dry stream beds covered the high plateau. Spotting the familiar vehicles I climbed from the car and stretched; campers, trailers, and a tent circled the fire pit.

"Anybody here?"

The dogs climbed down from the car, and I hooked the leash to Brutus's collar. The three of us followed the short path to the meandering meadow on the edge of camp. With each step dust billowed up around my high-topped hiking boots and coated the worn edges of my jeans.

Careful not to trip on the wiry clumps of grass, I made my way to a corrugated aluminum tank a few feet away. Water from an underground pipe trickled into the metal reservoir. The water was down several feet from last year.

Suddenly a wind gusted from the north. Shivering I hurried back to camp and gathered wood for a fire. When it was going well I searched the ice chest and found two pounds of hamburger.

I began cooking. Finally spaghetti sauce bubbled on the Coleman stove beside the tent. The fire sputtered and crackled with the addition of more wood. Warmth from the flames felt good. Leaning back in my chair I propped my feet on the fire rocks and watched the sun disappear from the needled tree tops.

During past hunting trips fear had never been my companion; my feeling toward others in the woods had always been one of comradery. There were always good-hearted people sharing the camping and hunting time with us. This year seemed different.

Darkness crept through the jack pine forest, and uneasiness crawled up the back of my neck. Beyond the fire in the flickering shadows leered the face with the gun.

"I will not be afraid," I whispered. "I will not be afraid. There's no one there— Brutus!"

Brutus lumbered over and sat down on his haunches beside me, and Brandy climbed into my lap, his legs hanging over the edge. The three of us waited alone. Fear crept upon me, but I ignored it.

About nine, a set of lights pulled off the main road several hundred yards from camp, eased its way through the trees, and stopped next to my car.

"Violet, what are you doing here?" Dave asked. He climbed from the truck and crushed me to him, his wool jacket scratching my cheek.

"I decided to join you."

"I thought you wanted to take classes this term."

"I did, but there was just no way I could get the work done and attend the trial too. I stewed and fretted about it, but made the only decision I could," I said.

"It sure is good to see you. I've been lonely without my lamby to cuddle at night."

"If I'd known I'd receive this kind of welcome, I would have come sooner." Nervous laughter gave way to calm, and I stared at the big teddy bear man.

"Where are the other?"

"They'll be back shortly. We ran a drive through a clearing over by Bear Flats. You remember where that is, don't you?"

I nodded.

"Well, we positioned your folks and Uncle Dan in his wheel chair at one end of the clearing and the rest of us had a good jaunt trying to drive the deer out. Unfortunately we didn't see a thing. Guess it was good exercise though. Here come your folks now."

Momma and Daddy climbed from the old stationwagon.

"Vi . . . I didn't expect to see you here," Daddy said.

I slipped my arms about his heavy jacket and hugged him, then Momma, noting how tired she looked.

"Don't worry, Momma, I already made dinner."

"Good, I wasn't looking forward to cooking."

The rest of the campers returned, giving me welcome. I felt warm inside for the first time in months. It was good to belong.

After cooking the noodles I brought two large pots of spaghetti to the table by the fire. Someone brought biscuits and someone else coffee.

It was like old times except for one thing. Ken was not there.

Still, I did not toss and turn that night. I slept till morning. Shaking myself awake I uncovered my face and peered from the sleeping bag into the darkness inside the tent. One thing I hated about hunting trips was getting up before dawn.

"You awake, honey?" Dave asked, switching on the flashlight and beginning to dress.

"Yes." I moaned and slipped my jeans and shirt into the sleeping bag to warm them.

"I just want you to know how glad I am you came," he said as he leaned across the sleeping bag and kissed me.

"I'm glad to be with you too, even if it is cold. It's good to get some sleep again. I love you."

"I love you too."

After breakfast we headed out through the silver shadowing light in time to see the sun dawn on the pristine forest. Tall ponderosa pine stood watch along the edge of the narrow road. Their long needles and reddish bark brought spicy color to the wilderness. The banks to the side of the road were peppered with old deer tracks, and chipmunks darted in front of the pickup. The air was chilly and crisp, the dust still frozen.

"I wish you'd carry a gun, Violet," Dave said, as he peered out the window of the pickup and scanned the bank for fresh deer sign.

"We've been over that before, and you know how I feel. I don't want to be responsible for the death of a poor deer."

Or any mammal. Especially after Ken killed those people. Guns were made to kill . . . animals and people. I don't even want to touch a gun.

Horror shot through me.

"The trouble with you is that you have a Bambi complex," he said. His voice was taunting. "I don't see the difference, since you eat them. That's kind of hypocritical, isn't it?"

"I guess it is."

"I don't understand how you can be so different. Your whole family on your dad's side hunts, including the women. A few of your mom's relatives do too. You just don't fit."

"Sometimes I wished I could be like them. It would be a lot simpler. But I can't. Guess I'll always feel a little out of step, like Thoreau's Different Drummer, you know . . . 'If a man does not keep pace with his companions, perhaps it is because he hears a different drummer. Let him step to the music which he hears, however measured or far away.' "

"I don't want a philosophy lesson," he said, irritation icing his voice. He glared over at me, the softness of early morning love replaced by detachment and disapproval, as it was so often lately. "I just want you to carry a gun. It makes no sense at all that you don't. And don't give me that bullshit about Ken."

Around noon we headed back. Lunch at hunting camp was mostly a simple meal, a couple of hot dogs stuffed between bread and a can of pop. The afternoon sun warmed the clear air and seduced the early risers into a lazy nap; then about four they headed out—"to be," Daddy said, "in the right place at the right time."

"Are you going to stay at camp this afternoon, Vi?" Aunt Dorothy asked. The two of us stood by the fire pit.

"Yeah, I'm kind of tired. Still haven't caught up on my sleep, and I thought I'd fix dinner."

"Then I'll leave Dan here. You can help him if he needs anything, can't you?"

"Be glad to."

"Good, I'll go out with Denise, Ted, and Dave. Where did your folks get off to?"

"Somewhere up by Pine Butte, I guess. I sure hope Daddy doesn't overdo it in this high altitude."

"He'll be okay. He has pretty good sense about taking care of himself. With your mom along they should be fine, and they have the CB radio in case they need help."

"I guess you're right. It's just that this family doesn't need more tragedies. I can't handle any more after Ken . . ."

"I know. It really shook us up too," Aunt Dorothy said, then headed back to her trailer.

Combing the edge of camp I loaded my arms with wood and headed back; I twisted several pieces of newspaper, placed them in the coals, and then put dry twigs on top. When they caught on, I added a few larger pieces. Ted wheeled Uncle Dan across the bumpy dirt to the fire, and Dave, Denise, Ted, and Aunt Dorothy piled into Ted's Blazer and pulled away from camp, dust boiling up behind them. When they were gone I added more logs.

"You're going to cook me out, Vi," Uncle Dan said, his eyes filled with the mischief I had seen in them so often. His brown hair was slicked back, accenting a slightly receding hairline. As a young man he had been a carpenter, muscular and tall. It was multiple sclerosis that crippled him.

"I don't want you to get cold. Besides, I'm building up the fire for myself too. I get cold just like Daddy. Although, I must say, I don't wear long underwear in the summer like he does . . . and he always wonders why he sweats so," I said. My face crinkled into a smile.

"I've noticed your dad's funny that way." Uncle Dan grinned.

I grabbed a marshmallow from the bag on the stump, jabbed the soft candy with a narrow stick, and lowered it close to the coals.

"You want one? I'll try not to burn it."

"Sounds good, if I can trust you not to poison me."

I grinned.

"You know, Vi, I've been sitting here thinking about Ken and the few years he came hunting with us. Of all the family except for your dad's brother Will, he was the best shot. I still can't believe it. I just can't believe he killed Kathy and Maurice and those other folks," he said; he rolled one side of the wheel chair away from the heat.

"I know."

"Your parents are a couple of the nicest people I know. If any person was down on his luck, your dad would help him out. Many's a time things were tight for Dorothy and me after I got sick. Your dad always made sure we were okay, had enough food and all. And your dad's not a rich man. He has had a hard enough time getting by himself. I just don't understand how Ken could have turned out so differently."

"Guess we don't know what goes on in someone else's mind."

"If it had been someone else, a stranger, I know what should be done. A person who kills another person except in self-defense should lose his life, but since it was Ken, my sister's son . . ." Uncle Dan's voice broke, but he managed to continue. "Why, I remember when he was a little tyke . . . playing with him, tossing him into the air. He was mischievous, but a good kid.

"That little fellow grew up and killed Kathy and Maurice. They were such nice people, good Christians too," he said, and dabbed the tears.

"It's different when someone you love kills someone," I said. "It makes you rethink everything you ever believed."

Seven days into hunting season Aunt Rose and Uncle George arrived in a small camper van and took their spot next to the fire pit. The following morning I stayed in camp with Aunt Rose; a visit with her always made me feel better. Allowing myself time to sleep in, I did the morning chores, then knocked on the window of the van. Her cheerful face peered through the dusty glass.

"Good morning, dear," she announced and opened the door. "Why don't you pull your chair up close." She perched herself just inside on the edge of the bed.

Seventy-seven wasn't a bad age to be. In fact, on her it looked good. She was a proud woman, and her bright brown eyes revealed an inner fire. Even her figure was still trim.

"I'm so glad you and Uncle George were able to make it."

"We were glad we could too, dear, even if we did arrive a few days late. With your grandma gone all these years, you kids are the only way I'm able to feel close to her. Your grandma and I were really close when we were kids. She and I were our father's boys and worked around the ranch."

"Grandma did farm work? She never seemed the type."

She nodded. "She and I were good friends too, and I really miss her. She had so many heartaches over the years with the deaths of three of her children and your grandfather's chasing after other women."

"You and Grandma were so different."

"She was always so worried about what was right and proper. She tried to live a good Christian life as she saw it. I did the same thing; but when my first husband began chasing other women, I would have none of it. Now I know there were those in the family who condemned me for my divorce, but I only did what I had to. I look at these things differently than some, I guess. I believe that if you're doing the best you can, God will understand. Even if the decision turns out to be wrong, he still understands."

"You think God is loving and understanding, and stands by His children, even when they make mistakes?" I asked, my voice quivering.

"Yes, honey. It's the only way I know how to figure."

"Maybe there's still hope for Ken—"

"If Ken can find God he'll have hope. Otherwise, there's not much left." She shook her head. "What got into him to make him do such a crazy thing. I can't figure it out," she said and scratched her head with long red fingernails.

"We heard about it on the news, you know," she said, staring through the pine woods. "I just couldn't believe it when I saw the name Andre flashed over the screen. My kids called about it too. They recognized the name and wanted to know if he was related. I went to Mother's old Bible and got Ken's full name and age. It was then I knew it was our Ken," she said, and tears stood in her eyes. "My sister Irene's grandson; it's just not possible."

"No, it isn't."

"Your folks seem to be handling it fairly well."

"Not really, Momma keeps blaming herself."

"There's nothing she could have done, honey. She raised you kids up right. After kids leave home, it's up to them what they do. If they have a good foundation, that's all their parents are responsible for. So, what Ken did was his responsibility."

I took a deep breath and slowly let it out. "I wish you could talk to Momma. Maybe she would listen to you, you being her aunt and all. Maybe you could make her see it wasn't her fault."

"I'll talk to her while we're here. I love your mother as much as if she was my own child. If I can help her I will. Do you know when the trial will be?"

"It starts on the twentieth of this month, as far as we know."

"If it would help I would be glad to go down with you, if my health holds."

"I'd like that." I touched her shoulder gently.

She smiled. "Good. Give me a call a few days before you leave to see how I feel. I hate to see you driving all that way by yourself. Dave isn't going, is he?"

"I don't think so."

Late that afternoon Dave and I joined my parents for the evening hunt. We climbed into the car and propped three unloaded guns against the seats, the barrels aimed at the ceiling. With Daddy driving we crept along the single-lane dirt road, and four sets of eyes stared out open windows at clearings, trees, and sagebrush flats. It was just light enough to shoot legally.

"Now, Vi, we're counting on your good eyes," Daddy said with some of his old zest.

"Okay, Daddy."

The car inched down the road and I scanned the thicket of trees to the left.

"Woah, back up," I murmured. "There, just beyond that row of trees. Do you see them?"

Leaving the doors slightly ajar the two men loaded their rifles, slipped up the bank and disappeared beyond the pine. Several minutes passed. . . . A shot cracked the silence, then another. Momma and I waited for the customary war whoop. Several more minutes went by. The men pushed back through the thick branches up ahead, unloaded their rifles, and climbed back in.

"Well?" I asked.

"It got away," Dave said.

Staring at the back of my father's head as he sped back to camp, I sensed something was wrong. Normally he would be talking about the deer he missed or another one in a similar setting on a hunt years ago. Instead he was quiet, and his face, in the rearview mirror, seemed pinched and sad.

Once back at the family camp Dave and I climbed out and walked toward the tent. When Momma and Daddy were out of range I asked, "Is anything wrong?"

"It was a doe. He's just sick about it. Doe season doesn't start until next week."

"Did he kill it?"

"Yes, so it wouldn't suffer. We didn't want to waste the meat, but we couldn't risk a ticket. In a case like that they confiscate your gun too."

When we got back to camp, I began to cook dinner. Grease splattered onto the back of the Coleman stove, and large hamburger patties cooked noisily in the cast-iron skillet over gas flames. Beside the stove on the table created by a wide board nailed between two trees, I sliced tomatoes and onions and absently stared past the privy and beyond my parents' trailer.

Death had come again, and this time it was my fault. The doe had died for nothing. If I had not spotted it, it would still be alive. It was another warm-blooded life, gone. It knew fear and pain and had nurturing needs just as did the people I loved. Daddy and I killed it. Ken had killed four people with his hunting rifle. How could anybody kill anything after that?

No more. No deer. No pain. No death. Never again.

When dinner was ready Dave and I filled our plates with fried potatoes and hamburgers, and joined the rest of the family by the fire. Flames shot high, licking cold out of the darkness. When I tuned in, the conversation was already in progress.

"I remember the time Ken came out hunting with us and there was that big storm," Uncle Will, Daddy's brother, said with a laugh. His gray-blue eyes danced as he pulled his black suspenders out away from his red flannel shirt, arching back the way he always did when he launched into a story. "Ken was just a kid . . . home from the army on leave, I think. We camped over by China Hat that year. You remember Lee?"

Daddy nodded.

"Lord, did it rain and thunder and lightening," Uncle Will said. "First time I'd ever seen it crawl along the ground. Poor kid was scared the lightning would strike him. He was hopping around all over the ground, and finally wound up sleeping in the car."

The rest of the family laughed.

"I remember the time Ken got his first deer," Bill, my cousin's husband, said. "A merry grin spread across his face and his eyes glistened." He leaned forward, and as he did so his belly folded nearly down onto the seat.

"He must have been about twelve or so then. Carried that forked horn out of that deep canyon, almost by himself. Of course he was a good-sized kid. He was as proud as any man."

Chapter Ten

Hovering clouds hid the top of the Coast Range as I made my way down Highway 38. The smooth, wet pavement curved along the base of the hillside and through the leafless December forest. Two months before I had driven this same route to attend the trial. That time it had been postponed. Splatters of rain swirled in and cooled my face. I shrugged my shoulders and tried to rid myself of the tension. The apprehension that had been with me for days was growing, along with bleak, unshakable thoughts of Ken.

It was dark and raining by the time I pulled off the county road and angled down the narrow driveway to the one place I could always call home. Careful not to trip over the cat dish and a bag of potatoes, I crossed the porch and pushed open the back door.

"Aunt Rose didn't come?" Momma asked. She held me longer than usual.

"Not this time. It's colder than it was in October when she came down, and her hip was acting up again. With the weather nasty like it is, she didn't want to travel."

"I kept dinner warm for you. There's a chicken

breast and a baked potato . . . and a little salad if you
want it."

"Thanks, I am hungry."

"Hi, Vi." Daddy shuffled in from the bedroom and
wrapped himself about me. "It's good to have you
home."

A couple of hours later found me alone in the bedroom. Momma had replaced the wallpaper a few since I
left home, but at night it looked the same . . .

I remembered when the room belonged to Ken, and
when my room was where the laundry room was now.
He was not afraid then, but after two years in the army
. . . I could still hear his voice perforating the darkness
his first night back home.

>   "Vidy . . . Vidy!"
>   "What?" I moaned, half asleep, not sure
> what was going on.
>   "Did you hear that?" came Ken's voice
> from the doorways.
>   I blinked myself awake and strained to
> hear a noise above the country silence.
>   "There it goes again," he whispered, his
> voice tense and excited.
>   Again I strained for several long moments.
>   "Don't you hear it?"
>   "No . . ."

He was so frightened. Several more times that night
he came to me, his ten-year-old sister, for reassurance.

Now I scooted into the crack between the bed and
the wall, tucking covers up around my face. It seemed
safer that way when I was little.

The house creaked. In the open doorway I saw the
man. He raised the gun.

No!

With a surge of courage, interwoven with terror, I

reached across the nightstand and switched on the light. Cautiously I padded into the kitchen and turned on that light, too. No one.

I snapped it off, returned to bed, and again placed my back against the wall. At least that way I was safe on one side.

Safety failed me the next day, though. The courthouse seemed more sinister than it had in October. Now, it was the enemy. Anxiety coated the lime-green walls as Momma, Daddy, and I waited in the hallway for the jury selection to begin.

A dozen or more people milled about, waiting; I paced in front of the small conference rooms.

Finally I found myself on the stairway landing, staring out at the courtyard and the vicious-looking clouds. I clutched the window sill and blocked the noise around me.

I prayed silently to a God, who in my heart did not exist, had not existed for months, even years. But maybe, just maybe . . . *Lord, if you're there please help us. Everything that is about to happen is out of our hands. We need your protection and guidance. Please send comfort and some kind of confirmation that You are there.*

I closed my eyes and waited . . . for some kind of miracle . . . to transform the moment, to make it a time of answers rather than questions. Nothing happened.

In the morning, rain began to fall, easily at first, then harder and harder.

Kevin McDonald strode from the judge's office and motioned me into a conference room. When the door was closed, he said, "I may call you as a witness, Violet. I'm not sure yet. So after the jury selection I want you to leave the courtroom." He leaned uneasily against the tall case filled with law books.

"I promised Ken I'd be there for him."

"I'll explain it to him."

"Are my parents going to have to testify?"

"As far as I know."

"Even my father? He could die on the stand."

"I'm sorry."

Back with my mother, I asked, "Momma, did Kevin tell you about testifying?"

"Yes," Momma whispered. "I just can't believe they're going to make your dad take the stand." She watched Daddy head toward us with the morning coffee.

"Ah, nothing beats a good cup of coffee, does it, Violet?" he said and stroked the top of my head. I smiled in spite of my anger with the court system.

"Here comes Denise and Billie," Daddy said.

"How are you, Billie?" I asked. I remembered Denise's discomfort two months before, when she told us of Billie's pregnancy. No marriage was planned. Apparently she did not want a husband.

"Me and the baby are doing just fine," she said, patting her stomach. She looked off in the distance. "Here they come with Ken."

He and the two guards were headed our way.

"Ken," I managed, when he was just a few feet away.

He jerked his attention from the floor and surprise jolted his face. Momma reached toward the son who broke her heart. He took her hands and held them. The rest of us did nothing. Then Ken and the guards went into the judge's office, and Momma backed into Daddy's arms.

"He looks awful," Denise muttered. "How did we ever let him get this far? We should have been able to do something to stop him." "Dear God, what?" I said.

Momma took out yarn from her satchel and started knitting in an effort not to think, to make the time more bearable.

"You aren't going in for jury selection, Momma?" I asked.

"I can't stand the thought of it," she answered.

"How about you, Daddy?"

"I'll stay with your momma."

"Is Aunt Elsa coming?" Denise inquired.

"She'll be along about 9:30 or so," Momma said.

A few minutes before the session began, Denise and I entered the room of paneled walls and empty seats. We inched our way along a couple of rows from the front and sank onto the seats. Tension and fear choked me; my throat felt dry and swollen.

"Maybe we came in too soon," Denise remarked as she fidgeted with her gingham blouse and polyester slacks, trying to smooth imaginary wrinkles.

"From the looks of all those people, the place is going to be crowded."

"I guess a murder trial attracts a lot of attention in a small place like this."

The jurors' chairs began to fill, as did the rest of the room. Ken, Kevin McDonald, and the prosecuting attorney entered through the side door behind the judge's bench. A gray-haired woman, the one we had seen several times during the past few months, stood at the front of the room and said, "All rise."

We did, and the judge came forward from the back of the courtroom and sat down.

"What did she say?" Denise asked, nodding in the direction of the woman.

"I don't know. I wasn't listening." In fact I was feeling dazed.

"Would Delbert Daniels please step forward?" the woman said.

Daniels took the vacant chair in the front row with the other jurors. I looked about the room. It was full. In the back sat a woman I had not seen in years. She had attended church with my family and the McCalls when we were kids. She was a little older than Ken. I nudged Denise.

"Cathy Simpson's sitting in the back row," I remarked.

"Wonder what she's doing here?"

"Who knows. She hasn't changed much, just gotten fatter."

When court recessed, Denise and I joined our aunt, who had been seated just inside the door.

"I'm glad you could make it, Aunt Elsa," I said as I hugged Momma's only sister.

"I'm glad I could come. I thought your mother could use the moral support," she said.

"How's it going, Violet?" Daddy asked when we met him in the hall. His voice was unsteady and his eyes wistful.

"I guess they selected most of the jurors yesterday. I didn't even realize anything was going to happen yesterday. Wish Kevin would have told us. Anyway, right now they're getting ready to select two alternates."

Daddy leaned against the wall. He looked beaten. When I was little he cuddled me, made me feel safe. Now when he needed it I could not provide the same comfort. It was not fair.

Aunt Elsa, Denise, and I returned to our seats. Ken and Mr. McDonald were already at the attorney's table. Ken was bent forward. He cradled his head and protected his eyes with his hand, as he did when he was feeling frightened. His curls were carefully corralled, the way he wore them in high school; but he looked too thin in his flannel shirt and slacks.

When the selections were completed and everyone left the room, Denise and I stood alone for a few minutes before joining our family.

"I can't believe that Cathy Simpson was selected as an alternate," she said. "There's no way she can be unbiased."

"Nobody who knew any of us could be. There's also a gal on the jury whom I went to high school with."

Court reconvened after lunch. The attorneys gave their opening statements, and the first witness took the stand.

"Would you tell us, Officer Hammond, what happened when you first encountered the defendant," John Murray, the district attorney asked.

Officer Hammond looked down at his statement and began to read. "I was driving down the river road. As I neared the area of Gaffney Lane, the sight of the reported shootings, I saw an individual walking toward Dayton on the river side of the road. He was dressed in dark clothing. The individual watched me go by.

"I removed my shotgun from the rack, laid it on the passenger seat and proceeded on. As I passed him I felt that I should stop and talk to the man. So, I turned around in Gaffney Lane. As I did this individual turned and raised his hands.

"I stopped the car about twenty yards from the man. His hands were still extended over his head. I stepped from the car and chambered a round in my shotgun. At that point I instructed the individual to assume a spread-eagle position face down on the ground. I approached him from his right and asked him what was going on. He said that he wanted the death penalty. When I asked him why, had he shot someone, he said yes. He said he knew he was wrong and he just wanted to die.

"When I questioned him further, he said, 'I think I killed four people.' Those were his exact words.

"At that point I instructed him to remain silent, not to say any more. By that time Officer Jerry Gibson had arrived and offered his assistance. We handcuffed the man and applied physical restraints. Then I advised him of his Miranda rights. When he got up he told me that his name was Kenneth Andre. I frisked him, but found no weapons. We placed him in the back of my patrol car and he agreed to go back up to where the shootings had occurred.

"I started back up Gaffney Lane at Mr. Andre's direction. He seemed nervous and was all wet, but his speech was clear. He seemed to answer my questions properly. So I did not believe he was under the influence of intoxicants or drugs.

"As we proceeded up Gaffney Lane the defendant, Mr. Andre, directed me to a residence just past the grade school. As we went by he said, 'That's my house.' He then said, 'Turn left.'

"I took the first left past his house and pulled up in front of a nearby house. As I got out of the car the defendant said, 'My flashlight's over by the telephone pole. Mr. Bennett is in the living room, sitting in the chair.'

"I saw the telephone pole, but didn't look for the flashlight. When Officer Gibson arrived, I stepped up on the front porch, peered through a window, and saw an individual in a chair reclined back. He had obviously been shot in the side of the head. This startled me.

"I grabbed the doorknob and it came off in my hand. I dropped it and climbed through a broken window to the left side of the door. Entering carefully I called out, identifying myself. No one answered. I felt for a pulse on the gentleman in the chair, but there was none.

"I proceeded cautiously through the rest of the house. In a back room I noticed a white female lying on her back beside a couch. Bits of a disintegrated telephone receiver were still in her hand. She obviously had been shot in the head at close range. I felt for a pulse, but there was none.

"At that point I rechecked the house, exited through the window, and returned to the patrol car. I told Officer Gibson that the two people in the house were deceased and asked him to stand by.

"I radioed a report of what I had found and requested assistance. Mr. Andre was still in the backseat, and I advised the office that he had admitted shooting the Bennetts.

"Since the defendant had stated he had shot four people, I asked him where the other two were. He directed me back up Gaffney Lane and down another one-lane graveled road. On the way the defendant stopped me and said, 'Hold it. Stop right there, by your left fender. That's where I dropped the rifle.'

"Before we arrived at the second residence I asked the defendant where the people were in the house. He said that they were in the kitchen on the back side of the house. He stated that he had shot them through the window. He said he had first shot Mrs. McCall, then when Mr. McCall came into the room, he shot him. He said he wasn't sure if he hit any of the children. He said that over and over.

"When I pulled up in front of the McCall residence, I climbed out of the car and headed for the house. A young woman ran out the front door toward me. She was very upset, seemed to be in shock an was hysterical. She said, 'Ken Andre did it' or 'My parents have been shot, Ken Andre did it. He's around here somewhere. You've got to catch him. Just hold me,' and she grabbed me like she'd never let go." The officer, his face grim, stopped, took a deep breath, and reviewed his notes.

He killed them. My big brother Kenny killed Christy's parents. It's horrible, just horrible.

I crushed my hands together and dug my fingers into my palms until they hurt. Cautiously I glanced over at Denise. Her eyes were riveted to the floor and tears ran down her freckled cheeks.

Officer Hammond continued reading, "I didn't want her to see that I had Mr. Andre in the back of the car, so I walked with her away from it. Then I asked her if anyone inside was hurt. She responded that her parents had been shot. When I asked if they were alive, she said she did not know, but they were really funny colored. When I asked if she was hurt, she said no."

The officer finished his direct testimony, and the cross-examinations began. Each attorney tried to score points.

Kevin McDonald had requested that I not be in the courtroom too long, and I worried about it. Being in there I probably was violating some kind of law, but I had to discover the details of the murders. Otherwise I would probably never know.

John Murray, the district attorney, seemed cold and dispassionate; his well-cut brown suit accented a lean figure. His nose was thin and straight with almost a hook at the end. That coupled with narrow eyes gave him a hawklike look.

When court was dismissed for the day, Cathy Simpson and the other jurors filed by.

"Did you see the expression on her face?" Denise whispered.

"She didn't even look at us. Maybe she hates us."

"I'm afraid this is going to be the longest two weeks I've ever spent."

Although the first day was over, we felt no relief on the way home or that night in bed as we tried to sleep. Now that we knew what to expect, there seemed more to fear.

The following morning we headed back to the courtroom.

"Officer Hammond, the tape we are about to hear was recorded just after you arrested the defendant, is that correct?" District Attorney Murray asked.

"Yes, I stayed with the McCall girl until a backup arrived. Then I made contact with the defendant and again advised him of his rights. I advised him that the tape was running."

"Would you say that he gave the testimony of his own free will?"

"Yes, he said that it didn't matter anymore anyway.
He'd just as soon be dead."
Feels like I've been kicked in the chest real hard.

After several minutes the tape began:
Officer Hammond: Can you tell me why you did
    it? What caused you kill these people?
Ken: Uh, well, I've been thinking about it for a
    long time.
Officer Hammond: Oh?
Ken: Yeah, in fact I told Teresa that she and those
    people down the street were driving me nuts.
Officer Hammond: Yeah?
Ken: 'If you and these people down the road
    succeed in driving me nuts,' I says, 'I'm going
    down there and shoot every one of the
    McCalls and I'm going to burn their house
    down.'
Officer Hammond: Yeah?
Ken: Well, she succeeded in driving me nuts.
Officer Hammond: Hum . . . you think you're
    nuts?
Ken: No, sir, I'm a very sane person.
Officer Hammond: You think so?
Ken: Yes.
Officer Hammond: You're talking fine. You're—
Ken: I sometimes get nervous.
Officer Hammond: You do? Well, I think you were
    a little bit nervous earlier, when I first caught
    up with you down there. Did you see the
    McCall girl, McCalls' daughter in there?
Ken: No, I didn't see her. You know, I told my
    wife that those McCalls were out to get me.
    That Maurice was trying to get me fired. You
    know, he was some kind of cheese with the
    company I worked for. And of course he tried
    to get my kids to go to church with him and

his family. I mean, he used that time to turn them against me.

Officer Hammond: You didn't want your kids to go to church?

Ken: Well, no, but I didn't do anything to stop them. I mean . . . I guessed they were old enough to make up their own minds about that. It's just that those McCalls and the Bennetts, too, were a bunch of hypocrites. Always talking about God and then the first chance they'd get they'd be trying to screw you over, stab you in the back or something. Maurice was the worst. [Ken raised his voice in angry hysterics.] I tell you, he wanted me fired. Then when Teresa and the kids left for no reason, well, I knew it had to be the fault of the McCalls and the Bennetts, turning my family against me with their lies. [His voice grew quiet.] So I devised me a plan.

Officer Hammond: Oh?

Ken: Yeah. I hid the gun so my parents wouldn't see me take it out. I'd been thinking about it all day at work, and I wasn't sure I'd do it, but when I got home and called Teresa and she wouldn't come home, well I knew I had to. They were a menace, those people, them and the whole lot of them down there at that church.

Officer Hammond: What is your religion?

Ken: I don't have one. I'm atheist. Now, I don't have anything against religious folks, I want you to understand. Whatever anyone wants to believe, that's their business. [Ken's voice became loud and shrill.] I just don't like hypocrites.

Officer Hammond: Is that why you killed them, then, because they were hypocrites?

Ken: Yeah, partially I guess. Mostly because they
     ran off my family. I didn't have anything left
     to live for. You see, we were raised really
     strict. There were a lot of things we couldn't
     do because of this church we attended . . . I
     never had any fun . . . Religion ruined my
     life . . . [Ken's voice broke and he began to
     sob.]

Grief clutched my heart; I had never heard him cry
before. He always took bad news with a straight face.
Now I clutched the arms of the chair, stared at the back
of his head, and blocked the rest of the testimony. Denise
was crying too. All of us had so many conflicting emotions.

Ken had not moved. He stared straight ahead.

At the next recess Kevin McDonald moved toward
me. My heart jumped and I tried not to feel guilty.

"Violet, I must ask you to leave. As I said before, I
may call you for a witness." He turned away.

When court reconvened and most of the people
went back in, I sat outside in the hall with my parents.

"Are those kids down at the end of the hallway the
McCall children?" I asked Momma softly. "It's been a
long time since I've seen them. The girl looks like
Kathy."

"Yes, Christy and Cal McCall. They've been here
quite a while," Momma said, her voice stiff with re-
pressed tears.

"Do you think they'll testify today?" Daddy asked.

"No. The court is still hearing the testimony of the
first officer."

"After all those kids have been through, it's too bad
they have to sit and wait," Daddy said.

Dejectedly I paced from the jog in the hallway to the
stairs, already tired of waiting. When I returned, five additional people stood down the hallway. The man and

woman appeared to be about my age. The children, two small blond boys, seemed to be about eight or nine.

Instantly I knew who they were from Momma's description the night of the killings—the Bennett children. Two of the adults would be the aunt and uncle with whom the kids were staying.

The couple tried to hold the Bennett children close, but the youngsters pulled away and huddled together on the side of the hall.

"You don't think they'll make those little guys testify, do you?" I whispered. "Doesn't the court care about them either?"

"I don't know, Vi," Daddy answered.

We were silent and strained to hear the conversation between the Bennetts, their attorney, and the officer of the court who had just joined them. I squeezed my father's arm and caught a sideways glimpse of him. His eye were filled with tears as he watched the two little boys. Momma knitted rapidly and looked at nothing else.

"The court has decided to allow the reading of the deposition in lieu of testimony," the officer said to the couple.

About a half an hour later the officer returned again and said, "The boys are excused now. The testimony has been read and accepted."

"Thank God," Daddy said.

"Yes. Thank God," I repeated.

Chapter Eleven

December nights are dark in the country and old farm houses creak with shifting winds and settling foundations. Beyond the walls, beyond the limits of time, four bodies robbed of life lay beneath blackened earth. Granite stones record names and years, and caskets of covered plywood mock the value of those who once lived.

Mine was the restless mind—a tortured heart caught up in murder. On the second night of the trial Ken's voice from the confession tape would not let me rest.

"After I shot Mr. Bennett I shot the door knob. The door still shouldn't open, so I busted out the window and climbed through. The boy and Mrs. Bennett ran down the hallway to the back of the house. The boy disappeared. I followed Mrs. Bennett. She picked up the phone. That's when I shot her. I remember she screamed first. Then I heard the explosion and there was blood everywhere."

The murder scenes and Ken's voice kept running on in my mind.

"Did you see the kids? Sure hope I didn't hit them. I used to play with the McCall children when they were little. Took them motorcycling and things. Oh, God, I hope I didn't hit them."

Pictures of bloody children and splattered brains did not let me sleep. For months now it had been so, as I tried to grasp the horror. My Kenny was a killer . . . a killer. What had happened to the big brother who used to call me Vidy?

"Kenny, wait up." Little feet scurried up the center of the mounded driveway and under a canopy of alder and myrtle. Ferns, salmon-berry bushes, and cloverlike plants covered the dark earth along the road's edge. She hurried toward her big brother. Her blonde curls danced in the shadows of late summer, and a shirt, half untucked, clung to her little body.

"Well, hurry up then, Vidy." Kenny grinned and allowed his four-year-old sister to catch up. He reached down and hoisted her to his shoulders. With her head almost touching the trees she held on tight. Trickles of sun splashed on her face.

"Where's the hive?" She asked as she nestled her nose his hair.

She loved his ebony curls, especially the ones that would not behave.

"Up by the road in that bunch of brush. Me and the Smith kids were up here last night."

They reached the end of the driveway and Kenny swung her to the ground. He pushed back the prickly bushes and there in the old alder tree found the conical nest.

"Are they going to bite me?" she asked.

"Nah. There's the opening. Look at that one. I didn't know they got that big."

"Kenny . . . you're going to make them mad."

"Stay back. I want to get closer." He climbed back into the salmonberries. The branches cracked and snapped, and his feet squished down into the moist ground. He broke a twig from the tree and poked the side of the nest.

"Oh shit, here comes one. Get back. Get back," he said, scrambling out of the brush.

"Ouch. It bit me. Kenny, it bit me," Vidy cried out. She chewed on her lower lip and tried not to cry. She did not want him to think she was too little to come along.

"Come here . . . let me see. You'll be alright. See this mud here? It's good for stings. It'll cool it off and stop it from hurting." He squatted down, dipped his finger into the mucky earth, and dabbed it gently on the swelling red skin beside her mouth.

"That's a big girl now. You're going to be alright."

He took hold of her pudgy arms and she snuggled to his big shoulder. "Would you like a ride back? Denise and I can bounce you in the blanket out on the lawn. You like that, don't you? . . . We got to go back to school tomorrow, so I won't be able to play with you as much."

"Can I go?"

"Not this year . . ."

Memory after memory flashed through my mind.

The white schoolhouse with steepled roof and belltower overlooked a valley of grass and tussocks. Farm families, some of them dating back to the pioneers, settled in houses up next to the tree line. Pastures with ditches and barbed-wire fences kept cattle in. Behind the school up on Blue Ridge, tall fir touched the place where God lived.

Down over the hill from the schoolhouse, a half dozen homes lined a graveled road. A country store straddled a channel of water where the slough met the creek. Some years when the rains came heavy and the water rose, residents wondered if the store would float away.

Across the valley dairy cattle already lined up for the evening milking waited amid pitted fields. The stench of manure and rotting silage drifted to the edge of the schoolyard on the warm September afternoon.

A dozen children stood on the front porch and in the dry grass below. On the bottom step, the one that came loose if you stepped on it wrong, Herby waited for his best friend.

"You got any money, Kenny?" he asked. He dug into his pocket and pulled out the coins his dad had given him that morning.

"A dime and two nickels," Kenny said.

"Good, that should be plenty. You coming Mikey? If we hurry we won't have to walk with the girls," Herby said.

"Did you ask Mrs. Parker if we could go?" Kenny said. He peered back inside the doorway toward the teacher's desk. It seemed kind of dark in there.

"No, just a minute." Herby hurried inside and soon was back. "She said it's okay. Let's get going."

He sped to the corner of the field and found the rutted trail that angled down the side of the steep hill. Kenny was close behind, followed by Mikey. Carol, Denise, and a half dozen other kids scooted down the path single

file, hanging onto bushes and trees to keep
from sliding.

"Those two nickels are mine, Kenny," Denise yelled.

At the base of the hill hidden in the brush
where he had stashed it that morning Herby
found his bicycle. He climbed on and looked at
Kenny. "You want a ride? Dad patched the tire
last night. It should be okay now."

Kenny climbed onto the back of the bike.
"Gee, I don't know. It still sits kind of low.
Maybe you can pump it up at the store. You go
ahead. I can run pretty fast."

The eleven-year-old boy pushed his foot
down hard to get the wheel turning, and
pumped as fast as he could down the dusty
lane. The dry wind felt good beneath his shirt.
He was going to have an ice cream bar. Beyond
that he was not sure. It depended on what
Kenny wanted.

Willis, a veteran of trees and trucks,
geared down and wrestled the vehicle around
the corner just up from the store. It was a good
load, about the best you could find in these
parts. Three good-sized logs. They would pay
him nicely for them. Yep, he was going to buy
Jenny that new wringer-washer she had been
wanting. With three babies at home there were
lots of diapers . . .

Herby was going good when he pedaled
out onto the main road. He looked back at
Kenny and grinned. A truck roamed into his
path.

"Herby look out—" Kenny shouted.

Boy and bicycle smashed into the side of
the truck. The driver slammed on the brakes

and dragged the boy along underneath for nearly five hundred feet.

"Oh God, dear God—" He jumped from the truck and yelled at the owner inside the store, "Call the ambulance. Dear God, I just hit the boy."

Hot dusty children raced around the corner by the teacher's house and down the road to the truck. Beneath it lay Herby and the bicycle, both of them crushed.

"You boys got to help me. We've got to get him out of there," the driver yelled. Two of the bigger boys helped Willis pull Herby to the side of the road in front of the store.

"Is he hurt bad?" The storekeeper hurried out and laid his grandmother's quilt over the freckled blond boy.

"Son . . . son, can you hear me?" Willis asked.

The boy did not stir, but he was still breathing. Willis ran his hands over the Herby's body, checking for breaks. "At least he's not bleeding. I couldn't stop. I just couldn't stop. He came pedaling out there, not even looking where he was going . . . How long is it going to take an ambulance to get here?"

"A half hour if we're lucky," the storekeeper answered.

When the ambulance was gone, the rest of the kids returned to the school. Kenny walked back alone. He could still see his friend crashing into that truck. . . . He could still see Herby's crumpled body beneath it.

That night he dreamed of crushing bones and death. He saw the tall stones in the old cemetery up the road. He and Herby snuck in there just last month. Now it would be Herby's name that glared back at him from cold granite.

The days went slowly after that but changes came quickly. A month after the accident the older kids like Kenny were sent in to Dayton to school, and in the cool of late October Kenny struggled in the shaded spaces of his mind.

It was almost raining that day when the bus stopped in front of the mailbox. Kenny grabbed onto the vertical rod by the front seat and swung around to the steps inside the door. He stumbled out of the old yellow bus onto the sharp rocks in the dirt road. Denise followed her older brother and listened for log trucks around the curve up the hill.

"You forgot to get the mail," she yelled at him.

He shuffled past the neighbor's big farmhouse and headed toward the driveway, ignoring her.

She pulled down the rusted lid and peeked inside. Nothing. "Herby's big sister, Sharon, got married."

"Who told you that?" Kenny asked.

"Carol. I don't know how Sharon could have done that so soon after what happened to Herby. They went away on their honeymoon and everything. I just don't think it's right. How can she be happy when he—" Denise's voice choked and she wiped her eyes on the sleeve of her new coat.

The long driveway seemed lonely and frightening as they walked silently toward the house. Denise clung to her books and watched the back of her brother's head. He never would let her close. Why wasn't he like other brothers?

When they reached the house, they stepped on the block of wood and up to the back porch. The door opened and heat from the pot-bellied stove met their shivers. Vidy was playing on the living room floor with her doll. Kenny dumped his books on the table and hugged his little sister. She was such a little thing, so warm and sweet. So unlike those boys he went to school with in Dayton.

Betty came in from the back bedroom and squeezed Denise. "How'd it go on your first day in town?"

Kenny went in to his bed and flopped face down on the woven spread.

"Son?"

"It was awful, Momma. Just awful. I don't know why they sent us in there. I hate that school with all those kids. They're bad kids too. Really bad kids. I bet not one of them goes to church."

"What makes you say that, honey?" Betty sat beside him and began petting his hair. Denise stood in the doorway just out of sight, twisting her braids and crossing her legs tightly because she had to pee.

"They were so awful. At recess the boys sneaked out to the end of the playground. That's when this boy took a pack of cigarettes from his pocket, lit one, and offered us all a smoke. Momma, all of them tried it. They were cussing and everything.

"They started talking about doing things to girls. One of them was bragging. He said he and the neighbor girl went out to this field. He said he pushed her to the ground and tore off

her . . . oh, Momma, they're awful kids.
There's not one good one there."

Betty spread her arms around the boy, but
he pulled away, huddled alone against the wall.

The organist was playing "What a Friend We
Have in Jesus," and the vestibule of the large
church was crowded. People greeted each
other and walked into the auditorium. A bal-
cony and a room for crying children overlooked rows of pine pews. A red carpet ran up
the center isle.

Denise found a seat with her friend Marcia
and Marcia's mother. Kenny, who was fourteen
sat with Larry, Marcia's brother, in the back
row. Betty and Lee with Vidy between them
settled on the other side of Kenny.

When the singing was over Mr. Kirkfield
moved from the seat by the baptistery, laid his
Bible on the pulpit, and addressed the congregation.

" 'Enter ye in by the narrow gate: for wide
is the gate and broad is the way that leadeth to
destruction, and many are they that enter in
thereby. For narrow is the gate, and straight is
the way, that leadeth unto life, and few are they
that find it.' "

Mr. Kirkfield pushed back from the pulpit
and grasped its sides. A tall man with an ath-
letic build, he surveyed the people. Somehow
today he must get the message across. It had
been weeks since anyone had given his heart to
the Lord. Maybe today was the day.

"The opening scripture is from Matthew,
chapter 7, verses 13 and 14. It was heavy on my
heart this past week as I went out into the community calling on the lost. The ways of the

world are wicked. And we, God's redeemed, must find a way to bring all to repentance.

"I look out onto the congregation and see evidence of sin. There are those of you who still smoke and drink. There are those of you who must turn from the evils of the dance. We all know the lust that abides in those halls of iniquity. We must look to God's laws to find our way.

"Turn with me now to Matthew, chapter 5, verses 27 through 30. 'Ye have heard that it was said, Thou shalt not commit adultery: but I say unto you, that everyone that looketh on a woman to lust after her hath committed adultery with her already in his heart. And if thy right eye cause thee to stumble, pluck it out and cast it from thee: for it is profitable for thee that one of they members should perish and not they whole body be cast into hell. And if they right hand causeth thee to stumble, cut it off and cast it from thee: for it is profitable for thee that one of thy members should perish and not thy whole body go into hell.'

"So, brothers and sisters in the body of Christ, I want you to look among yourself and find that which is evil and cast it out into the eternal darkness. There is no place in God's kingdom for the wicked. The world has plenty of room for these. Don't let sin ruin your life.

"And you, sisters, mark my words, unless you modify your clothing, you become the serpent unto man, like in the days of old when Adam was tempted by the woman and did fall into the lust of the flesh. And they were cast out of the garden and had to work by the sweat of their brows to produce sustenance. Keep your daughter from wearing the tight clothes of the

Jezebel, like this young one over here." He pointed to a flashily dressed girl in the second row. "Repent and turn to the Lord . . ."

The two boys sat quietly. Kenny's white cords were spotless and his hair perfectly combed. He was leaning forward, his eyes wide, staring at the minister, he was nodding in time to the minister's words not to ruin life. He whispered to his mother—"I must become perfect so Christ can love me."

The day before Christ's birthday the cold mists of winter drifted across the evergreen hills and dark waters of morning. The push of the tide crowded the inlets and sloughs that meandered away from the bay. Sucking mud flats were covered now. Only the coarse tufted grass on the higher ground and cattails along the edges remained aloft.

Up beyond the bridge where the slough and the river divided, three teenage boys slammed the front door of George's house. They hurried across the road, hip boots thug-thugging beneath them. Shadows crept beyond the bouncing flashlight. The shotgun Rex carried was carefully aimed away from the others.

They climbed over the short bank and crossed the grass-covered mud along the edge of the slough. Locating the wooden duck pram they pushed it halfway into the water.

"You guys climb in," George called out.

Kenny and Rex stepped in one at a time and sat down. George grabbed hold of the boat and shoved it out. Pulling his feet from mud and water, he climbed in and took the oars. There was room for only one person to row.

Tugging against the incoming tide, he

headed down the slough toward the two-lane
bridge. The wind was quiet; the swish-plop of
the oars was the only sound. Once beyond the
bridge he turned the boat toward the grassy island in the center of the bay. Soon they were
there.

Up the river beyond the big bridge and for-
ested hills the ebony night lightened to milky
gray. Kenny climbed quietly into the shallow
water. George got out as well and pulled the
boat along the edge of the channel that meandered through the center of the island.

Rex perched himself on the center seat. On
his lap was Kenny's old gun, loaded and ready.
Dawn was close.

"Up ahead, just beyond the edge, there's a
bunch of them," Kenny said. Quiet excitement
laced his voice. He was the best shot of the
three and he knew it. But this time he wanted
Rex to try first. Being from the East and all, he
never got much of a chance to shoot ducks.
Mallards were the most plentiful . . . He'd get
a few right off.

BOOM— George crumbled into the water.

"Oh, God," Rex said. He flicked out the
rest of the cartridges and laid the gun of the
seat.

"Help me get him into the boat," Kenny
yelled. "Can you stand, George?"

"Uh . . . I don't know. What happened?"

"The gun went off. We've got to get you
into the boat. Rex, put your shoulder under his
left arm. Can you lift your leg, George?"

"Oh . . . no . . . it—"

"You hit below your knee?"

"I guess." George looked dazed and about
to faint.

"Hang on," Kenny yelled. "I'm going to lift your legs. Rex, just kind of roll him in. Now get in the back and hold him up out of the water and start bailing."

"I'm sorry, George," Rex said. "I don't know how it happened. It just went off. I didn't mean it . . ."

Kenny rowed as fast as he could, tugging against the current. When they made it to shore, the two boys stepped out and hoisted George out onto the bank.

"Go call an ambulance . . . there's a house just around the corner," Kenny said. "George . . . does it hurt?"

"I . . . can't feel anything. Feel kind of dizzy—"

"Now don't pass out on me, you hear . . . don't pass out on me. Should've gotten rid of the gun. There's no safety on it. Should have gotten rid of that gun . . ."

Chapter Twelve

"Morning, Momma. Were you able to sleep?" I inquired, positioning my feet in front of the electric heater under the dining room table.

"Not very well," she murmured. She wrestled the frying pan onto the front burner and took out a package of sausage and some eggs.

"Me either. I kept hearing Ken—"

"Me too," Denise chimed in as she padded in from living room; a white terry robe was pulled snugly about her.

"I keep seeing those little boys on the porch," Momma said, her voice sore and distressed. "I just can't get them out of my mind, and seeing them yesterday so alone and scared . . ."

Two hours later found us waiting again in an institutional corridor. Dave, who had arrived late the night before, stood with me at the top of the stairwell.

"Thanks again for coming," I said.

"Finished my chores, so thought I'd come after all. Not much a person can do around the farm with it pouring down rain and cold like it's been the last few days."

He kissed the top of my head. Right Guard and Ivory soap emanated through his wool plaid shirt. His hair was neatly styled and his beard, a little too long for my liking, brushed the edges of an unbuttoned collar.

He seemed large beside me. Of course he out-weighed me by a hundred pounds. The pressure of his large hands was comforting through my sweater and wool jacket. By nine the hallway filled with jurors. They hung up their coats on the rack and entered one of the rooms. Witnesses congregated on smooth wooden benches and padded chairs; we all waited.

"Have Teresa and the kids arrived?" I asked.

Carrie, one of Teresa's friends who had been called to testify, nodded. "They're talking to the district attorney now. They may have to testify today," she said and turned back to my folks. "Like I was saying, the steel head were running. I cast my line out into deep water . . ."

Denise leaned against the opposite wall and listened to Carrie. Billie had vanished. At quarter after nine Denise, Dave, and Aunt Elsa disappeared beyond the doors. A number of other people, known and unknown to me, followed them inside.

My mind now prone to the worst imaginings frantically, vainly searched for escape. There was none, for on the dark wings of a nightmare, sweeping in and around a long hollow passage came . . . the McCall children, Calvin and Christy.

The two children and their Aunt Hazel rounded the corner at the far end of the hall and headed for us.

Oh God, they're here. Wonder if they blame us? I can't stand anything else.

My parents, a kind of unimaginable dignity about them, rose and greeted their son's victims, who brought with them the images of the dead. Momma's eyes were full of forced courage . . . and near panic. She touched Hazel's outstretched hands and the women grasped each other. Pain and compassion flowed between and filled the space around them. Daddy encircled the little girl

with pale skin and golden hair in his frail loving arms
and clasped her to his damaged heart. Then her brother
Calvin took Daddy's hand. The young smooth one
clasped the old and gnarled. No one spoke.

It was amazing, so different than I had imagined.
They understood we did not do it. What about Greg and
Jered, Kathy and Maurice's other children? Were they as
loving and friendly? And Kathy's brother Joel and the
other two brothers? Surely some of them hated us. The
idea made me want to climb inside myself and hide.

"Do you remember our youngest daughter, Violet?"
Daddy asked. He patted Christy's shoulder. "Oh my,
yes," Hazel, Kathy's sister, said, "She was a little girl
when I saw her last." She took my hand and held it,
smiling beyond the pain. There was tenderness in her,
tenderness I had noticed years before. And shattered
peace.

"I remember seeing the two of you playing with
Loni and Russ," I said to Calvin and Christy, "but it's
been quite a while and you were probably too little to
notice me."

Christy was a lovely girl. Silver-blue eyes and dainty
freckles on her nose, she looked just like her mother.
Seeing her, knowing what Ken had done to her, made
things more intolerable.

After some contrived conversation the orphaned
pair sat down beside my parents. I stood above the stairs
and gazed out the window at the other wing of the building.

*It was hard to know three sides of pain . . . the
killer's . . . the victims' . . . and my family's—the hidden victims. Three sides with so many faces, and all of us
plagued by dark memories.*

Caught up in horrifying images I slumped against
the half-wall over the stairwell. Another inhabitant of the
inferno moved in beside me.

My throat tightened. I took a silent breath and struggled to smile at Christy.

"Have you seen Loni and Russ?" she said in a frightened childlike voice. Like me she stared straight ahead.

"No, but they're here somewhere."

"I want to see them so badly," she said. "I've really missed them. Used to be over at their house all the time."

"Loni talked about you a lot."

"I wrote to both of them a couple of times and they wrote back. Loni was having a hard time accepting what her father did. She was afraid I would hate her. Why should I? It wasn't her fault."

"She was afraid it would destroy your friendship."

"I couldn't let that happen. I knew for years her father had problems. Seems like every time I was over there he was yelling at Loni or Russ for something. Mom said it was because he was angry at himself. I never quite understood that, but Mom said sometimes when a person is mad at themselves they take it out on other people. Do you think that's why he killed Mom and Dad?"

I began to shake, but my voice was soft and controlled. "Could be. It's called projection. It means you blame others for the things you cause yourself."

"When he walked by me yesterday I got really scared," she said. "I remembered that night . . . I heard a loud explosion. Dad, Calvin, and I were in the other end of the house. We all ran out to the kitchen to see what happened. Dad was first, then me and Calvin.

"I heard Mom moan. That's when the second shot went off and Dad fell. I started screaming. I remember I just screamed and screamed. When I finally stopped I went to Mom. She was all blue and funny looking. I felt for a pulse and there wasn't any. So, I went to Dad. He was trying to talk and blood was coming out all over the floor. He told me to turn off the lights, go into the bedroom, and hide under the bed. So I did.

"After a while I crept back in, knelt down beside him, and said, 'Daddy, don't die. I love you. Daddy, please don't die.' I leaned closer and tried to hear what he was saying, but I couldn't understand him. I stayed with him for a long time. There was nothing I could do," she said and her voice raised in quiet hysteria. "My daddy was dying and there was nothing I could do . . ."

I can't deal with this. There's been too much pain. Can't cry now. Must wait until I'm alone. Can't cry now. Can't.

"After a while Daddy died. I knew when it happened because he stopped breathing with sort of a gurgling sound. I didn't know what to do. I guess Calvin had gone for help. I was so scared. The house was dark and cold and I was afraid Ken would come back to kill me too."

"Then you knew it was Ken."

She nodded. "Yes, in fact Mom had warned me that afternoon when I got home from school to stay away from Ken's house because Teresa and the kids had left. She heard Ken screaming and carrying on the night before when he got home from work and found they were gone."

"Did you ever see him?"

"No, it was too dark outside, but Calvin did. He told me later when he went for help he saw Ken walking back toward his house. He raised his hands and told Calvin to call the police because he had just killed some people. Calvin tore out of there as fast as the car would take him.

"Anyway, I remember running back into my bedroom. I didn't know what to do. It was dark in there, so dark. I climbed under the bed and waited until I heard a car drive up. It was the police. I was so scared. I still am. And when I saw Ken in the hallway yesterday it really scared me. Uh . . . it's not right to hate someone, is it?"

I struggled for control. "Ken killed your parents and you watched it happen. He took your love and security. It must be terrible for you to bear."

She nodded.

"But," I tried to find words to comfort her, "it's important to try to forgive people who hurt you, because if you don't it does so much more damage to you than it does to them. But don't be too hard on yourself if you can't forgive him yet. Do you believe in God?"

"Yes," she whispered.

"Do you believe God knows when you need help and helps you with your problems?"

She nodded again.

"Then remember God is Love. He'll help you with the anger and pain. Do you pray?"

"Yes, but He seems so far away at times."

"I know. I have problems with that too . . . but you must try to have faith, a faith that Someone Else is guiding our lives, Someone much stronger and more knowing than we are."

I was surprised at my words and wondered if I believed them at all. At that moment, however, it did not matter what I believed. I just wanted to comfort her.

"I've had a hard time dealing with what Ken did too," I went on. "He's my brother and I love him but I can't understand how he could kill anyone, especially your folks. I've tried to understand what causes a person to do something like this. I don't have the answer."

"I don't either," she said tearfully. "When Mom and Dad were alive they made all the decisions for me. They told me what was right and wrong, where I could go and what I could do. Since then I've had to act like a grownup. I've been living with my older brother and he lets me make those decisions. It's hard. I just want someone to take care of me again."

A man opened a courtroom door and stepped into

the hallway, his eyes searching and his voice clear. "Christy McCall, please."

After more than an hour the doors inched open just enough for the small-framed girl to slip back through. Her frightened eyes stared bleakly at the corridor.

She was a child alone.

I needed to go to her and hug away the fear, but my body would not cooperate. I stood rooted to the spot.

Daddy, the father of the killer, had remained seated along the wall behind me. Now he shuffled toward her. He took her into his gentle arms and she clung to him. Guiding her away from the doorway and down the stairs to the landing, he held her. Clinging to him she sobbed in the safest place she had been in months. He bent his white head to her blonde one, kissed her hair and let the tears slide unchecked down his pallid cheeks.

God . . . why? If you're such a loving God, why did you let Ken break their hearts?

Each day we returned to the courthouse, anticipating the unacceptable. On the fourth day Momma and Daddy knew they would probably have to testify. They sat together, hands intertwined, and with pinched faces watched the door.

After a long morning and a brief recess, court reconvened for the second segment of the wait. Within a short time a man stepped out onto the polished tile and called, "Lee Andre, please."

Daddy stood up. He seemed more fragile than before. His legs housed in a loose pair of trousers shook slightly; I worried about his weak heart. Momma squeezed his hand in farewell. Her future looked bleak without the son who might be executed and the husband who could die anytime.

I stared at my watch. Forty-five minutes passed and my father was still inside the chamber speaking against his son. Near panic replaced worry. I paced and sat

down, only to rise and pace again. Momma looked frantic and for thirty-six more minutes we waited, watched,
and fretted. Close to noon Daddy stepped out looking
drained, hopeless, and defeated.

Momma ran over and clung to him. Years of love
and dependency melded together and arms who had
held each other often now reached for refuge. Theirs was
a love grown and nurtured for over forty years, the kind
the rest of us knew little about, comfort in a time of com-
fortlessness, someone to cling to amid tragedy.

I stood alone.

The hall filled; court had recessed for lunch.

"How did it go?" I asked Denise when she emerged,
her eyes looking worried.

"Dad was really nervous," she remarked, "but he
seemed alright. Of course you never know with him."

"Grandma, Grandpa," came a familiar voice from
behind. Loni, Ken's eleven-year-old daughter with long
brown hair and big brown eyes, hurried toward us. She
and her brother, Russ, hugged their grandparents.

"Aunt Violet, it's so good to see you," Loni said and
dropped her almond-shaped eyes in sudden shyness.
"They told us we weren't supposed to talk to anyone, but
we couldn't wait anymore."

"It's good to see you too, sweetheart," I said as I
embraced my brother's only daughter. I remembered the
letter she had written a month before:

Dear Aunt Vi,

I'm not happy here. Mom is gone all the
time. Russ has a job and works a lot. I spend
some of my time with my grandpa and
grandma. Grandma doesn't like me. When I
come up for the trial, I plan to stay there with
Grandma and Grandpa Andre. I won't come
back here. I hate it.

Carefully I had written a reply of love and encouragement, but I had no way of knowing how the letter had affected her.

In a round of hugging Russ sidled up to me and smiled a lopsided smile, the one that always made everything seem better. He was fifteen and nearly six foot with intensely brown eyes and hair that feathered back from his face. His denim pants and polo shirt fit him perfectly. He had always been particular about his appearance, the way his father had been when he was growing up. In fact, except for hairstyle, he looked a lot like Ken had as a teenager.

"Where's your mom?" I asked as the family group started for the main entrance.

"She's going to meet us over at the pizza parlor," Russ said.

We walked the few blocks, ordered several giant pizzas, and waited for Teresa. There was an atmosphere of uneasiness between the dark hickory walls. The red-globed lanterns broadcast flickering gloom.

It had been over nine months since I had seen the woman who had married my brother and been my sister for so long. I was Loni's age when Ken brought her home. We shared so many secrets as I grew.

What if she wants nothing to do with me because I'm Ken's sister? Maybe she thinks I've turned against her.

The door screeched open as Teresa and one of her friends came in. Teresa walked past the rows of tables and chairs.

There was something different about her, makeup maybe. Ken never let her wear it. Now her eyes were heavily lined and lavender eyeshadow matched her doubleknit pantsuit. She had been very heavy, but as she edged closer I saw she'd lost weight.

"Hi, y'all," Teresa said in a westernized southern drawl. She forced a smile but could not fully remove the worry from her face.

One by one we greeted her, then stuffed our nervous
stomachs with pizza. The conversations were light, too
light, and tension dominated careful exchanges.

I said little, reverting back to the behavior of my
childhood. Sometimes it was the least risky thing to do. I
was afraid to get her alone and ask what she was thinking.

With the advent of the afternoon session Momma
took her turn inside the closed room. Staring toward the
door, Daddy pulled a red hunter's handkerchief from his
back pocket and cleared his sinuses.

"Momma has been in there a long time," he noted.

"I know," I murmured.

"Wish they hadn't called her. She's so upset. It
brings it all back, having to relive it for them."

"How'd it go for you?"

"It wasn't too bad, I guess. I just told them what
happened, except what Ken said to me just before he
headed down to the McCalls. I got out to the road firs,
you know, just after he'd killed the Bennetts."

"What did he say?"

"It's something I'll never tell anyone, Vi." He closed
his eyes and rested his head against the wall.

Carrie Smith ambled down the hallway and seated
herself beside me.

"I thought you left after you testified. I didn't see
you at lunch," I said.

"I had some errands to run, but I couldn't let your
family face this alone," she said. "Besides, I always liked
Ken. He was so kind to me after I got my divorce. My
troubles seemed to bring out his compassion. He'd actually sit and talk to me instead of hiding upstairs like he
did when other people came to visit. A month or so after
he was arrested, he started to write to me."

"Did you write back?" My other self talked with her,
while I hovered above them.

"Yes. I knew he needed it."

"I'm surprised he wrote to you. He's been afraid they'd use what he wrote against him in court," I said.

"He mentioned that in his first letter. I guess he needed a friend. You know, I always felt sorry for him. It seemed that he had no friends, and I wondered how he got by without anyone to talk to."

"Guess he talked to his partner at work," I said.

"Yes, but I don't think they were that close, at least not from what he said in his letters. They never did anything together after work. Ken seemed to think that the man was dumb."

"He thinks everyone is. I'm the only one in the family he thinks has any brains. I guess that's because I graduated from college."

"He thinks a lot of you, Violet."

"He told me I was the only hope for the family, I was the only way we would ever get out of ignorance and poverty."

For the umpteenth time since Momma entered the courtroom, I studied Daddy. His gaze was still fastened on the door.

"Momma will be alright," I whispered and slipped my hand into his rough hairy one.

"I hope you're right, Vi."

Finally the door opened; Momma walked through and stood just outside. This time I rushed to her and slipped an arm about her. Her whole body was trembling.

"How'd it go?"

"I'm so afraid I said the wrong things," she whispered.

"What do you say we head down to the restroom?"

"Please."

Daddy eyes were desolate and broken. Momma stopped in front of him and grasped his hand. The exchange was brief; she hurried past him toward a place that held no eyes.

Alone in the small room we stood together. Momma lowered her face to my shoulder and tears surged up from the reservoir of pain. I held my mother, pretending to be strong.

"Hope I didn't say something that would make it worse for Ken."

"You told the truth. That's all you can do."

"What if I said it in a way that will make it worse for him? What if they send my boy to the electric chair?"

Preoccupation with that possibility plagued us all.

That evening my sister and I went up to the neighbor's pond as we had the first evenings after the killings. "I had to get away from everyone," she said as we trudged up the familiar road. "What finally did it was when Russ testified. He looked so scared. He sat up there in his jeans and jacket and tried not to look at his father. He just sat there and stared at the floor while they asked him all kinds of questions."

"What did he testify about?" I asked as I stepped into the wet meadow.

"Mostly about the Friday night before the Tuesday shootings. He talked about Ken threatening Teresa with a knife and the other times Ken threatened them."

"How about the McCalls?"

"He said Ken had been threatening Kathy and Maurice for years, so none of them thought he'd do it."

I shuddered, ignored the darkening fir, and scanned the murky water of the pond. A wet wind clung to my hair, and the small branches of alder trees pulsated in the fading light.

"Wish I had a drink, I'm so tense I feel like I'll shatter," I said.

"I wonder how long this thing is going to last. They present the same evidence over and over. It's horrible sitting through it."

"Dave said it's been pretty hard on him too."

"I suppose it has. It's helped to have him in there with me. Aunt Elsa keeps falling asleep."

"How can she fall asleep at her nephew's murder trial?"

"I don't know. I wish Ted would come down. I need him, but he just can't tolerate it. I'm having a hard time being here myself."

"Me too, but we can't let Momma and Daddy face this alone."

Saturday Dave and I planned to spend on my favorite set of cliffs, watching a winter storm crash pillars of water into jutting angular sandstone. Those plans were overruled. The morning of the sixth day found us again at the courthouse.

Carrie waited with the three of us, and after a few hours she and I grew tired of sitting and started down the hall. When we were well away from the others she said, "Your dad broke down the other day."

"Oh?"

"It was when you and your mom went to the restroom after she testified. After you disappeared around the corner, he put his face in his hands and cried and cried. I tried to comfort him, but there's so little a person can do."

"I've never seen Daddy cry much," I said hoarsely, my throat tight with unreleased tears, "except an occasional tear during sad movies."

"The poor, sweet man. I felt so bad. He looked so desolate and completely worn out."

"Violet, wait up." Kevin McDonald hurried toward us. "The prosecution is about to rest. Since they didn't call Teresa because of my opposition to spousal testimony, my next thought is that they may call you. I don't care where you go or what you do, just make yourself scarce. I have a feeling if you're not around they won't think it's important enough to try to find you. So disappear."

"For how long?"

"I'm not sure. Maybe for several days. I'll let your folks know this evening. Call them at seven."

Alone, I left the courthouse without talking to anybody else. I steered my car of faded red through the Kenton River valley toward Oceanside fifteen miles away.

A strange feeling invaded me, as if I belonged no where.

The dike road wound through the valley. On either side of me was water—a river on the right and flooded pastures to the left. Once out on Highway 101 that followed the coast, I found the small town and turned down Beach Loop Road to the point.

Drooping clouds lifted just enough to reveal an almost waveless sea. Minimountains of rock were encircled by a few feet of water. One rock jutted into the milky mist. Gulls and other seabirds lined the camel back of yet another hill of stone.

There was no turbulent surf to soothe me . . . no crashing storm to match my mood.

I considered where to go and discarded each option as it came to me, afraid the police would outmaneuver me if I went to some place predictable.

I started the engine and drove toward Dayton. There were few houses along the twenty-mile stretch. Only an occasional driveway cut into the dense evergreens.

Along the bay and a mile from the pillared bridge that spanned the river a covered shopping center housed twenty small shops, a large clothing store, and a drug store. I parked and walked across the puddled parking lot, keeping my head down hoping not to be spotted.

I stole through the shops wanting to buy something that would make me feel better.

Restless and lonely I kept watch for the police.

The floor of the entire mall was uneven. The base below the cement and brick had settled into the filled mud flat. I tripped along and finally entered a shop of jeans and hand-knitted sweaters.

"Will that be all, Ma'm?" the lady at the counter asked. She wrapped the two sweaters in tissue and slipped them into a sack, the white one first. It was a delicate knit that made me feel feminine and beautiful.

"Yes, thanks. I don't want my husband to skin me," I answered with a wan smile. I handed her cash, careful to avoid use of my identification. The newspaper was full of the details of the trial. Since I had retained my family name when I married, I did not want to risk questions like "Are you related to that killer?"

A man in casual clothes stood at the far end of the mall, another one down by the small photo booth. Maybe they were policemen in disguise.

As unobtrusively as I could I walked over to the telephone, deposited a coin and called my home.

"Hello, Dave, what are you doing there already?"

"The prosecution rested at two. You can come out of hiding now," he said and laughed.

"Thanks," I half-whispered and hung up.

Back in the car I leaned my head back against the hard plastic seat, all my energy gone.

Chapter Thirteen

"Can you tell me, Dr. Bradford, how long it was after the shooting incident that you examined the defendant?" asked Kevin McDonald. A lone panther in black pinstripes, he prowled before the defense table. From the corner of his eye he watched the judge and occasionally stared full into the eyes of individual jurors. Most of the time, however, he focused on the psychiatrist.

"I saw him twice, on March 21 and on March 28."

"Three and four weeks after the incident?"

"Yes, I believe so."

"What were your findings?"

Dr. Bradford pushed metal-framed glasses into place and began to read. "I found the defendant to have manifestations of extreme anxiety, extreme arousal, notoric evidence manifested by his skeletal muscles. He was also delusional and exhibited looseness of association. My examination revealed that the defendant has suffered from paranoia and other mental disorders for a long time and at the time of the shootings was under the influence of extreme emotional disturbance."

"You said, Dr. Bradford, that the defendant has had problems for a long time. Can you expand on that?"

It was Momma's first time as a spectator. Beside me

she perched forward on the seat . . . consumed by it all. Denise, Dave, Aunt Elsa, and I sat with her. Collectively we formed a defensive line behind Ken.

"During my examination of the defendant," the doctor's voice rose, "we discussed early periods of his life, his childhood, how he was raised, and after he left home. It was during the period of his military service that some of his problems began. Which, of course, fits the symptom picture—"

"The symptom picture?"

"Yes, of the schizophrenic. He was eighteen or nineteen at the time and in training as a paratrooper for the Airborne Division. He was excited about the assignment and looking forward to his first jump. The problems began then, and he had to be reassigned."

"Can you tell the court about that?"

"Yes. They were all in the plane heading out to the target area. That's when he heard voices."

"What do you mean voices . . . of the other men in the outfit?"

"No. Voices of people who weren't actually there."

Listening to the statements of the psychologists and psychiatrist was easier than listening to the other testimony. We too wanted to know what had happened to make the man we loved kill people who were loved by others.

Several rows behind us, Hazel, Kathy McCall's sister, watched and listened. Every day she had been there, trying to learn what had happened, trying to comprehend impossible events. Sometimes her nephew, Jered, was with her; sometimes she sat alone.

Dr. Bradford's clinical tone reminded Hazel of the doctors she had worked with, and her training as a nurse. Long years she had been away from her family working in the mission field. Though Kathy had written often and their relationship remained close, it could never make up for the years they had missed. She always thought there would be plenty of time to spend with her sister and brother-in-law, Maurice.

So many emotions had crowded her heart since the killings. Often there was no way to deal with them, but deal with them she did. She was not one to run from the things that needed facing.

From the back Ken looked like any other man, but he was not. He had robbed her of her loved ones. Anger, there had been some, even though she had prided herself on being in control of negative emotions. The ache and the sadness because of the deaths never let up. That sadness extended to Ken's family as well. They too were tormented by events they could not control.

Ken—he was so obviously paranoid, strapped to a mind unable to filter out erroneous assumptions. Evaluating it all, she could not hate him. In some ways she felt sad for him most of all. The Heavenly Father now cared for Kathy and Maurice. With God's help she and the others would find their way back to wholeness. But there seemed no helping Ken. She could only pray that God would restore wellness to his mind.

Our days were filled with tension as more people testified, then withdrew. Bound by love and tragedy we remained, and each evening of the trial we returned home exhausted in body and soul.

"Kevin thinks tomorrow will be the last day," I observed, padding into the wallpapered kitchen after changing to my jeans and wool sweater. Momma, still dressed in her court clothes, stood in front of the stove and toyed with a package of hamburger.

"I sure hope so," Denise sighed. She adjusted a large pillow beneath her back and snuggled into the living room couch like a sleepy five-year-old. "Tomorrow will be the ninth day and I've had it."

"Me too," Momma said.

"Want me to cook, Momma?" I asked.

"No, I need to do it. Just sitting all day listening, waiting, it's hard on me. Got to do something." She unwrapped the meat and with a farm woman's hands formed it into patties.

I trudged into the living room; Denise was there. I knelt on the cold tile in front of the bookshelf, the one filled with Ken's books. Scanning the titles I located a copy of one of mine entitled *Abnormal Psychology and Modern Life*.

I turned to the section on schizophrenia. "All three of the doctors who testified today said he was paranoid schizophrenic."

"I wondered about that," Denise said.

Tucking a foot beneath me on the vinyl chair, I took a seat at the dining room table and began to read.

> Frequently there has been a history of growing suspiciousness and of difficulties in interpersonal relations. The eventual symptom picture is dominated by absurd, illogical and changeable delusions. Persecutory delusions are the most frequent, and may involve a wide range of ideas and all sorts of plots. The individual may become highly suspicious of his relatives or associates. . . .
>
> These delusions are frequently accompanied by vivid auditory, visual, and other hallucinations. The patient may hear singing or God speaking or the voices of his enemies. . . . The individual's behavior becomes centered around these delusions and hallucinations, resulting in loss of critical judgment and in erratic, unpredictable behavior. . . . Occasionally a paranoid schizophrenic can be dangerous, as when he attacks someone he is sure is persecuting him.

"It sounds like Ken, doesn't it," Momma said. "Did he tell you about the voices at the holding facility in Dayton?"

I nodded.

"He kept talking about all those people who were plotting against him," Denise said. "I always wondered why he thought he was that important. Nobody gives a rat's hind side about him except us."

"Do you think he'll ever get better?" Momma asked.

"From what I've read there isn't much hope," I said.

"Any help that might be available won't be in prison. Prisons can make people paranoid under normal circumstances. It would take some kind of miracle."

I pulled out the green paperback I had recently gotten entitled *Criminal Code of Oregon 1980*.

"Each of the doctors," I said, "testified that Ken was extremely emotionally disturbed. I thought I'd look that up too. In ORS 163.115 of the criminal code book it says that

> a homicide which would otherwise be murder
> is committed under the influence of extreme
> emotional disturbance when such disturbance
> is not the result of the person's own intentional,
> knowing, reckless or criminally negligent act,
> and for which disturbance there is a reasonable
> explanation. The reasonableness of the expla-
> nation for the disturbance shall be determined
> from the standpoint of an ordinary person in
> the actor's situation under the circumstances
> as the actor reasonably believes them to be.

"Does it mean," Denise said, "that if he was extremely emotionally disturbed at the time of the crime, he isn't guilty of murder even though he killed them?

Killing someone is killing someone. They're just as dead regardless of the reason, and he's responsible."

I sighed heavily, technicalities and the law—we did not discuss them. There seemed no point. The law functioned beyond our knowledge and control.

On the last day of the trial Judge Jones began a short speech on the jury's responsibilities and the importance of what they were doing. Then he theatrically scanned the room and picked up his holy book. "In continuing this instruction I will read to you from the Criminal Code of Oregon:

163.115 Murder: emotional disturbance described; sentence required. (1) Except as provided in ORS 163.118 and 163.125, criminal homicide constitutes murder when:

(a) It is committed intentionally by a person who is not under the influence of an extreme emotional disturbance;

(b) It is committed by a person acting either alone or with one or more person, who commits or attempts to commit arson in the first degree, burglary in the first degree, escape in the first degree, kidnapping in the first degree, rape in the first degree, robbery in any degree or sodomy in the first degree and in the course of the crime he is committing or attempting to commit, or the immediate flight therefrom he, or another participant if there be any, causes the death of a person other than one of the participant.

"At this point I would like to say that if you find that the defendant committed the crimes while in the process of committing a burglary, then extreme emotional disturbance is not an excuse and you must find the defendant guilty of felony murder. If, on the other hand, you find that the defendant did not commit burglary and was in fact under the influence of extreme emotional disturbance, you must find the defendant guilty of manslaughter.

"As stated by this court several times during the trial, the issue here is not whether or not the defendant did in fact cause the deaths of the four individuals. The issue is his degree of guilt."

"Your Honor, I would like the record to reflect that I object to the giving of the felony murder instruction," Kevin McDonald said.

"Yes, I understand that," Judge Jones replied.

McDonald continued, "Your Honor, I know that the recent Reams case be against my position, but I believe it is the Branch case, an older Supreme Court case, which suggests that it is improper to instruct on burglary in the situation where the crime that he intended when he entered the house was murder or criminal homicide. According to Branch it would almost be a merger situation or something of that nature, so it would not be appropriate in a felony murder.

"I believe, Your Honor, that with the legislature and certainly going back to the common law, certain highly dangerous crimes were picked out, and if a death occurred in the commission of one of the delineated kinds of felonies, that it would be a murder. That is, the State would not have to prove intent. Now, that's the basic theory behind it.

"What we have here is the absolute reverse of that kind of situation. There was not a death occurring in the course of a burglary. If the facts as given by the State are taken at their face value, you have a collateral burglary occurring in the course of criminal homicide, which is what it amounts to. I would suggest to the court that felony murder should not apply."

Several rows in front of us Ken sat erect and for the first time stared into the face of the judge.

"What you're saying," the judge explained, "is that the defendant has to get the intent to do the burglary before he gets the intent to cause the death. If he gets the intent to kill somebody before he gets the intent to commit burglary, then he can't be guilty of felony murder."

"That's it, Your Honor. I mean, it is not consistent with the history behind the statute."

While the judge and the two attorney's argued the technicalities, I watched the faces of the jurors. They were impassive.

After the judge gave final instructions, the family returned to the hall. Momma sagged onto the chair beside Daddy and my sister; I stepped down to the landing.

"Guess Teresa and the kids returned to California after Russ testified," Denise said finally. "Wonder what the verdict will be?"

"God knows, I just wish it was over," I said. "I feel as though I'm going to explode, like my skin can't contain my body much longer."

"You and me both. Hope they don't deliberate all night," she said.

Within minutes the hallway congested with people, and the jurors, accompanied by "house parents," left for lunch. After the break they were again bottled into the room behind the judge's chambers. We sat there immobile.

"Wonder if they'll kill our brother," Denise said. Her voice sounded distant, as if she were talking to herself.

"I don't know. Guess that won't be decided until the sentencing next month. It's been a long time, all these months not knowing what they'll do to him. I still can't believe it. I keep thinking it's just not possible that Kenny did something like this."

The murmur of conversation between Carrie and my family was ignorable. Up the stairway a long spider web drifted out from the ceiling; the structure creaked with the sounds of an old building, and I shook from the inside out.

"From what Kevin said, the longer they are out, the better chance the verdict will be favorable for Ken," Denise said, looking at her watch for the umteenth time.

I looked out the window. Rain drenched a darkening sky as wind from the southwest drove it across the panes of glass. A slim young man dressed in a brown sports jacket and tan slacks descended the stairs and stood with us, yet apart, as though he did not belong.

"Miserable weather, huh?" he observed.

"I'm tired of it. There's been way too much," I said.

Denise muttered something and moved away. My first impulse was to follow her, but something made me stay.

"Are you covering the trial?" I asked, both curious about and afraid of the man.

"Yes. I'm Todd Wyatt. I work for the *Dayton Times*."

It was good to talk to someone not involved in my pain.

"What's your connection?" he asked. His face was nondescript, and he could have been anybody's brother. It was his eyes that drew me to him, so sensitive and blue.

I shouldn't say anything. He's a reporter. I'm not supposed to trust him.

"I'm the sister of the defendant."

He looked at me more closely "Bet the wait seems long for you."

"Longer than I ever imagined."

"Are you needing to talk?"

"I shouldn't. I don't want what I say to be printed in your paper," I said gravely.

"Look, this is off the record. I've just never had the opportunity to talk to a family member of someone charged with murder."

I sighed heavily. "The months since the shootings

have been the hardest in my life. I thought I had a tough time adjusting to my life some years back, but that was nothing compared to this . . . just nothing."

"Tell me about it."

Words long held in tumbled out. "I've felt victimized. I mean, I've suffered a loss; I've lost my brother. He'll never be the same again, even if he's allowed to live. I've lost interest in my career and my personal life. Sometimes I find myself just sitting, staring, and wondering what's the point.

"Before this I had a good relationship, had applied to graduate school, and life seemed okay again. Then Ken did this horrible thing and it all lost meaning.

"The events of the last few months have destroyed my faith. I'm scared. And friends? When I've needed them they weren't there. They didn't even care enough to call to see how I was.

"It has been hard, hasn't it?" he said sympathetically. I nodded. The mask I had been wearing for so long had been cast off in front of a stranger, one who could hurt me and my family.

Just as I was about to say something else, Dave slipped an arm about my waist and pulled me aside. "I think we should go for a walk," he said. He was brisk and businesslike, and he ignored the man beside me. Dave jostled me down the stairs and we headed to the other end of the courthouse.

When we were out of range he said, "What were you doing talking to that reporter? I can't believe you did that." Exasperated, he grabbed my arm, hurting me.

"I know, but I sensed it would be alright." I escaped his grip, opened the door to the courtyard, and stepped out onto the covered steps. It was nearly dark and rain whipped at us from round the end of the building.

"He could print what you said in the paper tomorrow."

"I didn't say anything that could hurt anybody.

Maybe it would make people understand that we're victims too, just as much as the families of the ones who were killed."

"He could twist what you said and make it sound awful. We were all sitting up there worrying about what you were doing, so I decided to do something."

Back inside, the courthouse was quiet and my watch read after 6:00 P.M.; the office staff had gone for the day. I stopped in front of the vending machines and scanned the selections, disappointed there were no M and M's, my favorite crutch.

"I'm going back up," Dave said.

After he was gone I sat on the bottom step. The step beneath me was waxed and smooth and felt good to my fingertips as I traced the tile blocks. A consciousness that must have been mine floated up to the ceiling and away.

There was no sound except for silent breathing, my own. My heart pulsed fear of what the next moments would reveal. I was the heart; I was the fear; mine was the pain.

There was no choice but to face that fear. So after a few more minutes alone I returned to my family. Time passed. We waited. Two hours later the jury returned to the courtroom.

"Have you reached a verdict?" Judge Jones asked.

"We have, Your Honor," the jury foreman said.

The judge took the sheets of paper from the foreman. "The verdict in Case No. 70-512 reads as follows: 'We the jury, being first duly impaneled to try the issues of the above-entitled case, hereby find the defendant, Kenneth James Andre, guilty of Manslaughter in the First Degree as to Katherine Virginia McCall.' It is dated the tenth day of December 1980, signed by John Hanson, foreman."

I held my breath of course, I had always known this moment would come.

"The verdict in Case No. 70-513 reads as follows:

'We, the jury, being first duly impaneled to try the issues of the above-entitled case, hereby find the defendant, Kenneth James Andre, guilty of Manslaughter in the First Degree as to Maurice James McCall.' It is dated the tenth day of December 1980, signed by John Hanson, foreman."

"I didn't know they'd have to read each verdict separately," Denise whispered. "I don't think I can stand it."

"In Case No. 70-514, the verdict reads as follows: 'We, the jury, being first duly impaneled to try the issues of the above-entitled case, hereby find the defendant, Kenneth James Andre, guilty of Felony Murder as to Doris Bennett.' It is dated the tenth day of December 1980, signed by John Hanson, foreman."

No. No! He could get the death penalty for that. They could kill my big brother. Feel dizzy . . . Can't breath.

In a sonorous voice the judge continued.

"In Case No. 70-515, the verdict reads as follows: 'We, the jury, being first duly impaneled to try the issues of the above-entitled case, hereby find the defendant, Kenneth James Andre, guilty of Manslaughter in the First Degree as to Richard Charles Bennett.' It is dated the tenth day of December 1980, signed by John Hanson, foreman."

The judge began another speech, but I did not hear it. Beside me my mother convulsed with quiet gulping tears. To her other side Denise masked her feelings, except for one small tear and stroked Momma's back.

When court had been dismissed, we waited for the jury to leave, then followed them out. The reporter looked as though he was about to say something to me, but I ignored him and lined up along the wall with the family.

The prisoner and two guards stepped past the heavy swinging doors and plodded toward us. Momma reached for her boy. Into her own she took the hands she had held for the first time forty-one years before, when they were fragile and new, hands now guilty of murder.

Next Ken held Carrie's hands and for the longest moment searched her compassionate eyes. They were brown, large, and tear-filled.

"Thanks for coming, thank you all," he said softly. "I couldn't have made it without you."

The guards took him from us.

Chapter Fourteen

Emotionally exhausted, Hazel sat down at the kitchen table and dialed the final number for the evening. She had saved the call to her brother Joel for last, knowing with him she could cry a little if she needed to. After all, they had both considered Kathy a friend as well as a sister.

Soon she could go to bed and huddle close to her husband. Just a little longer. Waiting for Joel to answer, she counted two rings—

"Hello!" Hazel heard Joel's deep, baritone voice.

"They reached a verdict. Three counts of man-slaughter and one murder," Hazel said.

"It's over then," Joel wearily said. All evening he had been pacing the floor. Now he felt like a deflated balloon. He lowered himself into the kitchen chair. He wished he could feel relief, but he could not.

"Except for the sentencing," Hazel said. "You know, I feel so sad for Ken's family. They looked so beaten and heartbroken. They've suffered just as we have. None of us is ever going to be the same."

"And you, Hazel, are you okay?"

She couldn't help smiling. He sounded like the psychologist he was studying to be. "As okay as I can be. I'm just glad today is over. I think I'll take a shower and go to bed."

When the phone call was over, Joel walked to the sliding glass door and stared out toward the river; the fog obscured the view. In the bedroom upstairs his wife was reading the Bible. At the other end of the house his two teenage children slept.

He stood there waiting, for what he did not know. Kathy and Maurice were dead. The verdict did not change that.

Shutting off the lights he climbed to the loft and told his wife the news. Then he lay in the dark, eyes wide open. Hours later he managed to fall sleep.

In his dreams he saw himself searching: Walking— he tried to look for her. Running—he tried to find her, the sister who had been his best friend and confidante. Kathy was not there, not in any of the places he looked near the home of their youth. He ran past neighbors' houses. Faster and faster he went through patches of trees. Finally, on the hill overlooking Dayton, he stopped to catch his breath. Stretching out below him was the sapphire bay. Ships roped to the docks waited to be loaded with lumber.

Thunderous clouds filled the sky, threatening to swallow the patch of blue over Harold's Peak. Soon the torrents would drench him. He did not care. He only thought of Kathy and how much he missed her. Rock-crushing pressure filled his chest. Even while dreaming he could feel nothing else, only intense loss.

Suddenly across a field of buttercups he saw Kathy, her amber-gold hair and luminous turquoise eyes. Encased in light she moved toward him.

"Kathy, you're here. You're not dead. All that pain was not real." He hugged her. He must never let go.

She guided him to a spot under their favorite maple tree. The two of them sat on the grass.

"Joel, my beloved brother, I love you." She touched

his cheek, the smooth-shaved skin. She looked into his gray eyes.

"Kathy, you are really here?"

"Yes, but not in the way you think."

"Are you dead?"

"The physical body you knew has died. I live in another place now. I have a new body. Do you like it?" For a moment she grinned, the impish way she had when they were children, and she played tricks on him.

It was that teasing that convinced him she was real. "It is you."

"Yes."

"What am I to do? How can I ever get by without you? There is no one to take your place. No one to talk to the way we talked. I need you. It's more than grief. It's far beyond that." He looked into the eyes he loved, eyes that knew all of his secrets, the things no one else knew, not even his wife of twenty-five years.

"Do you miss me?" His voice was wistful.

"Yes, but I feel your presence. I remember our special love. God gave us that love. We shall never be without it."

"You were always so wise," Joel said. "I never realized that until you were gone. I counted on your advice. When I got out of the ministry and started training myself as a psychologist, you supported me. So many in our church thought it was wrong. They thought religion and psychology were incompatible. But you stood by me. Kathy . . . how am I to live without you?"

Tears sprang to his eyes. "I feel so alone, even in the midst of our family—your children and mine, our brothers and sister. You're just not there, and I can't get over it."

"Look to each new day and know I am with you. Look to each night and know the Love of God is enfolded around you. You are never alone."

"I've had such a hard time understanding all this,"

Joel shook his head. "I can't understand how Ken Andre could have done it. We've gone to church with his family. They're good people. His cousin is my brother-in-law. I can't hate them. I can't even hate him. He just went berserk. What I keep asking myself is why didn't God protect you? Why didn't God heal Ken?"

"There are some things only He knows. Maybe I will come to know too, since the other side is a place of learning. I will tell you this—you can even help Ken heal. Every day ask God to wrap him and everyone you meet in Love and Light. Every day give thanks to the Father for the blessings you have. These two things will transform your life."

Her form began to fade. Joel tried to call her back, tried to hold on to her presence. He could not.

Instantly awake he sat up and stared at the curtains and knew he had lost her again.

He lay back. More memories came. He saw himself and his four siblings when they lived in the two-bedroom house on the hillside. His dad had worked hard, trying to be both mother and father. His mom was so often ill.

Smiling, he remembered when Kathy had led him into an afternoon caper.

Kathy, age eight, kissed her mother's forehead and looked into her eyes. Touching her Momma's hair she said, "I'll be home as soon as I can. I'm going to help Daddy make dumplings. You know, the way you showed me."

Her mother closed her eyes against the sunlight over the bed. "Could you shut the curtain before you go? I can't stand the light."

Leaving the house Kathy jumped down the front steps, catching up with her ten-year-old brother Joel at the edge of the road.

"We're going to be late for school if we don't hurry," Joel said. "The others have al-

ready gone. Let's cut across the Higgenbot-
toms' back yard. Mrs. Grouchbutt will never
know the difference. She's probably still
asleep."

Racing through the trees and overgrown
lawn Kathy clutched her lunch, tied into an old
dishtowel, and tried not to scuff her shoes. A
few more seconds and they would be safe. She
held her breath.

"You little bastards, get off of my lawn.
You kids are all alike. Get out of here. Get . . .
get!" Mrs. Higgenbottom picked up her mop as
if she would hit them and ran down the back
steps, stumbling on her dirty bathrobe. Hair
straggled from a scarf. Lines on her face
formed a permanent scowl.

"Hurry, Kathy, hurry," Joel called.

With a surge of energy Kathy reached her
brother and passed him, running the rest of the
way to school.

"I beat you. Ha, ha, I beat you."

Finding their classroom they settled into
their lessons. Kathy tried to concentrate on
arithmetic and then spelling, but her mind kept
returning to Mrs. Grouchbutt. Even during
lunch hour she thought of the old woman. Finally she developed a plan. When school was
out she, Joel, and their sister, Hazel, two years
older than Joel, stepped into the springtime air.

"Let's go through the field on the way
home," Kathy said. Delighted with her plan,
she skipped and jumped across puddles left by
the morning rain.

"Sure. You want to play fort?" Joel said.

"No, come on. You'll see."

Several hundred feet up the hill the land

leveled off. Pushing through the patch of salm-
onberry bushes, they stepped into a clearing
surrounded by fir and alder. Buttercups
danced above the grass. Wild iris grew in pro-
fusion along the edges.

Kathy picked some of each, holding them
carefully so she would not crush the stems.

"What are you doing?" Hazel asked.

"Come help, you guys. Pick as many as
you can."

Finally Kathy looked at her brother and
sister. "I think that's enough."

"What are they for?"

"You'll see."

Heading down the hill toward home,
Kathy stopped a hundred feet from her destina-
tion. "I'll take them," she said. She ran up the
steps to Mrs. Higgenbottom's front porch,
placed the bouquet on the painted boards, and
knocked. Quickly as she could she escaped out
the gate and stood watching from a distance.

The door screeched open. The old lady appeared. "You damn kids. I told you to stay away
from this house. I'll have the law on you."

Suddenly the old woman stopped. At her
feet the bouquet of flowers graced the porch
with purple and gold. Gently she picked them
up, saw the kids hiding behind the hedge, and
smiled.

Yes, that was Kathy, Joel thought. Impish and daring, but most of all kind, just like their father.

In the dream Kathy had said she was with him.
How could that be true? Heaven seemed so far away,
impenetrable to the human mind. He could not see her;
he could not touch her; he could not hear her. To him she
was gone. Could there be another reality, he wondered?

*   *   *

The next day atop the cliff at one end of the beach near an abandoned lighthouse, rain was in the air. Waves surged against the jetty.

Hiking over a ridge of sand and through tough grasses, the five McCalls—Jered and his wife, Patty; Greg; Calvin; and Christy—approached a vacant beach. Again his thoughts turned to the murder, but this time they revolved about Ken.

If only I could have been there, maybe I could have stopped him. Ken was my friend. If I had been there, maybe we could have talked it out. Thoughts of this kind had tormented Greg for months.

Down toward the cove a log with polished roots lay partly buried in the sand. Perching himself on one of the roots Greg watched the waves. Churning and spinning, the water hit the sand, breaking into brown foam. His two brothers stood apart, as if waiting, like him, for answers that did not come.

Removing his glasses Greg pushed a lumping of bangs from his forehead. The hair popped back to where it always lay, the cowlick sticking up on one side. He looked different than the others. He had inherited his father's angular face, not his mother's pudgy one. Tall and lean, he was built more like his father.

Pain starting in Greg's jaw shot to the top of his head; TMJ the doctors called it. He winced. It often made him grouchy and set him at odds with the others. Because of it he had said things to his parents he had not meant. Now the situation would remain unresolved.

At the funeral as he viewed his mom and dad, Greg realized there would never be a chance to say he loved them, or how much he appreciated their love.

Since then he had pushed himself into schoolwork and his job. Finding no way to deal with the grief, he buried it. On occasion he brought it out and looked at it, then stuffed it back into his subconscious. He remained isolated, alone.

Now, sitting near the ocean, he was glad to be with his family again. Glad for the sharing and the bond that existed. They were all he had left and they were precious.

Glancing down at the wave-sculpted sand he saw Christy and Patty huddled together against the log. A burst of wind took their words away. He turned back to watch the surf.

"Honey," Patty said, huddling her elfin body closer to her sister-in-law, "I know it's been hard sometimes, living with Jered and me. I hope you know Jered does love you."

"I know—"

"He's not trying to take your father's place. He's just trying to help you grow up the way your parents would have wanted." She drew the strings of the hood tighter, covering her short brown hair. Her large compassionate eyes closed momentarily. "He's being protective, and he's concerned about your schoolwork." Patty shivered.

"He bosses me too much."

"Try to be patient with your brother," Patty said, with a sigh. "I love you too . . . you do know that, don't you?"

"You told me before."

"I mean it. You can come to me with whatever bothers you. I'll do all I can." Tightening her arm around Christy's shoulder, Patty stared out at the horizon.

The horizon captivated Christy as well. *That's where heaven is. That's where Mom and Dad live with God. Please God, take care of them and me.*

Trying to picture what it must be like for her parents, Christy stared still harder. Until they died heaven had been a faraway place. People went there if they were good. Sometimes she and Calvin talked about it. He told her the things he was learning in Bible college. She missed him even when he was with her, because she always knew he would leave again. They would never be a family the way they once had been. Ken Andre had changed that forever.

Chapter Fifteen

Sun sliced through a clouded sky and touched the tops of the shifting dunes. In the distance a few gulls landed in the flooded estuary not far from the road. Brown cattails withered by winter stood midst the rising tide.

The mid-week traffic was light, since most of the working people had already made the morning trip. The loud whistles and rumbling trucks of the mill town were behind me. With heat turned high and window open I watched the road ahead and blocked the thoughts that kept trying to emerge. I was tired of thinking about Ken and the trial. Yet I could not seem to stop.

Passing over the coastal range and out on the freeway that ran through the Willamette Valley, any kind of stillness I had known evaporated. By the time I reached Eugene, which was half way home, I was panicked. Dave had called me just before I left home. He said the story of Ken's conviction was in all the papers. It was bylined by the reporter to whom I had spoken.

Headlines alternated on a signboard in my mind:
HIDDEN VICTIM BETRAYS BROTHER

MURDERER'S SISTER STATES
BROTHER RUINED HER LIFE
ANDRE CONVICTED OF MURDER,
SISTER TELLS ALL
CONVICTED KILLER CONDEMNED
BY SISTER

By Salem, another hour up the freeway, fear pulled me from Interstate 5 and down the four-lane street to Lancaster Mall.

I obtained the number from the operator and dialed the *Dayton Times.*

"I have a strange request," I said, "I am Ken Andre's sister. I was wondering if it's possible for someone to read the article to me concerning the Andre convictions."

"Well, I don't know," the man replied. "We are a business office here and we're very busy, but just a minute, let me see if I can find someone who has some time."

I waited.

"Hello, my name is Mary Woodward. I understand you're Ken Andre's sister and would like the Andre article read to you. If you will hold on I'll begin."

"Thank you."

"The article reads as follows:

ANDRE FOUND GUILTY OF MURDER, MAN-SLAUGHTER
One murder and three manslaughter convictions were returned Wednesday, ending the trial of Kenneth James Andre, age 41.

The defendant sat and listened as the verdicts were returned after an all-day deliberation by a Kenton County Circuit Court jury.

Andre was charged with murder in connection with the shootings of four of his neighbors last March.

Presiding judge Robert Jones set a sentencing hearing on the convictions for January 28, 29, and 30.

For the murder conviction, Oregon law mandates either the death penalty or life imprisonment. The first-degree manslaughter convictions each carry a 20-year maximum.

Andre was found guilty of felony murder in the slaying of 30-year-old Doris Bennett. The shootings of her husband, Richard, 32, Maurice McCall, 45, and his wife, Kathy, 43, were manslaughter due to the defendant's extreme emotional disturbance at the time the four people were killed.

Both the McCalls and Richard Bennett were shot by Andre as he was standing outside the windows of their homes, according to testimony presented during the nine-day trial.

Andre broke through the window of the Bennett house and followed Doris Bennett into the back room before shooting her, according to the testimony. The judge's predeliberation jury instructions indicated that such an entry is burglary.

A homicide committed during burglary is murder and emotional disturbance is not a defense in that situation, according to the judge's instruction.

Through a stipulation entered at the start of the trial by his attorney, Andre admitted he had intentionally killed the Bennetts and the McCalls. At that time Jones told the jurors they would decide if the defendant was guilty of murder or manslaughter.

After the jury was excused Wednesday, de-

fense attorney Kevin McDonald told the judge a
motion challenging the constitutionality of the
death penalty statute would be filed.

"Is that what you wanted to hear?" Mary Woodward asked.
"Yes. Was that all that was written about the trial?"
I said.
"Yes, it was."
"Thanks for taking the time to read it. You have no
idea how it puts my mind to rest," I said quickly, replacing the receiver before the woman could ask any questions. The churning in my stomach, the fear that I had
betrayed my brother, ceased.

The trial had ended a few weeks before Christmas. The
holiday was supposed to renew our hope for love and
peace in the world. For those of us who loved Ken, yet
hated what he had done, the season blatantly reminded
us that our reality negated hope. We endured that time,
spending it together, but our thoughts centered on the
events of the past year and how they had destroyed everything beautiful within our hearts.

When Christmas and New Year's were past Dave
started a new job. My classes began in January and so
did the heavy homework.

I pulled my chair up to the end of the counter next
to the cast-iron stove and felt heat radiate through my
jeans and tan fisherman-knit sweater. It was almost too
hot, but I was cold everywhere inside. So I read next to
the fire. The two dogs lay next to me.

It was not from a source of enlightenment I read,
but instead from a book filled with boring governmental
regulations and procedures. I sighed. It seemed totally
devoid of inspirational merit, and in my chaotic state of
mind I couldn't concentrate.

I reached for the phone and dialed Rochelle.

"Oh, Vi, look, whatever you need it will have to wait. I'm just on my way out the door to church. Got a meeting to go to."

My hand trembling, I dialed another number.

Several times since class ended the previous summer I had met Aaron, my professor, for coffee. During the first meeting we discussed the paper I had written about Ken. Thereafter, I would sometimes call when I was in Portland and we would meet in the cafeteria on campus or in a cafe nearby. In him I found someone to listen when I needed to talk. He was becoming a friend.

"Aaron, this is Violet. Are you free for lunch?"

"Is it really you? It's been weeks. I've been worried. I kept watching the paper for the results of the trial, but I must have missed it. How are you?"

"I've been a little neglectful of calling you. I just need some time to myself, I guess."

We met at a lounge on the edge of the Willamette River two hours later. Aaron poured a glass of rosé wine from the carafe and handed it to me. I stared out the window at the water.

"I want to know how you are," he said. "And I'm not going to be satisfied with a brush off or change of subject."

"Where do you want me to start?"

"Tell me about the trial, then how you are doing now."

Wearily I told him some of the depressing things that had been happening in my life.

"It sounds like you need to take a day or more and just unwind. Look at you, your hands are shaking, your eyes, in fact, your whole body is tense. What are you doing for this?"

"I'm thinking of dropping classes again."

"Are you sure that's what you want to do?"

I shook my head, "I don't know. I can't seem to make any good decisions lately. I'm three weeks into the term and I just can't concentrate on the work. I can't seem to think of anything but Ken and the sentencing."

He nodded, leaning forward watching me.

"I called Momma and Daddy last night. Momma was really upset. Ken's been raising all kinds of hell with them again, trying to get them to find him another attorney. Of course, they can't afford that.

"Momma talked for over an hour. It's not that I mind. I just feel guilty for not being there for her." The ache behind my eyes had gotten worse. I rubbed my forehead.

"Vi, try to relax a little."

I tried to smile. "I keep asking myself, why am I in school? Even if I complete the program I probably won't be able to get a job. The outlook right now for jobs in social services is dismal, and I'm not able to be anything but depressed. Who would hire me even if they had a job? I'm so discouraged, and I don't know how to help myself."

"When you get to the point where you can't take any more," he said, "give me a call. I'll take the day off and spend it with you."

"That's so kind of you, Aaron, but you've done more than you should to help me already."

"I want to," he said softly. His green eyes stared back at me.

On the way home I felt happier than I had in a long time. I turned on the radio and suddenly heard exciting news.

As soon as I unlocked the kitchen door and let myself into the house, I hurried to the phone.

"Did you hear the news, Momma?" I nearly shouted into the receiver. I pulled up a chair beside the dining room table and perched on the edge.

"What's that?"

"It's about the death penalty. It's been declared unconstitutional. Can you believe that? Oh, Momma, isn't that wonderful?"

"Really? Where did you hear that?" For the first time in weeks Momma's voice held hope.

"On the news on the way home from town. I can't believe it. There's only a week left until the sentencing. I just can't believe it."

"Oh, Violet, it's an answer to prayer. I've been praying so hard that Ken's life would be spared. Maybe now he'll have a chance to find God," Momma said. I heard a deep intake of breath. Then she went on, "But maybe someone will try to reestablish the death penalty."

"They may, but that will take a while. In the meantime, Ken will be sentenced and that sentence will hold true for him. They wouldn't be able to resentence him to the death penalty after sentencing him to life in prison."

"They wouldn't?"

"No."

"It's a miracle, just a miracle."

After I hung up I dialed Denise's number.

"Have you heard the news about the death penalty?" I said.

"Yes, just a few minutes ago."

"Isn't that terrific? I just talked to Momma; she was really relieved."

Denise sighed heavily. "Ted and I just had a fight about it. He believes in the death penalty. He says that Ken should pay for what he did. He says that he didn't give his victims a chance, so he shouldn't have one either."

"Doesn't he care about what would happen to Momma and Daddy if Ken was executed?"

"Yes, but he says Ken has to pay."

"I don't understand that. Will that make his victims live again? I don't believe in an eye for an eye."

"I don't either. Ted and I had a huge fight and he screeched out of the drive."

I sighed, "Is there nothing this thing doesn't ruin?"

"I don't know one," Denise said.

"How is Dave taking the news?"

"He isn't home yet."

Despite Denise's problem with Ted, I felt better. After I hung up I began peeling the potatoes. We would have mashed potatoes with chicken fried steak. I felt energetic for the first time in ages.

"Hi, Vi," Dave greeted me when he walked in half an hour later.

"Did you hear about the death penalty?"

"Yes," he replied soberly.

"I was afraid you might be upset. I know you're torn on that issue."

He nodded, "You're right about that, but when I heard about it, I just felt relief for your folks. This will make it easier on them even if Kenny really deserved to die just like his victims did." He turned away.

Chapter Sixteen

A winter storm hurdled sheets of water against the windows in the corner of the courtroom, blotting out the day. Inside the courtroom, Judge Jones's sonorous voice rose.

"It is the judgment of the Court that in Case No. 70-514, that is, in relation to the murder conviction of Doris Bennett, that you, Kenneth James Andre, be committed to the legal and physical custody of the Oregon Correction Divisions for the remainder of your natural life, with the minimum of twenty-five years before you are eligible for parole," Judge Robert Jones said. The judge's voice droned on, punctuated by bursts of thunder.

"In Case No. 70-512, the case of Katherine Virginia McCall, it is the judgment of the Court that you should be committed to the legal and physical custody of the Oregon Corrections Division for the period of twenty years with a minimum of a ten-year sentence, the sentence in 512 to run consecutively to the one imposed in 514.

"It is the judgment of the Court that in Case No. 70-513, that is, in the death of Maurice James McCall, that you be committed to the legal and physical custody of the Oregon Corrections Division for a period of twenty years with a ten-year minimum sentence, that sentence to run

184

consecutively with those imposed in Case Nos. 512 and 514."

A distant rumble, then a flash, and light illuminated the walls.

It seemed a bit theatrical. Things like that happened only in movies. But maybe . . . maybe God really was talking.

"It is the judgment of the Court that you, Kenneth James Andre, be committed to the legal and physical custody of the Oregon Corrections Division, in Case No. 70-515, that is, in the death of Richard Charles Bennett, for a period of twenty years with a ten-year minimum, that sentence to run consecutively to those imposed in Case Nos. 512, 513, and 514."

Ken, immobile, stood beside Kevin McDonald. There was no jury to hear the sentence, no gaping crowd, no hatemongers to insist he pay with his life. Only we who loved him, the attorneys, officers of the court, and the court reporter were present.

When court was dismissed, the four of us left the room. "He looks so alone. There's nothing I can do, no way to take us back to before the shooting," I said.

"I know," Denise replied sadly.

Again we waited in the hallway just outside. I slipped my arm about my mother's waist. Denise stood beside Daddy. This was all of my family now.

The guards brought Ken from the room and moved him quickly down the hall; my family and I followed. We stood a few feet from the elevator and watched it close on Ken's life.

We had lost him. I felt as if he had died, just as surely as his victims had.

We were about to head down the stairs when I spotted Kevin McDonald. "Do you know when they'll take Ken to Salem," I said.

He set his briefcase on the floor and rubbed his

well-groomed beard. "I believe tomorrow or the next day."

"How soon before we can see him?"

"A couple of weeks. He has to send you visitors' applications. You must fill them out and return them. The prison runs a check on you, and when you are approved you can visit. That usually takes a couple of weeks."

"Thanks, Kevin, for everything. I know this must have been hard on you too," I said. For the first time in months I tried to put myself in his place—a man responsible for defending a stranger who had committed such terrible crimes.

"It has been. I'm just glad it's over. I've spent so much time trying to do the best job I could, trying to make sure I explored every avenue. I'll be recommending that the twenty-five-year minimum be appealed. Ken can contact the state public defender's office once he's settled."

"You won't be handling that?" I asked.

"No. I've gone into private practice. The life of a public defender is just too harried. I never had enough time to devote to my cases. Many of them got my second best as I concentrated on Ken's case. Well, anyway, take care."

"One more thing," I said.

"Yes?"

"Why you didn't use the insanity defense?"

"A person using the insanity defense rarely wins."

"Why's that?"

"People think it's just an excuse to do what you want. My boss and the other attorneys in the office considered it, but we decided against it based on the conservative nature of this community." He paused and sighed. "Is there anything else?"

"Yeah, why didn't you mention the drugs Ken was

taking? You know, all the ones we found in the house, lithium, Valium, stelazine, librium, thorazine, and a couple of others."

"It would have worked against him." He nodded to the rest of the family and took himself and his fatigue down the stairs.

Once outside I took a deep breath and faced the western horizon.

God please . . .

But I had prayed so often, there were no more words.

It was mid-February before my application to see Ken was approved and I set out on my first trip to the prison where he was housed.

I drove past acres and acres of rain-soaked dirt that stood fallow, in the winter cold on the way to Salem. Small fruit stands had been closed since October, the gates padlocked shut. I turned up the heater. My eyes and heart ached.

Passing the little gift store and the creek that ran alongside the prison, I turned into the parking lot and stopped. Locking the car I made my way to the sidewalk leading to the main entrance. Fear rocked each of my steps, each of my thoughts.

Tall birch trees and closely clipped lawns lined the road. Residential-type office buildings stood on both sides. The fortresslike section of the prison at the end of the lane seemed odd and menacing.

It can't be me, Violet Andre, on the way to see my big brother, Kenny, in prison. This cannot be happening.

A lighthouselike gray building, with a guard staring out the window at the top, stood about a hundred feet from the entrance of the fortress. I passed it cautiously. Carefully I pushed open the sets of glass doors and stopped at the front desk.

"May I help you?" asked a polite dark-haired woman in a guard's uniform. A sign tacked on the counter read, "Positive identification required each visit."

"Yes, I'm here to see Kenneth Andre."

"Is this your first visit?"

"Yes."

The officer pulled out the application I had returned to Ken. "Sign here," she said, pointing to the bottom of it. The form included my name, social security number, address, and questions about criminal convictions.

A tall, stocky woman guard with red hair arrived and called, "Andre." I stepped forward.

"Remove your jacket. Take all the items from your pockets and place them on the counter. Step on this metal plate here and through to the other side."

She ran my jacket through an x-ray machine like the ones in airports, then returned it along with my keys and tissue; she then motioned me to go around the corner to the right.

"Wait on down at the end of the ramp."

Inside a glassed-in room with a panel of control switches and levers to the left of the ramp stood a man. A few more visitors joined me. After several minutes the red-haired guard who monitored the x-ray machine came over and waited with us before the door of bars. The man inside the glass room pushed a button and the door opened.

"Follow me, please," the same guard said.

We stepped into a holding room, and the man inside the glass room electronically closed the door behind us. He opened a door of bars and we stepped into a long hallway. Prisoners dressed in blue jeans and light-blue shirts passed through a lobby at the end of it.

The red-haired guard unlocked a solid door and urged us on in. "Have a nice visit," she murmured, and again locked us in.

I entered a long, rectangular room with vending

machines along the opposite wall. A fiftiesh balding guard sat at a desk at one end. Rows of vinyl lounge chairs faced each other with coffee tables in between.

Unable to spot Ken, I made my way to a pair of chairs in the corner. None of the half dozen prisoners in the room looked like "criminal types." Hairstyles varied as much as they did on the outside, as did sizes and shapes and bodies.

After fifteen minutes of clock watching I saw a door open along the side wall and Ken stepped through it. He peered around the room, then headed carefully toward me. His shoulders were hunched forward, his face gaunt and drawn, his eyes sunken.

Pain splintered through my body. I wrapped myself about him, but he did not respond. I backed away and sat down.

"How are you doing?" I asked in a hoarse whisper.

"Uh, okay, I guess," he said. "See that bald guy over there, the one talking to the lady in blue?"

I nodded.

"He's crazy. He stuffed his kid's head in the toilet and drowned him. Then he cut him up and ran him down the garbage disposal," Ken whispered.

"Are you scared, being in here," I asked sympathetically.

"Yeah, so I just don't socialize much. I understand that's the best way to survive."

"Isn't it lonely?"

"It's not bad so far. I've been resting up from the trial and the move here and writing letters to everyone who wrote to me before the trial."

Ken scrunched himself into the seat and covered his face as he had done at the trial and for so many years.

"I'm sorry I didn't bring change," I said. "I didn't realize there would be vending machines."

"It's okay. I sure could use a chocolate bar though. That's something I've really missed."

"Can't, you buy any here?"

"I can if I have money. I've asked Mom and Dad to send me some from my account, but apparently it hasn't cleared yet."

"I'll leave you some," I said, grateful that I could do something concrete. "I have ten dollars in my purse upstairs."

"I'd appreciate that, Vidy." He looked off into the distance and suddenly his face hardened. "The place is bugged," he said, agitatedly running his hand back and forth along the under side of the coffee table. "I don't know how they do it, but I've been told they listen in on all of our conversations. See those vents up in the corner?" I nodded, my pulse quickening as I watched him. "I bet there are microphones hidden in there." His eyes were glassy; I shuddered. "You may think I'm crazy, but I'm serious. You people on the outside have no idea what goes on in here."

I sighed. How was I supposed to answer him? I struggled for calm and began small talk about our family. At 11:30 the guard announced, "Visiting hours are over. Prisoners please step this way. Visitors remain at your seats."

"Thanks for coming," Ken said. His voice was matter of fact now. "I enjoyed the visit."

On the drive home a pervading sadness consumed me. Ken's tragedy had become mine also.

Back at home I waited for daylight to end. When night came, the lights in the house were turned off. Climbing under the heavy quilt, I snuggled down and slipped my arm about Dave.

I remembered when we were first together. He had been so gentle with me. Despite his strength his hands would envelop mine and his lips had been tender upon me.

"Burr, you've got cold hands. You're cold all over.

Back off," my husband murmured and pushed me away. "I'm not kidding, back off. You're an iceberg, and I don't need that, I've got a heavy day tomorrow and I have to get some sleep."

Chapter Seventeen

Troubled months of pain and confusion inched by slowly, like the stagnant waters of an oozing stream. Useless days led one to another. Purpose was something that did not exist. By summer things had not improved.

It was evening and still light out. Dave was across the street helping the neighbor with his sheep. Brutus waited in the front yard and barked at whoever happened past, especially those in trucks. Warm days had arrived and with them nomadic drivers.

The stillness and dusty smell of the old house bothered me. There seemed no way to get rid of it.

I walked nervously from room to room and stopped again at the dining room table. The phone rang and absently I reached for it.

"Will you accept a collect call from Kenneth Andre?" the operator said.

"Yes." I answered.

"Violet, I've been waiting all day to talk to you. You've got to get an attorney and reopen my case," Ken said agitatedly. "Just get me out of here."

I tried to talk softly, soothingly. "Ken, I wish I could but I don't see how I can, and I don't think an attorney will help. Even if the murder conviction is reduced, they'll keep you in there, unless you want to try for an insanity plea."

"I'm not crazy," his voice rose, desperate now. "Vidy, please, you can't let me down." There was a click and a dial tone.

Brandy, our large dog, thumped his tail against the woodgrain tile and continued to chew the worn bone. "Oh, Brandy . . ." I moaned, my emotions conflicted.

"This thing with Ken is a mess. I just don't know what to do." I paused. "There is nothing I can do. Not only that, but my relationship with Dave is getting worse."

Brandy nosed his way halfway into my lap. His wet tongue licked my arm. "Everything is wrong," I said, petting him, glad to feel his softness nuzzling me.

I walked into the kitchen, pulled a cola from the refrigerator, and emptied some ice into a glass. The ice snapped as the liquid poured over it.

I looked out the window. The barn across the street had numerous nests tucked under the eaves. Swallows popped in and out with bits of food for young gaping mouths. Nearly twenty hummingbirds lined up at the two feeders outside the house, buzzing and attacking each other. On the warm grass just off the front porch Brutus sat watching the road. Missy, the black and white long-haired cat, rubbed herself against him.

The moon in its quarter shape peeked through a darkening sky. Again Brandy looked up at me, his tail wagging with joy and adoration.

"All of nature is so precise," I murmured to my dog. "Even the astronauts agree with that. Some of them said it was hard to deny the existence of an intelligence beyond our own once they were out in space.

"I like what Momma says best. 'Someone sat up a lot of nights figuring it out.' I can see Him with His glasses on looking like George Burns, leaning over the drafting table adding the final figures to the sketches.

The master Creator is at work with love and a plan for all of us. If we'd only listen to the still, small voice within our own hearts, we'd find it.

"This has to be close to the way it is. He, She or It is there, is real and loves me. 'The truth is often hidden from those who seek it in impatience.' That's why I couldn't find It before. I demanded instant answers. The only answers that come, come quietly. I will find them if I listen, learn and, grow.

"It's all so simple."

Oftentime when I reached a new conclusion I expected everything to work out easily. After all, I had "the answer." Yet simple is not the same as easy, and the right answers often create changes it takes courage to implement.

The euphoria of my new belief evaporated in a week and a half. On a July afternoon amidst stillness and dreary skies, I dejectedly sank onto the couch. Above me the blonde boards in the ceiling offered no feeling of home or safety. They seemed cold and despairing, as was my life.

Beside me on the floor Brandy was asleep. His little mouth jittered, his voice gave muffled barks, and his legs ran in the excitement of dreams. He was all I had to talk to, but I did not want to waken him. Instead, the conversation, like many I had with myself, locked itself up in my mind.

Even with a God my life seemed pointless. He must have a special purpose for me, but what was it? I had searched for years and still didn't know.

Ever since dropping my classes six months before, I had tried to find a satisfying job, but nothing had worked out.

Okay, God, what do you want me to do? Show me.

How am I going to make sense of all this? Since there was no one to confide in, I closed my eyes and waited. Simply and without warning it came to me:

Write, put all your thoughts and feelings about the murder and its aftermath on paper. No one had been there for me, but I could be there for others who were like me, for the hidden victims.

I made a vow to myself that I would start writing that day.

In a different corner of Oregon another victim struggled with his own solutions. Attending church camp in the foothills of the Cascades, Greg McCall hoped to find peace and rest.

Overshadowed by a tunnel of alders, a creek sputtered toward the Willamette River. Rivulets of crystalline water hurried and meandered passed the edge of the camp, a camp where Greg had spent many summers with his family.

This summer was different. His parents lay in their coffins a hundred miles away, parts of their bodies exploded by high-powered bullets. Shot by Ken, a man Greg had considered a friend.

It was not possible. Everything that had embodied his life, all sense of security, had evaporated on that night, that awful night.

His mother—he could still see her sitting beside his bed at night reading him Bible stories, kissing his forehead before he went to sleep. Sleep was instantaneous then, but not any more. He wondered if it would ever be again.

His jaw clenched with tension. Pain shot through his shoulders. The all-too-familiar ache in his jaw and up the side of his head came back with a vengeance. He kept telling himself to relax.

Leaning into the trunk of an alder he gazed at the water. He considered the afternoon devotions and what Bill, the teacher, had said about God, and about the scriptures they had read. About the prayers. Prayers and God, that was all he had now.

His brothers and sister understood, but they were not there. So much of his life he lived apart from them. He had lived that way since starting college several years before.

With Cal off to Bible college and Christy still living with their brother Jered, who knew how they were really surviving.

Turning from the creek Cal headed toward the site of the campfire. Soon the group would gather for the evening sing-along. Maybe there he would feel as if he belonged.

Focusing on the dirt path, he did not see Carole, a college friend, heading out of the meeting hall. When she spoke to him he looked up startled.

"Oh, there you are Greg. Wasn't this afternoon's lesson great? I've been thinking about what Bill said. I plan to use his study method. I've attended church my whole life and never has anyone made it so clear. I need to start witnessing to everyone. God puts people in our paths for a reason. There are so many left to save.

"How are you, anyway?" She looked at his distraught blue eyes. "You were different during the discussion, unlike your Friday night self when we all get together to sing."

"I'm feeling empty . . . hollow inside," Greg replied. Maybe this was his chance to talk. He had always liked Carole. "I need to—"

"Oh, there's Beth," Carole interjected. "I've got to talk to her. See you at campfire." Not looking back, she hurried toward Beth.

Pressure contracted Greg's heart. Shuffling away from the building, he entered the shadows of the nearby trees. Beneath the limbs of a fir he crumpled to the ground and cried.

Grim months filled with tough classes and exams stretched before him. In two weeks he must face the second surgery to correct the problem with his jaw. This time there would be no parents to comfort him while he recovered, parents whose images he now saw in terms of the horror that had ended their lives.

As it grew dark people passed on the path twenty feet away; he blurred them out. Sitting on the ground, he propped himself against the ridged bark and idly stroked it. His thoughts turned to another time.

Greg walked up the short driveway, climbed the steps, and knocked on the old door. Peering in through the window, he could see no one. He pounded harder.

"Just a minute," called a male voice inside the house. Ken hurried down from his attic bedroom and to the door. Seeing the teenage boy on the other side, he grinned and opened it.

"Greg, come on upstairs. I got that radio working. You were right. It was that old tube, even though it tested out okay at first."

Greg followed Ken up into the bedroom and waited while Ken switched on the radio.

"Listen to that. Clear as a bell. It's a sharp set . . . and I was ready to throw it out." Ken's grin expanded to the wide, open kind. He looked Greg full in the face.

The look always surprised Greg. Ken was not given to open expressions. With most people he hid his eyes.

Pulling a book from the metal shelf on the far side of the room, he handed it to Greg. "This is like the book I have, only it's a later edition. I ordered it for you a month ago. It came in yesterday. Teresa picked it up when she went shopping."

Greg took the book and thumbed through the pages. There it all was, the things that fasci-

nated him about electronics. He and Ken had
talked about it a lot. "Thanks . . . I—"
   "It's a gift. Keep it and study hard. You've
got a real good head for this stuff."

Greg heard voices singing hymns around the campfire behind the meeting hall, friendly voices, belonging to
people he had known a long time.
   But comfort him they did not. The desolation that
encompassed his heart was beyond penetration. Pain en-
shrouded him.

Along the freeway were acres of burnt and stubbled
farmland. Across the valley at the edge of the hills a lone
tractor turned under the butchered grass. The tongs of
the plow spaded up dust.
   One hundred and seven degrees was unusually hot
for the northern part of the Willamette Valley even in
August. It was the humidity that made it so unbearable
and the fact that few of us had air conditioners.
   Whipping winds and heat blasted in through the
open windows. On the seat beside me was my brother
Ken's daughter. For months I had worried about her. I
did not know how to bridge the awkwardness that time
and tragedy had erected.
   "Did you have a good time at Denise and Ted's?"
   "Yeah. Aunt Denise and I went to the county fair.
And I spent time with Wayne and Jenny. Wayne's my
favorite cousin."
   "Did you get along with Jenny?"
   "She was really sweet to me." She pulled her legs to
her chest. White shorts showed tanned thighs.
   "I'm glad."
   Pulling my sweat-stained tee shirt away from my
breasts, I fanned myself with the taut fabric.
   "Loni," I said gently, "your dad wants to talk to
you."

"No," she answered firmly.

"Loni, whatever you say I respect your space."

"Aunt Violet!" Loni looked anguished, "I know he is my father but I can't stand the thought of speaking to him yet."

"I know, honey. I've felt that same way too."

"Really, Aunt Violet? . . ." She seemed about to say more, but then she turned away and stared out the window.

We drove into the mountains and home.

Night brought phantoms of darkness; we could not rest. Only the television lit the center of the room. Dave slumped into the leather chair next to the fireplace, his stomach resting on muscled thighs. He seemed absorbed in the program.

On the floor Loni leaned back on the huge pillow, a remnant of Dave's college days. Brutus and Brandy cuddled on either side of her.

"Do you want to sleep upstairs in the bedroom or on the couch here in the living room?" I asked. "If you sleep down here, Dave and I will be on the other side of the wall, but the bed upstairs might be more comfortable."

"I'd rather sleep in the living room."

"Ever since Daddy . . . I can't be near windows," she said.

"Okay, honey. Would you like me to place a towel or something over the windows in the door? Dark windows still frighten me too."

I closed the door, found some thumbtacks, and tacked a towel over the small windows.

"Thanks," she said as she nestled into the pillow. Soon she was asleep. When the show was over, Dave switched off the television.

"You think we should wake her?" he asked quietly.

"No. She might stay awake and be scared all night. Let's just put a thin blanket over her and leave on the light in the corner in case she wakes up."

"You think that's necessary?"

"Yes . . . it was her father."

After climbing into bed I stared into the country night for a long time. Beyond the window the face with the gun was back. Even with my eyes closed I could see him.

The following sunrise I woke when birds began singing in the apple tree next to the window. Listening to them cheered me. Dave went to work; Loni and I headed out to the Sandy River on the east side of Portland.

Alder and fir edged the bank just down from the tavern. It was a morning of breeze and sun, and moisture still clung to the grassy tufts along the road. Only a few other cars were parked next to the bridge. I pulled the inner tubes from the backseat and handed them to Loni. Grabbing the sun screen, I spread it over myself, then offered it to her.

"If I use that stuff I won't get a tan at all," she said. I laughed and looked at her. Morning glistened in her hair and the beauty of youth lighted her eyes. "At your age you don't need it, but wait," I laughed.

We tucked the tubes awkwardly under our arms and climbed down the bank. Standing on the round, smooth rocks next to the water, we looked at each other and grinned.

"The river is really low," I observed. "We might have to wade a lot."

"Good," she giggled.

Testing the water with my big toe, I inched in. When the water reached my mid-thighs, I climbed into the tube, butt first. We paddled out into the channel. Small waves lapped against my legs. The warm air felt good. Tilting my head back I gazed up at the powdery morning.

"Aunt Violet?" Loni's arms and legs dangled over the sides of the tube. Settling her head on the back of the tube she twirled around and looked at me.

"Yes?"

"Do you think, uh, we'll run into any rapids?"

"Only small ones. The water's low this time of year."

The course of the river left the road and we floated past homes set in the fir and alder, back from graveled beaches.

"Aunt Violet, look. There's a rope dangling out over the river. I wonder how you get to it?"

"See that steep trail up the side of that rock?"

"Yeah, boy that would be fun," her face lit up.

"Want to try it?"

"Uh, no," she murmured, her face serious again.

We passed a big bend where the river stood deep and still.

Loni's mood improved again.

"Look at the mother and baby ducks!" Loni giggled. "I sure hope nothing eats them."

"Here come the rapids. Hold on." We were drawn into the swirling, churning water.

Loni loudly laughed. "I just hit my rump on the rocks."

With a solid grip on the sides of the tube I spun around and nearly hit a large rock. A partially submerged log appeared and I almost slammed into it. White water covered me. Soon we were in smooth water again.

"Wow, that was fun," she said. She cupped her hands behind the tube and propelled herself out into the current.

We were alone on the river except for the ducks, both domestic and wild. I pulled a Diet Coke from the netting tied to the side and offered it to Loni. Then I took one for me. The biting liquid tasted good.

More gentle rapids and spaces of still water and we were at the Troutdale bridge.

"There's Rochelle over there." Loni pointed to a

woman in a black one-piece bathing suit at the edge of the beach.

"How was the trip?" Rochelle asked as we climbed from the water.

"It was really fun. You know, I didn't say anything before, but I was scared," Loni said.

"Aren't you glad you went anyway?" I asked.

"Yes."

"Loni, here are the keys to the car. I was wondering if you could run up and get the paper plates. I forgot them," Rochelle said and unloaded the cooler.

"Sure." Loni hurried up the bank.

"I brought Loni along," I said quietly, "to help her understand tragedy doesn't have to mean the end of everything."

"Good idea. I always seem to think it does."

We both laughed. Then I went on, "I'm worried. Ken's going to call tonight. He insists on talking to Loni, and that I take her to see him. Loni isn't ready; so it leaves me in a spot."

I stretched my legs on the rocky ground and leaned back on my elbows, allowing the sun to baste me.

She shook her head. "There's not much you can do. Ken'll never understand, but you may be able to help Loni understand her father," she paused, "and you may not."

I shook my head. "I can't understand him myself. All I know is that his mind doesn't function right." I turned away.

"It still hurts doesn't it?"

I turned toward her again and met her gaze.

"Just as strongly now as it was at first. The shock wore off, but the hurt is forever." I looked over at Loni. "Seeing her, I wonder what she's feeling. Except for saying she doesn't want to speak to her dad, she's not telling me and I don't know how to ask. I don't want to intrude."

"Maybe you should," Rochelle observed softly.

The arrival of evening brought us home again. When dinner was over, I opened the dining room window, then joined Dave and Loni on the lawn chairs in front of the house. It was still fifteen minutes before Ken could call. My stomach gurgled and bucked.

"It sure is muggy," I said. "Feels like a thunderstorm."

"Aunt Violet, can we go to the river again tomorrow?"

"Sure, honey."

The phone rang. After the third ring I called, "Would you get it, Dave?" He stared at me.

"I guess . . . but I hate to be in the middle."

"Where do you think I am?"

Finally he came back out.

"He doesn't believe that Loni doesn't want to talk to him. He insists on talking to you, Violet. I don't know what else to say."

I went inside. "Hello, Ken."

"What's the big idea of not letting me talk to my daughter? Dave said she'd gone for a walk. You knew I was going to call. I haven't seen her since the trial, and I haven't talked to her since before I was arrested. I insist that you let me talk to her."

"She isn't ready. Ken, please," I pleaded.

"Loni wants to talk to me and you aren't letting her. The whole mess of you are conspiring against me. You're worse than those McCalls. Let me talk to my daughter!"

"I'm sorry, but I have to respect what she wants."

"You're just as bad as Mom and Dad! I can never get them to listen to me or do what I want. You're all ignorant. Absolutely ignorant!"

"There's nothing I can do. When Loni is ready she'll talk to you, and when she's ready I'll bring her in."

"Why have you turned against me too?"

There was nothing more to say. The conversation

was over. Afterward I walked over to the bar, made myself a screwdriver, and chugged down half of it.

"Pretty rough, huh?" Dave asked when I rejoined him and Loni.

I nodded.

"It would have been easier on you if I had talked to Daddy, wouldn't it?" Loni asked.

"Yes, honey, but I don't want you to do that until you're ready, not even for me."

"Thanks, Aunt Violet," Loni said. I smiled wanly and felt tears rise in my eyes. "I wish I didn't have to go back next week. I wish I could stay with you forever," Loni said, her lip quivering.

"I wish you could too," I answered.

Chapter Eighteen

Loni had gone back to her mother. I was lonelier than ever. The mountain mornings grew misty with rain and cold wind. It was September. Colorful flowers that came in the warm days were beginning to die. Leaves of maple and alder were fringed with yellow, and sunburnt grasses filled the ditches.

"I don't know, guys," I said and looked at Brandy's wagging tail beside me as I peered out the garage at the orchard; "I just don't know."

Even the birds were quiet. The red-tailed hawk and her young had ceased their flying lessons. Only the ants refused to rest. On the huge mound under the group of fir along the fence they toiled, getting ready for winter.

"Maybe I should have been born a red ant. Then I'd know what to do," I murmured. I went into the house, walked to my office, and began a letter.

Dear Ken,

You, Denise, and I were given a very special gift. I had to leave home to discover it.

Now fourteen years later I have come to value this gift more than all others. The gift I speak of is our parents.

As a child I didn't know that I had something special. I thought all parents loved their children. Sure, I sometimes thought them unfair, like all children do, but I was wrong. I have learned over the past few years that although they are not perfect, they did the best they could. And no one can give more than his or her best.

In the time since your arrest Momma and Daddy have done everything they possibly could to make things easier for you. They have run errands, seen attorneys, sent you money when you needed it, and visited as often as they could, twice a weekend before you were sent to Salem.

They managed in spite of the fact that their health has not been the best. I have been afraid the strain would be too much for Daddy's heart, and that Momma would have a nervous breakdown. I wonder how Momma goes on day after day with her constant headaches.

I am asking you to be as gentle with them as possible. They love you more than anyone else does. So please be kind. Their well-being is in your hands.

Remember that I too love you and will do what I can.

Love,
Violet

I folded the letter, slipped it inside the envelope, and licked it closed. Taking the two dogs with me, I went outside and put the letter in the mailbox. When the flag was up on the mailbox, the two dogs and I walked down the road toward the back of the property.

A week later his reply came.

Dear Violet,

When I read your last letter I couldn't believe my eyes. I had to reread it to be sure that I hadn't imagined it. How could you have said such hurtful things to me? Don't you know that I am helpless and cannot defend myself. They read all our mail before we get it. They will see that you have turned against me. That will not look good for me when I go before the parole board.

How I treat Mom and Dad is my own business. If I want to tell them what I think, then that is what I will do. So butt out. They are incompetent country people. Sometimes they can't seem to do the simplest things. So I tell them how to correct it, that's all.

You are saying that I am responsible for Mom and Dad's ill health. I just can't believe that you have turned against me too . . .

Dismayed, I finished reading the letter and called my mother.

"Oh, yes," she said, "we've already been told how you betrayed him. Just a few weeks ago you couldn't do any wrong. Now he thinks you've joined the mafia group where he used to work and that all of you are trying to make his life miserable."

"He said that?" I took a deep, labored breath.

"I'm afraid so. He still wants you to go to the appeal, though."

"If he thinks I've turned against him, why does he want me to look out for him at the appeal?" I said.

"I don't know, honey. I never can figure him out,"
she sighed.

The appeal took place in October in Salem, Oregon.
I picked up Aunt Rose at her home outside of Oregon
City, and the two of us traveled to the state capital.

Justice, marble, and tall-ridged columns—the building that housed the Court of Appeals was built as though
each depended on the others. All the officers therein did
not await our arrival. No one knew we were coming except Ken.

A dark-wood banister edged the steep stairs, the
kind I still wanted to slide down. Scanning the halls of
marble, I located the elevator. With a few halting lurches
Aunt Rose and I arrived on the third floor.

Around the perimeter of the courtroom, red paisley
covered Victorian couches sat below a ceiling that
arched into a dome of stained glass. The room was deco-
rated in gold with mahogany trim. At the front of the
room a desklike bench accommodated seven high-
backed chairs. The core of the room contained five tables
and a lectern.

"Do you know what's going to happen?" Aunt Rose
asked. She wiggled on the couch beside me and looked
around like a curious child.

"No, Momma and Daddy talked with Ken's public
defender, but they didn't learn anything."

People in business clothing cluttered the space
around us. With the exception of a man and a boy along
the opposite wall, my aunt and I seemed to be the only
nonprofessional members of the audience.

"Where's Ken?" Aunt Rose asked.

"I don't know. I thought he'd be here."

A buzzer sound. "All rise."

Everyone stood except Aunt Rose. Three judges, a
woman and two men, emerged through the doorway behind the bench. Someone in the back of the courtroom
said, "Ladies and gentlemen, the judges of the Court of

Appeals. Hear yea, hear yea, the Court of Appeals is now in session."

When we were again seated I studied the schedule of cases. Ken's case was number forty-five of the seventy-five cases to be heard. I concentrated on the attorney at the lectern who was discussing merits of a case. With calloused speed the judges flipped through the briefs and ruled on each one. Soon it was Ken's turn.

"Case number forty-five. The State versus Kenneth James Andre," the judge said.

A young blond woman with a long aquiline nose wearing a black-wool suit took possession of the lectern. "Your honor, I would like to point out that this case involves the issue of the constitutionality of the twenty-five-year minimum that is before the Supreme Court at this time," she said.

"I'm aware of that case. Andre will be held over for Reams," the judge firmly announced.

"Case number forty-six?"

When the last of the cases was heard, the judges dismissed the court and disappeared through the center door. I cut through the crowd of attorneys.

"Excuse me," I said to the woman who had spoken on Ken's behalf. "I'm Ken Andre's sister, Violet Andre. I'm afraid I didn't understand what the judge meant when he stated that Ken's case was held over for Reams."

The woman set her briefcase on the floor and smiled. "I'm Delores Howard. There's a case before the Supreme Court right now that challenges the constitutionality of the twenty-five-year minimum for murder. Reams is the name of the individual who has challenged that law.

"A final decision regarding a change in Ken's twenty-five-year sentence will depend on what happens in the Reams case."

"Is it possible that Ken's sentence will be reduced?"

"If the court rules that way, yes."

Knowing what I did about Ken's state of mind, did I want that to happen? I took a deep breath. "I'm afraid I'm quite ignorant of the system."

"That's understandable. I'm surprised to see you here. I didn't expect any of Ken's family to be present."

"Ken asked me to come. And I felt I had to. It doesn't seem like each case gets much consideration."

"The judges read over the cases before they come to court each session."

"How can they possibly remember what was in each case?"

"They manage," she said. She slipped her hands into the pockets of her suit jacket and smiled. "If you would like a copy of the brief, stop by the public defender's office. Do you have any other questions?"

"No, thanks."

Back at the car Aunt Rose said, "I wasn't able to hear much of what went on. Could you tell me what happened?"

"They heard seventy-five cases in four hours. Justice can't be done that way. There's no way a person could remember everything he or she needs to on that many cases in such a short time."

Aunt Rose shook her head. "I don't see any point in the appeal anyway. They're wasting everybody's time."

"I really appreciate you coming," I said.

"I'm not sure what help I was."

"Having you there helped. I was scared, not knowing what to expect and all."

Before leaving town I stopped at the public defender's office and picked up the brief. It was about a half-inch thick and faced with a title page of blue paper. Climbing back into the car I handed the brief to Aunt Rose.

"Do you want to read this?"

"What is it?"

"It's sort of a summary of Ken's case as it was presented today."

She examined the document as I drove her home.

"Listen to this," she said, proceeding to read. "As
they arrived, two individuals came out from the Andre
residence. It was a man and a woman, and the woman
said, 'Ken is out there with a gun. I'm sorry. I'm sorry.' "
Aunt Rose stopped and stared at me. "You think that was
your folks?"

"Yes," I nodded slowly. "It must have been awful
for them," I added, almost to myself. "My God, they
were right there when it happened. How have they stood
it all these months?"

"A lot of prayer, I guess. Lord knows, that's all
they've had."

"But when you're alone with your thoughts in the
middle of the night, God seems so far away."

"That's why they have each other, dear. God lives in
the heart of each person. When you act in a loving way to
another, it is God within you providing the love."

I said nothing. The next morning I went to the
prison to see Ken. There were only a few other visitors
there.

"Didn't the attorney contact you with the out-
come?" I asked and watched my brother fiddle with
some candy bar wrappers, arranging them in neat stacks
parallel to the edge of the coffee table.

"No, I guess I should have figured it would be like
this. I only met with her once. I've had very few letters
from that office to let me know what was happening. It's
all a plot, of course. I'm sure you can see that by now."

I stared at him.

"I guess I'm going to have to try a different way to
get a new trial. They're sending me the transcript within
the next week or so. I plan to read it over bit by bit and
see if I can find any errors. There's got to be a way to

change the one felony murder conviction to manslaughter."

I didn't trust myself to answer.

"I have to get out of this place," he announced. Again I was silent.

He talked until visiting hours were over. When he stood to go, I stared briefly into his desperate eyes and tried not to cry.

"Thanks for coming to let me know what happened."

I hugged him, and this time he did not stiffen. His stricken look, his sunken eyes stayed in my mind on the drive home.

It was still so difficult to see him like that. For months I had tried to decipher the look. Desperation controlled a part of him, but it was more. It was almost as if he was lost . . . that was it. Kenny had lost his way within the rat mazes in his mind. Each hall he took led to a dead end, or in a circle. No way out existed.

All those years ago at church, Sunday after Sunday, the minister preached about the "lost," about how we were supposed to save them. To us it was as if they had the plague or something. But all "lost" really meant was "can't find your way." All "lost" really meant was the look in Ken's eyes.

When Easter Sunday came round Momma and I went to the chapel. We sat together surrounded by her congregation. The auditorium was filled with white lilies, pink azaleas, and purple hydrangeas.

"On this special Sunday I'd like to talk about forgiveness," Pastor Young said. "It's something I have struggled with for years, and most often I fail miserably, even when the other person is sorry. But what about when the other person is not sorry?

" 'Father, forgive them,' Jesus said, 'for they know not what they do.' He asked the Father to forgive His killers before they killed Him, before they were sorry. Obviously in His heart He had forgiven them. If He can forgive His own murderers, how much more should we forgive the wrongs people do to us. But too often we nurse our anger instead.

"The words in the Bible are given to show us a better way to live. Not only did God provide us with the right way to do things, like this example with Jesus, but He shows us the wrong way. He did not hide the frailties of His people.

"Look at David. He had people murdered, as is the case with Bathsheba's husband, yet God forgave him. You see, that's what Easter is all about—forgiveness. It is a time of hope and promise and God's eternal love."

"You might say, but Jesus is special, the Son of God, and it was no sweat for him to forgive these people. After all, He is Divine and He was just doing what He was supposed to do. Jesus is a part of God.

"Yes, Jesus is a part of God, but then so are we. Each one of us was created in the Image of God. Each one of us has the Divine heart flowing within. Jesus was given to us as an example of what we can be. God did not create us inferior with no way to attain perfection; each one of us is capable of that perfection.

"A good start is with forgiveness. Forgive all who have harmed you. Let go of the negative energy . . . then watch the Love and Beauty awaken within your soul."

I listened, I heard, but I could not as yet seem to do what was asked. Still I vowed to try.

Chapter Nineteen

My family and I drove down Interstate 5 into the barren lands of central California. Finding our way to the wrong side of town in a desolate part of the state, we drove into the dilapidated trailer park. The car tortoised along the dirt road until we saw Teresa's trailer. The yard between the single wide trailer and back of the neighbor's home was heaped with rotting boxes. Rust stains oozed down from the front window. Half-broken wooden steps were shoved up against the side of the house.

"Grandma, Grandpa," Loni yelled as she hurried across the packed dirt of the side yard. "Aunt Violet, Aunt Denise, I'm so glad you're here."

"Me too, honey," I answered. "Is your mom home?"

"No. She had to take my other grandma to the doctor. Mom should be back soon though."

"Where's Russ?" Denise asked and began fanning herself.

"He's at school practicing. He thinks he's really smart now that he's graduating from high school," Loni said, sarcastically.

"Your brother being a pain?" I grimaced at my niece.

"Yes, especially with the honors he's won. He even got a letter of congratulations from some senator."

We entered the living room and Loni self-consciously moved several boxes from the couch.

"Is your momma still cleaning houses?" I inquired.

"Yes, she works for an agency now."

A short time later Teresa sidled through the doorway. Her face was still pretty, but she had gained weight again. Huge breasts stretched the knit fabric of a homemade green-plaid blouse. Black leather shoes, frayed and run over on the edges, strained against large feet.

"Hi, y'all," she called out and hugged each of us.

I felt uncertain and shy in front of the woman who had become my sister years before. She dropped her purse onto the kitchen table and pulled out a cigarette.

Ken wouldn't let her smoke. Maybe this is defiance after the fact.

"Loni, did you fix the iced tea?"

"Yeah, Mom."

"Get everybody some. Sorry I couldn't be here when you arrived. I had to put Momma in the hospital today. Ever since Daddy died she hasn't felt good. We just thought she was lonesome. Her heart's big and she can't get a breath. She won't let anyone but me tend to her . . ." She took a drag and sat on a chair, overflowing the sides.

"I didn't get to the store," she said. "Violet, could you take Loni and get some chicken. You guys must be starved." She grinned tiredly and pulled money from her purse.

Driving past empty lots of bare dirt, abandoned gas stations, and crumbling buildings with Loni beside me, I felt disconnected and dazed.

"How's school been, honey?"

"I'm not doing too well. I can't concentrate."

She had been such a good student in the schoolhouse next to her Oregon home. Now from what Teresa had told Mom, Loni was close to flunking, and rumor said she had been running away regularly.

"You don't like your teachers?"

"It just doesn't interest me." She fidgeted a little bit and stared out the window away from me.

"Do you like it where you live?" I said.

"It's better than where we lived before . . . the guy Mom lived with drank too much. The neighbors here seem real nice. Mom said I can even get a dog. She wants a big guard dog to protect us. I do too. I still get scared."

"Just remember, honey, if you need me, I'm here. Call me collect—"

"Thanks, Aunt Vi." Her eyes reflected the same shyness and hopelessness I felt.

But as we talked, every once in a while I saw there the naive optimism and enthusiasm of youth. "Perhaps," I murmured to myself, "she would be alright."

After a dinner of crispy chicken and home-baked biscuits, we headed to the football stadium for the evening ceremony. A layer of pollution dusted the nearby houses and school buildings. Insects gathered over the newly watered lawn.

"Do I look all right, Grandma?" Russ asked as he straightened the graduation cap on his newly styled hair and zipped the red gown. He squinted at the sun and stared with anticipation into the proud eyes of his grandmother.

"You look just fine, honey," Momma said.

The group of us squished across the wet lawn to the stadium. After we found seats, Russ went to locate his classmates. I scooted over the wooden benches and leaned across Loni and her boyfriend to Teresa.

"Is your family coming to the graduation?" I asked.

"Momma was, but now she's in the hospital," Teresa said.

"How about your brother, Rich?" I said. "I hoped to see him."

"No, he didn't attend his own graduation; so he's not about to attend anyone else's," she sighed.

"And the rest of your family?" Denise inquired. She wiggled uncomfortably on the hard seat.

"No." Teresa scanned the field for Russ.

It seemed odd that none of her family planned to attend. It was such a good way to show Russ they cared. For him it was especially important after all he had experienced because of his father.

Expectant relatives and friends rustled to quiet as a speaker stepped to the platform. The graduates marched onto the risers. Sun sparkled on the hair and robes of the young people. Shades of pink painted the summerlike sky.

Russ sat with the others. I resisted the urge to wave and call his name. Slipping the pictures I had taken a half an hour before into my purse, I balanced the Polaroid on my knees.

"Russ is going to get several awards," Teresa said. "He's done real good in school since we've been here. He's in the top three percent of his class."

Momma leaned over Denise and Daddy and whispered, "Violet, would you walk down to the platform and take a picture of Russ when he receives his diploma?"

I moaned. "Why don't you do that, Momma?"

"Please, would you do it for me? I'd feel really funny up there in front of all those people."

Slipping in front of the row of legs I headed down the steps. Once on the field I hurried to the front row just below the platform. As students received their diplomas I kneeled on the grass, out of the way of the flashing cameras.

Finally Russ's row approached the platform. Inching closer I found a spot below it and sprawled on the grass, hoping my red dress would not be stained.

Several minutes later Russ stepped up to the podium. I stood to one side and flashed several pictures.

"Hurry up," he whispered, holding the grin.

I clicked the last one, turned around, and noticed Momma ahead of me. We returned to our places.

"I thought you weren't going to take any," I whispered.

"With you up there it was easier. I couldn't resist. He's my grandson, you know. I just wish Ken could see his son . . ." Her voice caught and tears spilled from her eyes.

"Yes, we are very proud of the boy," Daddy said and dabbed his eyes with a hunter's handkerchief. "It's been a hard road for them all."

When the ceremony was over, I hugged Russ until he complained. "Aunt Violet, you're squishing me to death."

"I'm just so proud of you," I said.

Ken is in his cell in Salem right now. He should be here as Russ becomes a man. He always told me how special Russ was to him. Always bragged how good he was at fixing cars and things.

Kenny, look what you've done, now you have to miss this. Oh, God. I will not cry now. I will not.

"Doesn't Russ look handsome, even if he is my big brother?" Loni said.

"Yes, and for that matter you're very beautiful. You turned into a woman while I wasn't looking."

Loni sparkled. "It was so nice of Grandma and Grandpa to buy me a new dress. I've outgrown everything I have."

After the celebration dinner at Huey's Steak House with more pictures taken, stories told, and comfortable laughter, we headed into the night toward the cars.

"Thank you for coming, Grandma," Russ said. He bent his head to his grandmother's shoulder.

The light over the parking lot accented the tears in

Momma's eyes. "I know this must have been a hard trip for you with your heart and all. You being here means a lot," he said to his grandfather.

"I wouldn't have missed it for anything, Russ." Tears glistened in Daddy's eyes . . .

To each of us Russ expressed love and appreciation. His eyes were moist, as were ours.

Finally it was time to tell Teresa goodbye.

"Goodbye, big sister," I whispered.

"Goodbye, little sis. Take care of yourself."

Chapter Twenty

Sun hung above the Pacific coast and found a place to penetrate the fog. On the beach two gulls picked at the remains of last night's hot dogs. Cal and Christy McCall awakened with light rays in their eyes.

"Christy critter," Cal said, grinning at his sister's sleep-puffy face, "let's put the sleeping bags in the car and walk up the beach."

"Alright." Fully clothed she climbed from the bag and rolled it up, figuring her blond hair was probably a mess. She smoothed it with dainty fingers tipped by pink polish. A glance in the rearview mirror told her the touch of mascara she had applied had not smeared. She grimaced at the freckles on her nose. Getting rid of them had proven an unachievable aim.

With an arm around his sister's shoulder, Cal walked with her toward the surf. Just three inches taller than she, he had finally given up on growing. He guessed he would have to settle for short and dynamic, rather than tall and commanding.

"How's it been going?" he said. "I worry about you."

"Okay . . . I'm okay."

"Have you made any more friends?"

"A few in choir. I really like to sing. I remember when Mom used to sing with Uncle Joel. It makes me feel closer to her."

"Have you been down to see Uncle Joel and Aunt Bitsy?"

"Not since the family reunion in February. I've been going to school and singing. Some of the kids have invited me to do things with them. It's better than at first. With all the publicity I thought I'd never find any friends."

"I had a hard time too."

"But you're always so friendly and everybody likes you. Everybody wants to be your friend," she said.

"When I've needed someone to be there, everybody is busy. I try to realize that they have their own problems, but I get so depressed sometimes."

Picking up a sand dollar, he sailed it toward a mound of seaweed. The breeze caught it, pulling it upward and over the mound.

"I'm glad you're here," Christy said. "We always used to talk about everything . . . but now . . ." Tears choked her and she gulped them back. "I try to talk to Jered and Greg about it. They miss Mom and Dad too. But they weren't there when it happened."

He nodded. "It does make a difference."

"Do you still have those awful nightmares about Ken?" Christy asked.

"No, I've stopped."

"Do you get mad at him?"

"No, it doesn't do any good. How about you, do you still get frightened when you see men on the street that look like him?"

"I can't seem to help it. It makes me scared, like it's happening all over again."

"Things have to get better, you know," Cal said, feeling protective of his little sister. "I refuse to spend my life feeling like I do now."

"Do you feel scared?" She looked at his profile, the way his nose turned up like Mom's. Grief hit her again.

He shook his head. "Mostly it's like I've lost everything that matters."

"Me too." She sighed and decided to change the subject. "Have you decided what to do about your major?"

"I'm going to be a minister."

"Really? You sure you want to do that?"

Her voice sounded like their mother's. In fact she reminded him more and more of Mom; the familiarity brought pain to his heart.

"I was thinking about it before Mom and Dad died. I always admired Uncle Joel for dedicating his life to helping people. I want to do that too." He looked searchingly at his sister. "You still want to be a nurse like Aunt Hazel?"

"I think so."

Cal rubbed his forehead and asked softly, "Do you hear from Loni or Russ?"

Their eyes met. The four of them had been such good friends, together nearly every day. Now all that had changed.

"Once in a while. I'm worried about Loni. She sounds awfully unhappy. I'm afraid the way she's feeling she'll get into drugs and stuff. I miss them both. We used to have such fun."

"You've never thought of doing drugs, have you?"

"I would never do that. It's not right," she said and quickly changed the subject. "Have you met any girls?"

"There's a really neat girl, Janet, whose just a friend. Sometimes I'd like it to be more. It would be nice to have someone to hold—"

"I think I miss that most of all. Have you seen much of Greg?"

"Some. We still have a good time together."

Christy smiled, feeling better just being with him. "Let's go to McDonald's and have a sundae.

"For breakfast?"

"Why not?"

"You're on."

Dave's and my homestead, purchased with old money and new hope, was beginning to look better by the summer.

The sprawling blackberries along the fence had been chopped out, the roots poisoned and removed. Behind the house the Roosevelt privy, that we found stuffed with an old mattress, had been burned. Even the wooden fruit dryer was gone. It had been a season of hard work. And we had fought our way through it.

Feeling hot and sweaty I untucked my striped work shirt and focused on the current project.

"If you don't hold the auger a little at an angle," Dave said, "when the bit drills into the ground, it will angle back the wrong way."

"That doesn't make sense," I murmured.

"Here, let me show you." He climbed down from the tractor, and angled the auger away from the back of it. "See, hold it like this. Right on that mark."

I tried to do what he said and grasped the bar. He lowered the bit to the ground and engaged it. "Put a little weight on it," he snapped.

Nodding I leaned my stomach against the bar and gripped it. When it had chewed a hole two and a half feet deep, I released my hold.

"That wasn't so bad, now, was it? A lot better than digging the post holes by hand, don't you think?"

"Yes," I answered disinterestedly.

"I'd like to finish this line along the side of the house at least. Then we can set the posts before dark. Ready for the next hole?" He readjusted the brim of his ugly brown hat and looked back to me.

"Yep."

With few problems the two of us completed the holes along the house.

For the next few days we worked on erecting a fence around the yard and orchard. By the afternoon of the sixth day we had set most of the posts.

As we worked Dave said, "You should feel lucky you have a husband who lets you play at writing."

"What?" I asked, my mind elsewhere.

"If you had been paying closer attention, you would have heard what I said," Dave retorted, his voice loud and angry.

"I was paying attention." I clamped my jaw shut and spoke past clenched teeth. Steadying the post, I glanced back at the line we had just set. The wind shifted the grass on the knoll above us.

He took another scoop of dirt from the wheelbarrow and shoveled it in around the post, then tamped it in with the metal rod.

"What do you mean, lets me play at writing? Do I have to ask your permission?"

"I'm the one who pays the bills, remember. I'm the one who's working around here. I'm the one who allows you to do whatever it is you do. Any other husband would make you earn your own way."

"Oh, is that right." My voice grew quiet. "I don't tell you what to do, and I don't expect you to tell me what to do. What I'm doing is important.

"We've worked late every night this week because I know this house is important to you. But now I need to get back to my writing. It's nearly three o'clock—"

"I don't care if it's three or eight! If we keep working, we can get the last line done before dark. We can start stretching wire tomorrow."

He glared at me and examined the post he had just set. "I don't give a damn about the fucking book you're writing, you understand?"

He backed the tractor into position and lowered the bit, ready for the next hole. I grasped the bar, careful not to meet his eyes.

"Ready?" he asked.

"Yes," I said, my lips taut.

The bit started twirling. When it had chewed nearly a foot of earth, I heard the familiar snap.

"Shit!" He dismounted and examined the drill bit. "I broke another bolt. Damn it all to hell! Well, missy, you're going to get your way after all. That was the last bolt. I've got to go into town and get another one and some cotter pins. We might as well stop for the day. You're excused."

Without looking at him I crossed the sloped lawn and headed for the house. I closed the door quietly and went to the bedroom. Sitting on the edge of the bed I pulled off my heavy work boots; standing up I stripped off my sweaty shirt and pants and walked into the bathroom.

As I stepped into the shower and turned the water on full force, I wondered when and how I would ever cleanse my life of all the grime and pain, which filled it.

Chapter Twenty-one

Summer ended and with it many of my illusions about my marriage. The other aspects of my life that I had refused to examine now demanded attention . . .

Fall has always been for me a time of change and metamorphosis. Despite all that had happened this October was, to my surprise, no different. Crisp air turned foliage to a dead brown and storms dislodged red, yellow, and brown leaves.

A fantasy wind promised snow in the high plateau of central Oregon and again the ritualistic hunt dominated the thoughts of my family. Wooden-stocked guns and cartons of bullets awaited the time to kill.

Dispersed amongst the sage and pine lodged in campers and tents, my family stalked white-tailed deer while I prepared for departure. It was time to return home to face my fear of the night stalker, Ken's ghost. Facing it was the only way I knew to conquer it.

"Are you sure you have to go, Violet?" Daddy asked. Dressed in his heavy clothes even in the warm afternoon, he rested against my dusty car.

"Yes."

"You'll miss me getting that bug buck," he smiled.

"You can tell me about it when you get back." His

shoulders made a nice place for my cheek. As I nestled there, he stroked my hair. When he backed away I saw his tears.

"Be careful on the drive home, Vi."

"Don't worry, Daddy, I will."

With drooping shoulders he shuffled back to the fire pit, carrying with him a father's eternal defeat.

"Sure you won't change your mind?" Dave asked. He sauntered over from the fire, a coffee mug in his hand.

"I must do this," I said with quiet determination.

Gravel popped up from beneath the tires as I drove from the highlands toward Highway 97 south of La Pine, struggling with my fears. Back home I scanned the evening sky and headed into the house, allowing the dogs to enter first just in case.

"Well, kids," I said after unpacking, "if there's anybody in here, you'll have to let me know. I'm not going to look this time. Don't know what I'd do if I found someone. Hopefully, no one will murder me while I take a shower and wash off the scum."

Entering the kitchen, they began to bark. I lifted the new blind and peered out. Our neighbor Kent Brown, from across the road, was walking toward the house.

"Hi, I brought your mail." He handed me a stack of envelopes. "I wanted to check to make sure you're okay and to let you know if you need me, I'm just a phone call away."

"Even if it's two in the morning and I'm scared?"

He chuckled, "Yes, my wife is afraid too and sometimes so am I. Just call if you need me."

"Thanks," I said watching safety turn and walk the other way.

Gray-white light flickered from the television by the living room door. A make-believe cop drew down on an artificial thief. I punched the remote and tried to find a show that was Disney harmless.

Death surrounded the room, penetrated my thoughts. The night stalker paced beyond the walls and entered the hollow spaces in my mind.

No. This time it would not control me. I was determined. I got up and went to bed without showering.

Huddled on the mattress in the place where Dave slept, I refused to look at the blackened hallway. Instead I forced my face into the pillow. On the floor beside me Brandy moaned. Brutus began snoring. I managed to sleep, waking every couple of hours. Finally it was morning.

Outside, the sky seemed radiant and cheerful. I stretched, reached over the side of the bed, and hugged Brandy.

"We made it, kid. I actually slept by myself last night."

I had to tell someone. Suddenly I thought of Aaron, my sympathetic professor. Four hours later found me in a lounge sipping a glass of chablis. On the Willamette River below the large window, boats bobbed against the moorage. Feeling safe for the first time since I left camp, I wiggled back into the loveseat.

"Boy, did I have to hustle to get here on time," Aaron said. He skirted the tables and perched on the edge of a couch opposite me. "I think we should find a table so we can spread out the pages of that article I've been working on. I hope you don't mind, but I really would like your advice."

Seated beside him facing the river I felt the attraction accelerate. His presence was disorienting.

"I'll go over some of my notes that you might not understand. The rest is self-explanatory. The first page starts a little slow and I don't know what to do with it . . ."

Black neatly trimmed hair curled up away from his temples. His skin, a vibrant brown, was beyond beautiful.

"Aren't you going to have any wine?" I asked in the middle of one of his sentences.

"I think I will."

Sipping the wine, we continued to work for some time. An hour or so later I was feeling heady.

"You know something?" I asked.

"What?"

"You're going to have to feed me or I'm going to be very drunk."

Fish and chips at a nearby restaurant stopped my head from floating. When we were finished he drove me to my car.

It was dark behind the building, too dark to see his eyes. A street light silhouetted him against the window.

"Oh, my," I said almost to myself.

"What?"

"I think I'd better leave."

"Please don't," he whispered.

"I . . ."

My internal alarm sounded and I struggled to silence it.

"Violet . . ."

The muscles of his leg draped over mine and his fingers slid to forbidden places. The alarm in my mind grew louder, and screamed. Confused and dizzy I pulled away, opened the door, and climbed out. "I've got to go Aaron . . . I . . ."

I climbed into my car and sped away.

Chapter Twenty-two

Winter came. Pulling eggs from the refrigerator, Patty McCall set them to boiling. Down the hall she heard Christy turn off the hairdryer and leave the bathroom. Patty's tousle-haired husband was in the back yard, pulling weeds from the flower bed. She loved to watch him, his wrestler's build bulging through the tee shirt, and his little-boy eyes focused on the task.

The vacuuming needed to be done and the tub scrubbed. Glad Christy had volunteered to clean the living room, Patty planned the rest of the day's tasks. Christy was helpful and easy to get along with. Sure she and Jered argued at times, and she thought him too strict, but it had worked out fairly well since she had moved in.

Forgetting how long the eggs had been cooking, Patty took them to the sink and dunked them in cold water. Discovering one of them was not done, she placed it in a bowl in the microwave. Just a little more ought to do it. She set the microwave to whirring and began to load the dishwasher.

BOOM— A sound like a shot exploded behind her. Startled she looked into the microwave. Bits of the egg had burst all over the inside.

Someone was screaming. In the living room she found Christy crying hysterically.

"Honey, honey, it's alright. It was only an egg. You're okay," Patty said as she tried to hug her. The girl did not seem to hear. "Christy, you're safe. It's alright."

Still, there was no response.

Violent sobs shook Christy's body. She felt terror. Again it was that night; her parents lay bleeding on the floor. Again she heard her father's words to run and hide. Unaware of Patty she huddled in the corner behind the chair. Tears and pain ruled her mind. There was nothing else.

Running from the room and out the back door Patty searched for Jered. There had to be something they could do. There had to be a way to pull Christy from her pit. Grief was one thing . . . this was something else.

She spotted him behind the shed.

"It's Christy. She's hysterical. I can't get through to her."

"What happened?" Jered's normally calm manner became concerned and worried. On the way into the house Patty explained: "It sounded just like a gun. I can't believe I allowed that to happen."

When they entered the living room, Christy was still sobbing. Kneeling beside her, Jered tried to comfort her. For an hour and a half her tears continued, until exhaustion took over. Until nothing was left.

Guiding Christy to the couch, Patty sat down with her. "It's okay now. We're here. You're safe."

They spent the afternoon together, watching television, saying little. Dark came and the two watched Christy carefully. After she had gone to bed they took turns looking in on her. Finally satisfied she was sleeping, they climbed in bed themselves.

Jered cried then, as he had right after the murders. Though he tried not to dwell on the crime, it remained a part of him. He never allowed it to dominate his life. He never allowed it to make him bitter. A person had choices. A tragedy could ruin his life, or he could become stronger. He had worked toward the second choice, but in some ways he had made no progress at all.

Beside him, Patty shed her own tears, tears for her parents-in-law, tears for herself and her loved ones.

When the ache subsided they fell asleep close to each other.

In the McCall family Jered had assumed much of the burden and responsibilities left by his parents' death. He was the oldest son . . . executor of his parents' estate, Christy's guardian, and chief fix-it man for his parents' rentals.

On this frigid February day Jered leaned on the shovel and looked out over the pasture near his parents' house. He moved closer to the pasture, squinting. Slowly the herd of elk stepped from the trees and out beyond the orchard. A bull elk raised his nostrils and sniffed the wind. Further into the pasture he moved to graze, his antlers nearly touching the ground.

Whispers of Jered's father's voice floated in on a memory. Dad pointed to a cow elk and then her calf, tucked in behind a tree. Glancing over at his parents' house, Jered saw his mother's ghost watching him in the window. Tears climbed to his eyes. He and his father had watched the herd many times.

It had been his parents' dream place, one they could finally afford. Forsaken now, it waited for a new family. Unfortunately, no one came to claim it. The For Sale sign was nearly faded. The lumber economy of the coastal region seemed permanently slumped. No one could afford to buy.

Jered picked up the shovel and dug around the water pipe, trying to locate the source of contamination. The renters had complained about dirty water for weeks. With each shovelful he splattered himself with mud. He inserted the shovel one more time, hearing the scrape and crunch of the rusted metal. Water spurted from the pipe. Searching under the old house and every place he could think of, he found no shut-off valve.

Exasperated he looked at the spurting water. If he wanted to swear, now would be the time. He did not. What was he to do? Dad had been a handyman. Not him.

Hurrying to the shop he looked for a clamp; most any kind would do. He fumbled through the contents of drawer after drawer; finally, searching a bottom drawer he found a clamp that might work. He kept working. With the onset of dusk he needed a flashlight. He located one in the glove box of his car and hurried back to the broken pipe. Mud gushed beneath his boots.

He slipped the clamp around the pipe and tightened it. In a few seconds the leak stopped. Tomorrow he would have to find a more permanent solution.

Muddy and wet he picked up the tools and headed for his Aunt Hazel's. The responsibility weighed on him; he ached to be free of it. The following night he had to be home for Christy's concert. Nothing would keep him from attending, not even the needs of the renters.

The next day went better than he had hoped. He made it home in time to dress and rush with Patty to the auditorium. They found seats in the middle, ten rows back.

Group voices sang happy and sad songs, lively and dull. Midway through the concert Christy stepped to the microphone and into the light. There was strength in her stance and clarity in her voice as she sang "Amazing Grace." Looking out over the audience she articulated the words, seeking to express the meaning of the writer.

"It's beautiful," Patty observed.

"I'm so proud of her," Jered said. "I just wish Mom and Dad could hear her. I wish they could be here." Tears crowded the corners of his eyes, but he choose to ignore them. Chose to ignore the clutching tension in his throat.

When Christy had sung the last words, the orchestra put away their instruments, and she stepped backstage and hung her robe on the rack. The music instructor, Mr. Wilcox, hurried to meet her, clasping her dainty hands in his own.

"Beautiful, Christy, that was so beautiful," Mr. Wilcox said.

"Thank you—" She blushed.

"You have a gift. You're one of the best students I've ever had."

Members of the choir congratulated her. Nancy, one of the most popular girls in school, rushed past the others and waited until Christy was free.

"That was wonderful, Christy," Nancy said.

"Thanks—" Christy answered slowly, her stomach churning.

"Say, I was talking to your friend Yolanda in history class yesterday. She told me about your parents. That must have been hard."

"It was awful. I saw it happen."

"Good Lord."

"I wish they could be here now." Tears boiled up and trickled down Christy's cheeks.

"How long ago was that?"

"It's a couple of years now."

Nancy patted Christy's hand, "Tell you what, I saw Yolanda around here a few minutes ago. Why don't you and Yolanda join me and my friends at the pizza parlor. Some of the cutest guys in choir are coming. I'll see you in a half hour, okay?"

"Yeah." In wonderment Christy watched the beautiful redheaded girl walk out the door.

She had made a friend, someone who hadn't run away when she heard what had happened to her parents.

Christy smiled, her heart uplifted by Nancy's invitation.

Snow swirled around the campus and outside the corners of Calvin's room. It brought back memories. The faces of his parents swept by, and then by again as the blizzard, rare in this part of Washington, increased in force.

His desk, covered with notes and research material from his trip to the library the day before, repelled him. Picking up his guitar he strummed the song he had been working on for a week. It seemed pointless.

He tried to find positive feeling within himself, but he found none. He had no home, no place to be other than his room on the Bible college campus. In many ways he wished the numbness of the first few months was still with him. During the trial when he had testified, he had not felt anything. It made the scene easier to bear.

Now lying on the bed he let the tears come, one at a time. The ache swelled. Sobs, jarring, devastating sobs, broke loose from inside. For hours he cried.

Daylight had become midnight when he could no longer weep. He switched on the light and stared up at the spider, poised in its web, in the corner of the ceiling, awaiting a victim.

Chapter Twenty-three

The kitchen floor was still wet when Dave's muddy feet trudged in.

"You are to stick around. I need your help this afternoon," he said. Turning from the sink where I was cleaning the mop, I could only stare at him. "I'm going into Woodburn to get those fruit trees. I got a call this morning from the nursery. They just got them in."

"What time will you be back?" I asked.

"Maybe three. That'll give us a couple of hours before dark. Do you think your royal highness can spare me a little time for once?" I nodded. "Just what were you going to do that's so damned important," he snapped.

I stared at him. "I was planning to repair your jeans and plaid shirts this morning. And to write for a little while." I kept my eyes lowered. "But if I wrote now instead, I could get that out of the way by the time you got back. I think—"

"I don't care what you think. I need those jeans and I'm down to two shirts."

"I'm trying to find a way so that both of us can get what we need," I said softly. "I can repair the clothes tomorrow."

236

"Tomorrow I expect you to help me with the trees. I want to get them in before it freezes again."

"I plan to write tomorrow too. I could do it in the evening, but you like me to watch television with you. That leaves morning or afternoon. I have to have some time to put my thoughts down on paper. You know how important it is to me."

"This place is more important," he snapped. "I want you to be proud of it too."

"How can I be, when you won't even put my name on the deed. You don't have to put my name on the investments. I don't care about that. But if I am to live and work here like it's mine, then I would like my name on it. The way it is now, I feel like your poor relation."

"There you go again. Who do you think you are?" he said dourly. "It's my place and I am planning to put your name on it just as I said. The question is when. And that's up to you," he said turning away, "when you earn it."

I wrung out the mop wearily, climbed the farmhouse stairs to my office, and took out my notebook. My mind seemed dry. When the words came, they were not what I expected.

Beyond Tears

> It was not the first time he had hurt me,
> There had been many times.
> Times when with a word or an action,
> He revealed his lack of belief in me.
> The difference this time
> Was that I had exhausted all resources,
> All options trying to solve the problem,
> And it had not worked.
> So the hurt was different this time,
> Hopeless,

Deeper,
And beyond tears.

After I finished the poem, I called Rochelle and
asked her to meet me that afternoon. Then I drove to
Southeast Portland and wandered about the mall; I
looked at the kittens in the pet shop and after a while I
perched myself on a stool in the corner of the pizza parlor and waited for my friend.

"I have an excuse" were Rochelle's first words
when she hurried through the door.

"That's quite an opening," I said.

"I'll get some coffee and tell you about it."

When she returned, she said, "You'll never believe
this, but someone hit me as I was pulling out of the parking lot at work."

"I guess I was just born to wait for you."

"How are you, Vi?"

"Awful. Dave and I just can't get along anymore.
Even before the Ken thing his insensitivity hurt me, but
at least there was affection between us."

"And now."

"Now there's nothing but his ego. Maybe I need
someone else. Someone different."

"If you and Dave have problems, move out. Tell him
you have something you need to work through. If he
loves you he'll wait."

"It would confuse him."

"Move out while the two of you can still salvage
your marriage, before too many ugly things have been
said."

"Right now I'm too tired to try anything. I just want
to go home and stitch up my wounds. The pain with
Dave is just auxiliary. The base pain is Ken."

"You mean it hurts more because he is your brother
and brothers are closer than husbands?"

"No," I answered, exasperated. "Murder is more serious than marital problems or any others I can think of, short of war. It hurts like hell to have a member of your family kill someone! It hurts more than any stupid divorce or lack of security."

"Vi, if you don't get your head together you'll end up in the street. I saw it clearly after you started talking about it. You'll have nothing."

I shook my head. "I have nothing now."

"You have a roof over your head. Besides, if you divorce he'll fight like hell for his money. His family has the bucks to do it too. My family knows his family. Money is loyal to itself."

"Oh, for Pete sake. His dad is harmless. Everyone just envies him because he's so rich. The law wouldn't leave me with nothing. We've been together for a long time. I'd be taken care of."

"All I can say is you'd better be careful. It's absolutely ridiculous for you to risk losing everything."

Chapter Twenty-four

Early morning seeped into the house. I stepped from the cubbyhole of a shower and tucked a towel about me. Dave was seated on the bed changing his shoes.

"Well, what little items are on the agenda for to-day?" he asked sarcastically.

"I have that hair appointment that I told you about. You're going to Salem aren't you? I thought when you get back we could spend some time together. I baked your favorite cake and I know how you like roast . . ."

He shook his head. "That probably won't work out. There are some supplies I want to get and I have to do the grocery shopping. I'll be back about seven or eight tonight."

Sliding open the dresser drawer I peered inside and frowned.

"What's a matter?" he asked.

"I'm running out of underwear."

"Is that all. You think you need a different set for every day of the month."

"Look at these." I picked up a couple of tattered bras and dangled them in front of him. "I only have one that's in decent shape."

"Who's going to see them anyway?"

240

"That's not the point."

"What happened to the last money I gave you?"

"That was over three months ago. Even with the best of budgeting it had to run out. I wish you'd deposit a certain amount in my account once a month. Then I'd be better able to plan."

"I thought we settled that."

"No, we didn't. You decided. The problem still exists, and it will until you either provide me with expense money on a regular basis or I get a job."

"I thought you didn't want a job," he said. The tone of his voice changed from dominance to insecurity. "I thought you wanted to do your creative thing."

"I don't want a job until I have my degree, but I need money I can count on."

"The piece of fluff wants an allowance."

"Just because I'm not a farmer doesn't mean I'm a piece of fluff. This is a partnership, not a dictatorship. Partners share."

"I should open a joint account too, huh, and share my money? Well, the money is mine. I'll do with it what I want. Don't you forget that."

When Dave had gone, I flopped onto the bed and stared at my bare feet. The dining room phone seemed to beckon me. I thought of calling Aaron, who was waiting only an hour away . . . one hour.

I made the call.

I put on a fitted pair of western slacks, a soft, silky cream-colored blouse, a leather jacket, and brown boots.

It was on the darker side of the lounge that I found Aaron, the light of one red candle on his face.

"I'm glad you called," he said.

"One of my appointments canceled this afternoon, so I have some free time."

"I didn't plan to."

"The last time we talked you were so against it."

"I know."

"What happened?"

"I got to thinking and I just decided to call," I said, not wanting to repeat my argument.

The first glass of rosé wine slid easily down my throat, followed by the next one. The embossed wallpaper seemed darkly red; the mellowing effects of alcohol tingled inside me. The sweet fragrance of Aaron's pipe tobacco floated through the room. His eyes held a look I had never seen in them before.

"Yes?"

"Aaron, I want to be with you but I can't seem to." I sighed, then went on: "I keep hearing this warning voice in my head. Then I'm afraid I'll lose everything if I make love with you."

"We'll go back to the friendship we had before."

"Can we do that?"

"Do you think all I'm interested in is another notch on my belt? If that was all I wanted I would have given up by now. We've known each other for several years. Nothing has happened thus far and I'm still here, aren't I?"

"Yes," I said. Pain cut through my heart. "Dave just doesn't seem to care about all I'm going through." Tears fell down my cheeks.

"What I don't understand is why for nearly three years I've had to face the situation with my brother alone."

"You don't have much of a support system, do you?" he said, biting on his pipe. A hickory-apple smell filled my nostrils.

"Why do people become so involved with themselves that they don't take time to help?" I asked emotionally. "I've been there for a lot of people, even when I was running on empty. But they don't even bother to call. I have to tuck the pain related to Ken into a hidden place that allows me to get by."

"I've been giving your situation a great deal of

thought," he said. "A lot of things have happened in your life. Any one of them would be hard to deal with, but you've had to deal with a bunch of things at once. Most people wouldn't be able to handle that."

"I'm not handling it."

He smiled, a warm, genuine smile.

"I think you're coping fairly well."

"I've got to figure out what to do at home. I don't want a divorce, but things aren't good there."

"I think you might be better off on your own," he said, his eyes meeting mine.

"I'd never find a job," I noted.

"Yes, you would. Let me explain what I've been thinking . . . There's the situation with your brother. That in itself is incapacitating. There are very few people who can understand what you've been through. Most therapists wouldn't even know how to counsel you.

"Everybody is draining you—your parents, your brother, Rochelle—and your husband just doesn't seem to give a damn.

He nodded and went on. "He doesn't believe in what you're doing with your life and doesn't like the intelligent, creative person you are. You feel rejected on the base level by the person closest to you.

"Then there's the lack of support from your friends. You give, but they rarely reciprocate. When you find a way to release your frustration, that is torn from you by the words of someone who calls herself your friend but is never there for you. Violet," Aaron said, his eyes compassionate, "you've done well to hold up for so long."

"What am I to do now?"

"I'm not sure. You're in a box."

"I'm so tired. Why do I always have to be strong?"

"You don't. When friends come to you, tell them to come back another time because you're out of energy. You're like a battery everybody draws from, but no one puts back anything to recharge you. If you continue this way, you will be a dead battery unable to help anyone, especially yourself."

"I think I've reached that point."

"Then stop the drain. If you can't recharge, you can at least keep any more from being taken. You are not superhuman. You don't have unlimited resources."

"I'm angry. Why am I not allowed to be human?"

"You are. You're a lovely woman who gives too much. Sometimes people like you go to the opposite extreme and become bitter, giving to no one, but that's a lonely way to live."

"I do get lonely."

"Violet, I know you do. I want to help you." He stared at me, his eyes warm, gentle.

"I've got to go," he said finally. "I was supposed to be back in my office twenty minutes ago. "Call me. If you need me, no matter when it is, I'll be there."

Chapter Twenty-five

The room at the inn waited for us. Aaron unlocked number 56 and let us in. "Would you like more wine? I brought a bottle."

"No, thanks."

Arms of a gentle traveler enfolded me. Lips that had spoken so many times of understanding kissed the wispy hairs at the edge of my temples.

"Even this feels good. Nervous?" he asked.

"A little."

"Me too. You've never seen all of my skin and I've never seen all of yours."

Soon naked skin met naked skin and feelings of awkwardness evaporated.

For that moment we had no guilt. Aaron's touch lifted my heart to a higher place. The room was shadowed, but they were shadows of comfort—a comfort I hadn't found in any other relationship.

That day in January brought my first real relief since the murders nearly three years before. By May Aaron and I had become closer, spending as much time together as we both could manage.

In the high country trillium pushed up through the humus beneath tall evergreens. Across the road from

Dave's farmhouse lambs frisked and jumped on the hill-side. Cream puff skies caught me in a pageant of spring fever.

With the eagerness of a ten-year-old child with a new bicycle, I called my playmate.

"Ah, my favorite lady," Aaron said. His baritone voice projected compassion. "You got home okay the other day?"

"No problem."

"Good. I always worry about that. Say, Chuck and I are going fishing tomorrow. We'd love some female companionship. You remember Chuck. We went out in his cabin cruiser with him and his girlfriend a couple of months ago."

"Yeah. It was great."

"Think you can manage it?"

"Yes, I'd love to. Dave's going to be out of town tomorrow and the next day. Where are you going?"

"Up the Clackamas."

Several empty vehicles sat in the graveled parking lot next to the old powerhouse. Turning generators and spilling water sprinkled the river canyon with a whirl of sounds. Within a few minutes of my arrival Aaron and Chuck parked beside me in Chuck's Continental.

The three of us grabbed the fishing gear from the trunk and passed through the opening in the concrete wall. On the other side were a boat launch and the res-tive waters of the reservoir. A dirt trail arched up the bank and through scraping brush. Two small docks joined to the land by bridges floated out from shore. Passing both of them we hiked along the mud, trying not to slide into the water.

"Vi, you going to make it alright?" Aaron, who was leading the way, looked back toward me.

"I'm part mountain goat." I grinned and patted his arm. "Maybe you're the one who needs help."

"Let's see you climb this bank without falling on your butt," he laughed.

"You're on." I eyed the dirt, grabbed the base of a small tree, and pulled myself up a few feet. Stretching a leg as far as I could, I placed my foot just behind a large protruding root and half crawled the rest of the way up the bank. "Do I win the prize?"

"You are part goat. You can have whatever you want." He twitched his eyebrows and grinned.

We followed the path for several hundred feet, over horizontal trees and past patches of poison oak. Remnants of a campfire lay to one side of the river bank. Mashed grass and decaying leaves made their bed beneath the leafed-out alder trees. Spots of sunlight slipped through.

When poles were rigged and baited hooks dangled in the water below red and white bobbers, we perched beside the water and listened to the stillness.

"My dad used to bring me here," Aaron murmured.

"It's a nice place," I observed. "Reminds me of places my father used to take me."

Chuck closed his eyes and hunched back on the partly bare earth. Aaron poured wine for me and opened beer for himself and his friend. We sat together at the base of an old alder, his hand over mine.

"Sometimes when I go to the river I take Brandy," I said. "He's such a special dog."

"He has a special mother," Aaron said.

He cast and recast trying to find the right spot. After a few hours he moved the pole to the other side of a clump of brush, removed his shoes, and waded out a few feet. Minnows darted around the submerged bottle of wine in the root hollow next to shore.

Standing on the bank behind him I watched his shoulders. I loved them. They made me feel safe, and safety was a newly found commodity.

"Are you willing to get your feet wet?" he asked.

"Sure, what do you need?"

"I want you to come here."

I waded out calf deep and stood beside him in the cool water of the manmade lake. His arm slid around me until his hand capped my bare shoulder.

"I like your bikini," he said. "You have a beautiful body. But it's more than that. I just like to be with you. Like I said before, you really are a special lady."

I'm falling in love. Dear God, this is what I've been afraid of. I think he feels it too. Where can we go with this?

Around the front porch light, night bugs danced. Missy, the long-haired cat, sat below them watching.

The house was silent. Dave had fallen asleep on the couch, and the dogs cuddled in the center of the living room carpet. Scavenging through the makeup drawer in the bathroom cabinet, I searched vainly for the fingernail file.

I was startled when the phone rang.

"I admitted your dad to the hospital today," Momma said.

Oh God. "How bad is he?"

"Almost as bad as when we put him in the hospital five years ago. He can hardly breathe and has lost so much weight. I just can't get him to eat," she said.

"I'll be there in five hours."

"There's not that much of a rush."

"First thing tomorrow then. Have you told Denise?"

"She'll be down tomorrow too."

"Good. I'll leave after breakfast. Today's your anniversary, isn't it?"

"Yes," my mother sighed, "forty-six years."

I went into the living room and told Dave. He hardly looked up. "I plan to stay down as long as they need me." He made no comment.

The following day my watch read one o'clock when

my car crossed the bridge over the bay. I sped past the welcome-to-the-city sign and the holding facility where Ken had been held before the trial.

Hemlock Hills Medical Center, a contemporary structure with no architectural charm, existed on the side of the ridge up from a filled marsh. An older subdivision and a few medical offices brought civilization to the semiwooded area.

Hurrying through the lobby I stopped at the desk and asked directions. The elevator was slow, too slow. Tension and near panic rode with me to the second floor and accompanied me down the maze of hallways to room 245.

Denise was seated on a vinyl couch outside a door at the end of the hall.

"Dad and Mom are with the doctor now," she said, motioning me to sit beside her.

"How does Daddy seem?"

"He's really thin and he looks so tired. I'm really afraid this is it," Denise whispered, pulling and twisting a strand of hair. "I'm afraid he won't be with us much longer. I've felt it since Mother's Day."

"Me too."

"What are we going to do with Momma?"

"I don't know."

Nurses and housekeeping personnel moved in and out of the patients' rooms.

"She's never lived by herself," she said.

The doctor came out of Daddy's room and shuffled down the sterile hallway. Denise and I hurried after him.

"Dr. Goodman," I said, "I'm Violet Andre, Lee's youngest daughter. This is my sister, Denise. Could you tell us how Daddy is?"

"I'm afraid the medication that worked a miracle on your father several years ago is no longer doing its job. It was a long shot at the time, but it worked. He's been taking three times more medication than most people can tolerate. At this point we are looking for alternatives.

"As I told your mother, we could transfer him to Sacred Heart in Eugene. They have an excellent cardiac unit. However, since I'm consulting regularly with the doctors there, I don't think he would get better care there."

"Will he get better this time?" I asked.

"That depends on whether or not we can find a substitute medication his body will tolerate. We can hope." His eyes were sad as he walked away.

"Looks like we were right," Denise said softly. She stared beyond the window at the hemlock bending with the gusts from the bay.

Momma opened the door. "Hi, Violet," she said, giving me a long squeeze. "Good to see you. Daddy's back in bed now. You can come on in."

Walking past the empty bed next to the door, I found my father amidst sterile white things.

"I'm so glad you're here, Violet," he exclaimed. "Thank you for coming."

The white gown he wore clung to my daddy and the muscles in his neck protruded with each movement. I stood beside the bed and enfolded his hand, tears in my eyes.

Momma and Denise looked in through the doorway. "We're heading down to the cafeteria to get something to drink. We'll be back in a little while."

When they had gone, Daddy said, "I couldn't take your momma out for our anniversary. I really feel bad about that."

"Momma just wants you to get well."

"I suppose you're right, Violet, but I've never missed before."

"Forty-six years is a long time. How have you managed it?"

"Love," he whispered. "To stay married for forty-six

years a person has to learn patience. You have to learn to give and take, learn not to get mad and say bad things to each other. That's what Momma and I have tried to do. It wasn't always easy, but there was never another woman I wanted. She's been a good woman, your mother. I've never been able to provide her much, but I did the best I could."

Unable to say anything, I sat at the end of the bed.

"I was never able to give her all the pretty things she wanted, and I guess I was selfish sometimes."

"You love her."

"Without love, without your momma, it would have been a lonely life. Love is the most important thing in this old world. Remember that, Violet."

He slumped forward, removed the oxygen tube. "I don't think this stuff is doing me a bit of good. I don't think those doctors know what they're doing."

"They're trying to help you breathe better."

"They say my heart is really enlarged. That's partly why I'm having so much trouble breathing. The oxygen is supposed to help reduce the size of my heart, but I don't know, Vi. I don't think it's going to work this time."

I love you. I love you. You can't die.

A few hours later I managed some time alone and called Aaron from the lobby.

"We can't meet tomorrow," I said. My voice was weak and the receiver shook. "My daddy is in the hospital. He's very ill."

"Oh, Vi, I'm sorry. Are you okay?"

"I'll manage. I always do."

"Call me when you get back home. I'll be praying for you and your dad."

When I hung up I sat in the silent lobby for a while contemplating the day and what Daddy had told me.

Love, the kind Daddy talked of, was all I wanted, a love that eased my loneliness. A love that tucked me in and made me safe. A love that erased negativity. For the next ten days we kept a vigil at the hospital night and day. Daddy seemed better. We were all exhausted; we went home for rest.

"It's good Loni and Russ came," Momma said. Her face anguished. She removed her shoes and leaned back in the easy chair beside the overloaded bookcase.

"I'm glad the children got here safe. You talked to Dr. Goodman today, Mom?" Denise asked.

"Yes. Daddy's coming home tomorrow. He'll need oxygen, and he'll be confined to either the bed or the couch," Momma said. Her voice was almost hopeful.

"Is the medication working?" I asked.

"They can't be sure," she said.

"How long do you want us to stay, Momma?" I asked.

"For a couple more days. Until I'm sure he won't have another attack."

On July 4, Independence Day, Daddy was home lying on the couch. On the opposite side of the room a hymn book was propped against the upright piano. I walked over to see the page they had turned to. It was a hymn we had sang as children. A half-remembered version of "The Old Rugged Cross" played in my mind.

On the floor beside her grandfather, Loni toyed with a strand of yarn in the homemade rug. Beyond the French windows the sound of tires on rocks greeted the country afternoon. A Toyota sedan stopped behind Russ's car.

Loni went to the window and peered out. "It's Christy . . . Christy McCall," she said. Clasping her hands she skipped about the kitchen.

Christy knocked at the open door. She hugged her two friends and said, "It's so good to see you!"

Blond curls framed her sweet, innocent face and a few freckles dusted her nose. She straightened her blue blouse and smoothed the ruffles around her neck.

She ambled in to the couch where Daddy was propped against pillow.

"Hi, Mr. Andre. I've been hearing you were ill." Gently she petted his hair with long feminine fingers.

"Hi, honey. I feel better just seeing you." His voice was breathy and gasping but his eyes lighted up seeing her.

My mind spun backward. I could see them in my mind, Daddy's silver head bent to hers as they stood on the landing outside the courtroom after her testimony at Ken's trial. No wonder she touched him so.

"It's good to see you," I said. Tears muffling my voice. "What have you been doing with yourself?"

She plopped down at the table between Loni and me. Her eyes conveyed friendliness. "I'm living in an apartment by myself in Eugene. I begin nurse's training this fall . . ."

There was so much I wanted to ask, but I was afraid my questions would reopen the pain. Still, I wondered how she could live alone, how she dealt with the fear.

We talked small talk for awhile. Then she left with Russ.

"That girl amazes me," I said.

"Me too, Violet. How she can have a normal life after what Ken did to her folks and how she can still care about us, I'll never know." Daddy's words choked his voice and he dabbed away his tears.

"I just hope she can be happy."

"She really deserves it," Daddy said.

Chapter Twenty-six

Grains of fall sifted through the wind. Bent needles and fractured limbs were scattered beneath the pine tree, and brown maple leaves woven into the wire fence above the house, the results of an unexpected storm. A hazy afternoon sun stood low in the sky. Tugging several package from behind the seat, I backed out of the car.

Brandy wagged his way across the grass and plopped a stick at my feet.

"How you doing, boy?" His friendliness was the most reassuring thing I had seen in weeks. I picked the stick up and heaved it toward the center of the yard. Clutching the packages, one containing a new shirt for Dave, I boosted open the kitchen door with my hip.

Dave and an attractive thirtiesh woman with long auburn hair sat at the kitchen table. The two of them scanned a sample management book.

I made myself a cup of tea and joined them, trying to see the book. Dave closed it with a bang.

"You get first bid on the timber, right?" he asked.

"Yes," she replied, glancing at me with narrowed eyes.

"It looks good to me. As I said before, I don't see

how I can lose. When do you think you could have a plan drawn up?"

"Probably by the end of the month," she said. She smiled, her eyes on Dave. I felt strangely excluded.

"Sounds good."

"I'll get back to you in a week or so. Now, will this agreement be made out in both your and your wife's names? Is the property under joint ownership?" She looked at him oddly.

"Yes," I interjected.

"No," Dave said, "only mine." I recoiled as though I had been punched. Dave ignored me.

"Well, then," she remarked smiling again, "I'll let you know when it's completed."

He followed her out to the truck, and they talked a few more minutes. I remained at the table staring at my tea.

My husband came back inside and poured himself another cup of coffee. Taking a seat at the other end of the table, he studied the literature.

"Who is she?" I asked.

"She's from the Publisher's Paper Company," he said quietly.

I nodded. "I thought you added my name to the property."

"I decided to wait," he replied.

"Why?"

"I just decided to, that's all."

"I thought it was settled. I thought I was a partner now." I tightened the muscles in my legs to subdue the shaking anger.

"Look, I decided to wait. I thought I'd see how you did on the fence and the rest of the work around here."

"You mean I have to earn it?"

"If you want to put it that way."

"It was embarrassing, you know, learning about it in front of that woman. You could have at least told me."

"I didn't think it was necessary." He gave me his how-dare-you-question-me look.

"Do you ever plan to put my name on it?"

"We'll see. I thought I'd use it as a lever."

"A lever?"

"Yes, for when you're finished being a writer and it doesn't work out. That way I can get you to do some real work around here like you're supposed to."

Leaving Dave to his selfish plans I trudged from the house. Taking the weed-covered road that led to the back of the property, I pulled on tree branches and long shafts of dead grass. My tears fell.

There were still some held inside the next time I met Aaron several days later. We met at a dilapidated A-frame cabin on the road to Estacada. It sat back between some tall alder and next to a small creek. Behind it a hill covered with thick underbrush offered all the seclusion anyone could want.

"This place belongs to one of my father's friends," he said as we stepped from our cars. We climbed the steps onto a rickety deck. He ran his hand under the edge of the siding until he located the key. Leaning his shoulder against the swollen door, he inserted the key and shoved the door open. We went inside.

"Clarence used to have big barbecues. He and Dad brought their women here."

"And now you do?"

"My friends and I have had a couple of parties here. Clarence lives in Palm Springs most of the time. I haven't talked to him in a couple of years."

The kitchen cabinets were constructed of ugly old boards. The air smelled of rotting wood. A sliding glass door fronted the small living room. Near the kitchen wall a black pipe, attached to an old Franklin wood stove, rose to the sloped roof and out a sealed opening. An armload of wood sat in a firebox next to the wall.

"Sorry, it's so cold," he said. "I'll build a fire."

When the fire was going Aaron pulled a chair up next to it and I sat on his lap. "You seem quiet. Are you okay?"

"I feel weird."

"Come here, maybe we can make it go away." He kissed my neck and massaged my body. On a cot in the corner of the kitchen we made love. Cold damp sheets spread beneath us. On the ceiling above Aaron's head a long-legged spider waited beside a maze of carefully designed webs.

I pretended to enjoy Aaron's attention, but my mind could see nothing but tears falling from inner eyes. Negative feelings invaded me. I wondered how many others had used the bed since the sheets had been washed.

Finally we dressed and found the creek. The small bridge needed repair. A couple of planks were missing.

"The best times with my father were fishing," Aaron said, absently staring into the ruffled water. "And even then he acted impatient with me. Never made me feel I could do anything right."

We stood together and alone.

That evening I called Rochelle and we arranged to meet for lunch later in the week.

Stuffed calico pig bodies and bundles of dried flowers filled decorator boxes on the papered walls of the Gresham Restaurant. Cloth napkins and blue wine goblets sat on the wooden table between Rochelle and me as we waited for lunch.

"I think I must be going through an early midlife crisis or something," I said.

She chipped at the cracked red polish on her fingernail and said, "What makes you say that?"

"I was reading a book last night, and what it said fits. It talks of seeing a black void at the end of the tunnel. That's where I am. Since Ken got into his mess, it seems that it'll never get better.

"I keep searching and finding nothing. I'm discouraged with everything. I'm afraid of dying. I look in the mirror and worry about the little lines I see on my face. I worry about my marriage and if I would be better off alone. I've been watching other people and for the most part they don't seem happy either. They just make do."

"I think you're being pessimistic."

"I call it realism."

"Have you seen Aaron lately? He always makes you feel better."

"I thought you didn't approve of our relationship?"

"I don't, but since you're going to do it regardless of what I think, I thought maybe he could help."

"Recently he seems to be a little withdrawn. His own marriage is difficult. I think he's in love with me, he seems so enraptured and . . . then he seems distant. Maybe it's just me. I'd like to think there is happiness somewhere, or at least peace of mind, but I can't find either."

"You're just under a lot of stress after Ken and with your dad so sick," she said.

"That's part of it. I don't know what I'm going to do if he dies, but it's more than that. Everything I do makes things worse, not better. And then there's Ken. I need to write to him again, but every time I sit down to do it I stop."

That evening I started another letter to my brother. Blackened keys hit sheets of white paper and words formed into sentences. The plunk-plunking of the Smith-Corona was anything but restive. After an hour Dave joined me in the office.

"What are you doing?" he asked.

"Writing to Ken. I've been dreading it."

"I didn't know you had problems with that."

"I always do, and this time's worse. I'm usually careful not to say anything that might upset him, but now there's no avoiding it."

"How's that?"

"I got a letter from him yesterday. He demanded to know why I haven't hired an attorney. I thought I explained that well enough, but I guess not. So now I'm telling him that no matter what he does, he's not going to get the answers he wants."

"Did you tell him that spending money on his case would be like throwing it down the toilet?"

"I can't say that."

"You're right, he's definitely not going to like it."

"He keeps telling everybody what a bad person I am anyway. He's written a lot of stuff to Aunt Rose about me."

Within a few days I received a call from Aunt Rose.

"Ken took you off his visitor's list," she said.

"He must have been really upset by my letter."

"He was. He said you were the worst one and that you were turning everybody against him. Pooh! He's not right in the head. I just tore up the letter. I won't respond to things like that. Anyway, he wanted me to tell you, so now I have."

"I guess that's that," I observed morosely.

"Pretty soon no one will have anything to do with him, if he keeps running everybody down."

In the three months since Daddy's heart attack I had traveled to visit my parents twice a month, spending three or four days each time. Each time he seemed worse. Early on Saturday afternoon just after Labor day I watched the ocean down from a jetty about fifteen miles from their home.

Sand sprinkled the tops of my leather shoes as I kicked my way down the beach. A layer of powdery clouds covered most of the sky. The tide left a narrow strip of wet sand, and minute birds scampered before easy waves.

It was the same place I had visited with Rochelle a month before; I could still feel the moisture soaking through the knees of my jeans, and coarse granules clinging to my fingers. That day I had gone to the beach to escape grief; this day I had come to face it.

I slipped my hands into pockets below my fisherman-knit sweater and continued toward the lighthouse. The wind wisked hair into my face. A gray and white gull circled above me and landed just beyond the breakwater. I raised my eyes to the streaks of blue and watched as they shifted and changed with the ocean sky. It was then that I began to pray:

Lord, please help me. I'm so afraid and I hurt so bad inside. Help me understand and accept Daddy's death when it comes, and my own. It's time for me to let him go. Help me grow from this experience rather than be crippled by it.

Focusing on the sand just ahead, I scuffed along the vacant beach. I reached an outcropping that protected a cove. Back against the vertical cliffs stripped logs and smooth rocks were piled against the weather-worn brush. I sat down there looking for a while at the sea gathering strength from nature. A gust burst 'round the sandstone outcropping. Particles of light shimmered into my body. It was as if I felt God's presence within me, saying, Your daddy will be all right here! My heart rose. Finally it was time to go.

Hunting season found me holding my father's hand in the living room of my youth. It was the first season he had ever missed. Momma was out at the barn feeding the cows.

"So, you decided not to go hunting with Dave and the rest of the family this year, huh, Vi?" Daddy hoarsely asked from his spot on the couch. The skin molded itself to the bones in his face; his eyes were sunken into the sockets. He squinted because he said light hurt them.

"I'd rather spend the time with you. And I couldn't miss Momma's birthday, you know."

"Thank you." His voice was heavy with love. "I wouldn't have held on so long if it weren't for your momma. I worry about her. I don't know what she's going to do when I'm gone, but this whole thing is such a struggle. Every position I put myself in is uncomfortable. My heart is so large that it's pressing against everything."

"Does it hurt a lot?"

"I'm afraid so, Vi. I hate this oxygen tube around my neck. Mostly I'm just tired of fighting. Maybe the Lord has a better place for me."

"I know he must, Daddy," I said, tears rising in my eyes. A few hours later I drove back to the house of my husband. Once there the peace I had made with Daddy's departure dissipated.

Dark shades of dawn covered the orchard and two-story house where Dave and I lay; he was sleeping. I lay awake. A faded moon barely shone in the western sky. A coyote across the road in the tree-lined draw lifted its head in a watchful cry, and on the floor beside me Brandy moaned in sympathy.

The telephone rang. Afraid to answer it, I stood listening to it ring one more time.

"Momma?"

"I think your dad is gone," she said. Her voice seemed calm.

"No," I whispered.

"Russ is in working on him now, has been for about fifteen minutes. I called the ambulance, but I don't think they can do any good."

"Are you okay?"

"Uh, I'm okay, I guess. Now, I don't want you to speed on the way down. Both Russ and Denise are here. Denise came down last night."

I woke Dave, who mumbled condolences. "Can you come with me?" I asked plaintively."

"I have too much to do tomorrow."

Dave didn't look at me.

"I'll come later—as soon as I can."

I hurried into my clothes, left Dave in the kitchen, and headed alone down the asphalt and away from the place that was supposed to be home. Rain gushed from the sky, and the car's wiper blades raced to keep up.

Arriving at my parents' several hours later, I paused before the closed door, trying to gain the courage to enter the house that would never again shelter my father. Grasping the metal knob, I pushed open the door and stepped into my mother's hug. I felt her grief.

"I'm glad you're here," she said.

The house seemed hollow as I made my way to the dining room and sat down in the seat where my daddy had often nodded off to sleep. I could still see him sitting there, his silver wavy hair nestled in his hand.

Grief hovered over me, but I pushed it away. I would not allow myself to feel it. I would not allow myself to fall apart when Momma needed me to be strong.

Denise entered from the living room and hugged me. She said nothing, only stared with clouded eyes. The old house creaked and the refrigerator roared, but we were silent.

Where are you, Daddy? Is your spirit still in the room looking down on us one last time?

Looking past the French doors into the living room I thought of Daddy standing at the end of the room and gazing out at the pasture as he so often had. I could still see his blue overalls and sweatshirt and that kind, thoughtful look in his eyes.

I walked to that window. Misty clouds hid the slough and all that was beyond it. I peered out toward the pasture, but I could not see him, did not feel his presence.

A pickup truck pulled up. Elsie, Daddy's niece, and her husband, Bill—our hunting buddies—got out and knocked on the door.

"Hi, honey." Elsie's dark eyes radiated love.

Bill's normally smiling face was serious now. I allowed his arms to engulf me. His large round body felt comforting and safe. A tear slipped down my cheek and soaked into his cotton shirt.

"It's hard isn't it, honey," he said softly. "Your daddy was a good man. We'll all miss him."

"Yes," I whispered hoarsely.

We visited quietly for an hour or so. When they rose I walked out with them and closed the door behind me. I jammed my hands into my jeans and stood on the edge of the porch, rocking back and forth.

"You call us now, if you or your momma need anything," Elsie said.

"Don't you worry, honey. We'll look after your momma. She's a fine woman," Bill said, scratching his chin. "We've tried to be here more often since Ken got into his mess. It was real hard on them. Harder on your dad than he ever admitted. It broke his already worn heart, I'm afraid."

After they went home Denise joined me on the back porch. "Can you tell me how it happened?" I asked.

"Dad woke up around six this morning. He said something to Mom and they went back to sleep. Next thing Mom knew Dad was shaking hard. He took some gasping breaths and then stopped breathing.

"Russ did CPR on him until the ambulance got here. Poor kid just wouldn't give up. I relieved him some." Denise shuddered and rubbed her lips. "Daddy was already turning cold and his skin had a strange texture. I can still feel death on my lips. It's something I'll never forget." She gave a shaky sigh and walked away toward the house. I decided not to follow. She probably needed time alone.

Half-looked-at photograph albums, sorting papers, staring out at the slough and trees across the way, pacing from room to room, thus went the first day without my daddy.

Evening came and the clock read nine. I looked forward to climbing onto the hide-a-bed and retreating into oblivion.

"I was thinking where we'd put everybody," Momma said, already in her robe. "Russ is staying in Violet's old bedroom, though I don't know if he'll be back tonight. Denise is in the trailer. Herb should be arriving late; so he'll take the hide-a-bed. Violet, you can sleep with me. Okay?"

"Sure, Momma," I said, trying to sound pleasant. I had imagined myself in the living room across from the glowing picture of Jesus. Instead Momma's brother would be sleeping in my spot. Inwardly I groaned, desperately needing time alone.

"I think I'll turn in," Momma said.

"I'll be along in a while. I'm not ready, yet," I answered.

After Momma and Denise had gone to bed I sat at the dining room table and stared at the dark living room.

Oh, Daddy, I'm not ready. I'm not ready!

Chills quivered through me. I turned up the space heater and put my feet in front of it. The house creaked. Emptiness reverberated through my brain.

Daddy, I love you. Why did you have to die? I thought of all the times through the years when Daddy had said that someday he would pass over. The true meaning of his words now possessed me.

Finally I entered the bedroom and Momma switched on the light. She must have done that for Daddy all these years, I thought, a simple courtesy she could never perform for him again. How hard it must be for her.

"Thanks," I whispered.

"You're welcome," she replied, her face showing her desolation.

Laying between the blankets I shuddered. Daddy had died that morning in the very spot I now lay. His body had touched the blankets the way mine did. His last breaths had entered the same air space. Eyes glued open I stared up at the ceiling. I stiffened my body to control restless muscles.

Later I could let down the shield. For now I would be and do whatever my mother needed. That was the way it must be.

"You okay, Momma?"

"Yes," she whispered, but her words were hollow and I knew she said them only to protect me.

Rolling over I scrunched my face against the bed. The mattress seemed to reject me. I felt stripped and isolated.

There was no Dave to hold me. Earlier when I called him he had said he would be down as soon as the chores were completed. What chores? What could be more important than consoling the ones you loved?

On the morning of the funeral in slumber room number three of the funeral home I saw Daddy for the last time. Except for his hands he looked normal. His fingers were arranged stiffly on his chest. They were the only real sign he was dead.

Peeking out from inside his blue shirt was his long underwear, like always. Over the shirt was a plaid blazer, the same one he had worn to Ken's trial. Now he wore it in the death pose. White hair rested on his final pillow.

Easing in beside me Dave said, "It's hard to be in your parents' house without him. It's too empty. I didn't even know if I could come in and see him. I've never seen a dead person before, but I am glad I came. Your dad was the kindest man I've ever known. . . . He'd gotten so thin. They did a good job filling out his face."

On that barren afternoon from the privacy of the family room I watched people enter the chapel. Beside the casket along with the others was a heart shaped arrangement of long stem red roses from Bill and Elsie, Elsie's siblings and their families.

Oh, God, they love him too. They love him too.

Seated between Dave and Russ I adjusted my black suit jacket and matching pin-stripped skirt with shaking hands.

On the other side of Russ, Momma sat without tears. Her face was red and puffy the way it had been after the murders. Denise and Ted were next to Dave.

Uncle Herb, Momma's brother, stood next to the organist. In his vibrant voice he sang Daddy's favorite song.

> ". . . Beyond the sunset, oh glad reunion,
> With our dear loved ones who've gone before,
> In that fair homeland, we'll know no parting,
> Beyond the sunset forever more."

Russ slipped his arm around Momma and squeezed hard. Except for his hair, he looked like his father's twin. Ken . . . He should be with us as we said goodbye to Daddy.

Thoughts of Ken forced thoughts of two other funerals three and a half years before. Many of the people attending Daddy's funeral had attended services for the McCalls and the Bennetts. Were they thinking about the murders too?

For a time the minister said nice things about Daddy. When he was done everyone filed out and I greeted close family and old friends. Wandering out to the entry hall I tried not to stumble in my high heel shoes.

Dave had vanished. I had no energy to move, no energy to search for him.

Suddenly Laura, my brother-in-law Ted's sister, saw

me and walked over. Hugging each other we sobbed but did not speak. Within moments she moved away.

Uncle Herb picked his way through the crowd. A knitted beret covered all but a fringe of grey hair. Around his neck hung a beaded cross.

"I wonder how Momma is going to survive?" I said, pulling at the ripped edges of my fingernails. "I'm so worried about her. She's never lived alone before."

"She'll be fine," he replied with a gentle smile. "Your mom's a strong woman."

"Do you remember much about her growing up?"

"I'm six years younger, so it's hard to give a good perspective, but she's always handled her heartaches pretty well. Even with Ken, she keeps supporting him even when he hurts her. She has an inner strength which helps her cope with changes. She's pretty special."

"I wondered if I'd feel guilty because I wasn't there when Daddy died. In a way I feel better, I don't think I could have handled it."

Uncle Herb looked searching at me. "When death comes close allowing you to watch, don't turn away. It's an intimate moment, special and Divine. Death is nothing to fear. It's a release." He kissed me and made his way to friends of his childhood who like us were leaving. It was over.

The days after the funeral crept by. The others except Russ had gone; he and I remained with Momma. Each night I lay beside her thinking how my father had lain there for so many years. How alone she must feel. Each night I ached inwardly for relief and escape. Instead of running away I controlled my own grief and comforted the woman who taught me how to love.

On the tenth day I headed for home and stopped in Dayton at my cousin's auto shop. Holding a sack of spare parts, I stepped up to the counter.

"Is Will around?"

"Just a minute. I'll get him," the man said.

"Hi, cousin," Will said, entering from the garage. His hair was graying, but like most of the Andre men he showed no signs of losing any. "What can I do you for?"

"I need to return the parts Russ didn't use when he tuned up my car last week."

He calculated my refund. "On your way back up to Molalla now?" he asked.

"Yes." The two of us walked to my car. "It's time for me to go home."

"Is your mom alone?"

"Russ is staying with her, thank God. He has been since Daddy got sick. Denise is coming back down this afternoon. She'll be down for the rest of the week.

"It was hard to leave Momma."

"Denise is coming down?"

"Yes, she and Momma plan to work in the flower beds. Bill and Elsie and some others will be over to help Momma cut up those trees that are down on the hill. It'll give her something to do. How's your dad? He's the only one of the older Andres left now."

"Not too good. We went hunting last weekend and he kept pointing out places he and your dad got deer over the years."

"Daddy's death brings back the whole thing with Ken."

"I was thinking about that at the funeral," he said.

"I wonder how Ken took the news about Daddy," I murmured. "It must have been hard facing it alone, but I guess there's no way I can comfort him, since he still won't let me visit. He tears up my letters."

"I thought about visiting him," he said. "A friend of mine in Salem said he'd go with me, but I just can't. It's been so hard on me. I was closer to the ones who died than I was to Ken. We all used to go hunting together until Ken. . . . Anyway, I just can't go."

I was surprised by his openness. We had never really talked before.

"This whole thing has been hard on everybody," I said. "For my own peace of mind I had to forgive Ken, not that he'll ever know. I still don't think he's sorry. I had to forgive him for hurting Momma and Daddy too. I'm still working on that because he's continued to mistreat them. And I had to forgive him for messing up my life.

"You need to do it too. Not for Ken but for yourself. Hate eats away at a person." My words seemed stark in the midmorning light. "I guess I'd better get on the road. It's a long trip."

I pulled out my keys and started around the back of the car. My cousin caught me mid-step, pulled me into a bearlike embrace, and held me tightly. Our innermost feelings, love, and pain were communicated without words.

Chapter Twenty-seven

Butterflies don't live in the California desert. At least I have never found any. It is a place where trees refuse to grow and scrubby bits of grass tenaciously grip dry hillsides and flatlands. In the city things are different. Pumped water and air conditioners make life almost bearable, for those who can afford such luxuries.

Teresa and Loni lived on the wrong side of town. The dirt around the ramshackled trailer park seemed harder packed. Dented cars were pulled up to hallway-sized houses. Across the street a fat man wearing a dirty tee shirt slouched in a lawn chair. An open can of beer sat beside him, near it was a twelve-pack of empties. Momma and I got out of my car and slowly walked to Teresa's; as I touched it the door flopped open, hitting the side of the trailer.

"You're here," Teresa said. "I wasn't expecting you until tonight. Come on in. Loni and Pete are still in bed. Breakfast?"

"No, we ate first thing," Momma replied.

"It may have done me good to stop smoking, but I've gained another fifty pounds I didn't need."

"Teresa lit a cigarette and sat down at the kitchen

270

table. "Make yourselves at home. Loni," she yelled, "they're here."

Sleepy-eyed Loni padded down the hall rubbing her eyes. She hugged us both, then dropped to the couch and scrunched her eyes shut.

"You stayed in a motel last night?" Teresa said.

"It was midnight when we got into town," I said. "So we figured we would find a place and see you this morning."

"It would have been no bother. I was up late anyway, waiting for Loni and her boyfriend, Pete, to get back from the county fair."

"By the way, I'd like to visit your brother, Rich, while I'm here," I said.

"He lives just a few miles from me. I'll give him a call. Did you see him when you were here for Russ's graduation?"

"No, and I regretted it."

"I need to check on my momma," Teresa said. "She's been in and out of the hospital a lot lately. Now she's home again. I thought maybe you'd like to come along. Momma likes to visit."

"I'd like that," I murmured. Her home was in a row of small cottages with lawns of dead grass and dirt. We visited Teresa's mother for most of the day. Shortly after we got back, Rich appeared on the edge of the doorjamb.

"Hi, foxy lady," he said, his grin wide and friendly.

"Hi," I responded.

"I've developed a little bit of a belly since I saw you last. Haven't been working out like I used to. Just sitting back and letting middle age take over. My God, but you're stacked."

"It helps to exercise." I said.

"So I see," he answered staring at how my breasts stretched out the French-cut tee shirt I wore. I blushed.

"Hey, if you've got it, be proud of it," he said with a

smile. Rich sauntered out to the yard and leaned against Teresa's car. I followed him.

"My cousin Bill is across the street visiting my older brother. I thought I'd come along and get a look at you," he said.

"How are things for you? I've wondered about you so many times!"

"I'm surviving. I've still got that job with the county parks department. I don't like it very much but—"

I interrupted, "In this economy you best keep your job."

"I know, I know. Next thing you know we'll be involved in another war."

"I'm afraid so too. When I think of all the guys our age who were messed up by Vietnam—"

"I'm one of them. Sometimes I still want to take the gun to my head, but those times are less frequent now. I killed hundreds of people." He pulled his baseball cap farther down and peered beyond me. "A couple of things have haunted me. I remember drawing down on this man who had survived the barbed-wire barricades. They loaded them with drugs, so they wouldn't feel the barbs ripping their skin.

"Anyway, I aimed at this guy and pulled the trigger. The force blew off his arm, the one holding the gun. Green stuff poured out of the stump . . ."

I shuddered. "Green stuff?"

"From the drugs, you know. He just reached down, retrieved the gun from the arm on the ground, and kept on coming. That's when I had to kill him."

"It must have been horrid," I said.

"It was. I was in most of the major offensives you heard about. Afterwards I had to take this bulldozerlike machine, dig trenches, and bury the bodies in them. The bucket had large grasping tongs. I lowered the bucket to the bodies, scooped them in, and closed the tongs. Sometimes the tongs cut the bodies in two and parts fell back to the ground as I lifted the bucket.

"I can see it as clearly now as I ever could. It was a horrible war. Then when I got home I was called a baby killer."

"You were ordered to do it."

"And all for nothing. We killed all those people for nothing." Rich's voice was even, matter-of-fact, as if his emotions were burned out. "Sometimes even after all these years it gets to be more than I can stand. When I first got home I came close to blowing people away after arguments, like those other vets you hear about. Especially when I got home to find that my wife, whom I hadn't seen for a year, was four months pregnant."

"That was pretty lousy of her."

"Her lover kept coming over and telling me how good she was in bed. I almost killed him. For months I was a mess. I felt like killing all kinds of people and I seemed to have no control over it. If it hadn't been for Uncle Virgil, I would have done just that. You remember Virgil?"

"Yes."

"I'd spend my weekends with him and we'd talk. He'd been in World War II, so he knew. I owe my life to him." He took a chug of beer. "That's why when Ken did what he did, I understood. I knew I could have done something like that. I cried when I first heard, just sobbed. Ken and I used to be close, you know. He wasn't close to very many people, so that made it more special.

"When he and Teresa lived down here for a while, he'd take me fishing. We were just kids then and we had a good time. That's why it hit me real hard when he killed those folks, but I understood. For some reason he'd had too much." There were tears in his eyes . . . and mine.

For a while we silently observed the darkening sky.

"I was disappointed you didn't make it over to the house this afternoon," he said. "I don't live like Mom and the rest around here. I've got me a real nice house in a nice section of town. I've worked hard for it."

"I could go over now."

"Uh, I don't know. I think my wife is probably drunk by now."

"Does she drink a lot?"

"Yes. I used to, more than I do now."

"How's your marriage?"

"I live for my girls. She gets so jealous, thinks I'm out playing around all the time. Hell, I haven't been with another woman in the thirteen years we've been married."

"Did you play around on your first wife?"

"No, I guess I'm just too straight, although I've had plenty of opportunity."

"You're an attractive man."

"Thanks." Rich grinned, some of the old mischief in his eyes, mischief I had seen when we were kids.

"I don't know if Teresa ever told you this," I said, "but the reason she took me with her, the year I was sixteen and met you and your family, was so that you and I would fall in love and get married."

"That would have been fine with me," he said.

"You were engaged at that time," I laughed

"I was at that. I should be getting home." He looked across the road as if searching, then back at me. "Violet, you're a beautiful woman. I always thought you were. I want you to know that I love you and I always will."

"I love you too."

He gave me a gentle squeeze, then abruptly backed away.

"It's been good seeing you. I think I'd better go now before I get myself into trouble."

He turned and crossed the road, looking back to wave only once . . .

Entering the crowded kitchen I wrapped my legs around the chair legs, sat down next to Teresa, and began stuffing my mouth with grapes.

After I swallowed them I asked, "where's Momma?"

"She was tired and went to bed."

"I had a talk with Rich. He said he understood about Ken because of what he went through himself in Vietnam."

"There's no excuse for what Ken did," Teresa shook her head, "none."

I sighed and changed the subject. "Where are Loni and her boyfriend?"

"Shopping. They said they'd go to a movie and be back late."

"How's Mom doing?" Teresa asked. The air conditioning unit stuffed in the side window covered our voices.

"She's doing things on her own now. Taking trips up to visit Denise and me, drives the whole way by herself too. She even bought new calves."

"That's good," Teresa murmured.

"And Russ?" she asked. "I've worried about him."

I shrugged. "Well, his staying with Mom has been a blessing for her. I know he's not ready to see Ken. From what Momma says, Ken still can't understand why neither of the kids has visited him. Has Loni written to Ken?"

"Not that I know of. Until he stops writing letters running everybody down, she doesn't plan to. How are things for you and Dave? Loni said when she was up there last, the two of you weren't getting along."

"Not good. I've tried everything I can think of."

"Think you'll get a divorce?" The weight and pain of sad years shifted over her face.

"Eventually. He treats me like some disobedient

farm-hand kid. What he wants me to do is to build fences and do the dirty work on the place. He's impatient and domineering. It's a mess!"

"You said in your letter that he's never supported you through the thing with Ken."

"He doesn't understand my need for his support in anything at all. It's taken him all four years to finally tell his family about Ken, four years after the fact."

She nodded. "Ashamed, I guess."

"Which one did he tell?"

"Frank, the brother just a year older than him. The family talked Frank into treatment for his alcoholism. When Dave went down to a family conference about it, he told Frank about Ken and all the drugs Ken took. He said he wanted Frank to know where substance abuse could lead. So I guess Dave's made a step. But it's not enough."

"How's your sex life?"

"It's hard to have passionate thoughts about a husband who doesn't consider my feelings. He's killed the beauty in our relationship. He's killed everything positive."

"Violet, you know my concern is with you not, Dave. You be sure and take care of yourself. He's not poor. You've planned your life like you would always be with him, and no one else. He never wanted you to work, so I'm sure you don't have anything put aside. You take care of yourself, little sis."

"Think you will ever get married again?" I asked.

"No, I lived with another guy for a while. But he turned out to be a drunk. Anyway, Ken burned me out. I'm better off on my own."

"Loni stopped running away?"

"Yeah, since Pete has been living here . . ." A glazed look came over Teresa's face and she quickly changed the subject. "Well, it sure is hot. I want you to sleep back in my bedroom with Mom. I'll sleep out here on the couch. I'm a bit tuckered out. I'd like to turn in."

In the bed beside my momma in a room stuffed with furniture and boxes I worried about Ken's children and his ex-wife through the night.

Chapter Twenty-eight

Another summer spun into fall and then to winter. Years had passed, yet those who had been hurt and were still hurting because of Ken's crime still struggled to make sense of their lives.

Fear had so many faces. By confronting and trying to dissolve one, another whole set sometimes had to be reckoned with.

Parking my car in the hot sun I entered the government building which housed offices for parole board members and searched for Rex Hutter's office. One narrow hallway led to another and soon I arrived.

Anxiety reached up from my stomach and choked at my throat. I ignored it. Now was not the time to let it control me. Now was the time to gather information. Buttoning the jacket of my best suit I entered room 102.

"I'm Violet Andre. Is Mr. Hutter in?" I asked the overly thin woman behind the desk.

"You can wait for him in his office. He stepped down the hall."

In a few minutes a slim thirtiesh man with red hair and business eyes sat down behind his desk. "You said on the phone you had some questions about your brother

Kenneth Andre. I looked up his case and gathered a few facts. What was it you wanted to know?"

I took a deep breath. As I spoke my voice quivered. "What are the chances of my brother getting out of prison early?" It was a question that had hung in my mind since before the trial.

"Let's see here . . . with the minimums, we are looking at consecutive sentences amounting to forty years," he said.

My lips tightened. "What I—what my whole family wonders is if there is any chance he will be out in just a few years? I keep hearing of cases on the news. In fact there's that guy who shot the mayor of some large city. He was out in five. Could that happen with Ken?"

"You're probably referring to that case in California. It was all over the news. The problem with California is the way the laws are written. There are too many ways for clever attorneys to get around them. It's caused the legal system there all kinds of headaches."

"Are you saying that can't happen here?" I asked, desperately hoping his answer would be no.

"It's very unlikely. The wording of our laws is much more precise."

I broke in, "I've heard that the length of sentence the judge imposes doesn't matter. I've heard that the parole board sets its own time limits." In my mind it seemed the judicial system had too many gods, each of them clamoring to be first.

"We do the best we can," he curtly said. "We consider every case and its individual merits. Sometimes justice can be served in a lesser amount of time."

"Does the shortage of jail space make a difference? My family and I are worried. It's a hard thing to say, but there are a number of us who are afraid he'd come after us if he got out."

"You think he might kill you?" he said, his face showing concern.

"We didn't realize until he was in jail just how destorted his perceptions were. Where he is, he's unlikely to get better. I love him. I want what's best for him. In fact I'd be willing to help him any way I could, but. . . ."

"In cases like your brother's, it is different. In any case where there are multiple deaths the case is handled very carefully. Your brother is obviously crazy. It's unlikely that he will ever get out."

I looked searchingly at him. In the late sixties my belief in government had disintegrated. Vietnam and all the scandals since that time had given me reason to be cynical. Since the murders my negative opinions had been further concretized. Still I wanted to believe there was goodness and honesty in everyone. It was a source of ongoing conflict inside my head. "On the average how long does a person in Oregon actually serve for one murder?"

"Sixteen years."

"Do families of the prisoners usually come talk to you about it?"

He scratched his chin. "Once in a while. If they do, they are usually convinced that their loved one is not guilty. He could be the axe murderer and have chopped up people all over the country, but he's told his little old mother in Iowa that he's innocent. So she believes him. She comes to us and asks that he be released to her custody. Mostly that's what we see," he said, watching me. His manner seemed kind, yet practiced. "That isn't the case here, is it?" He added.

"No." I shook my head. "We don't want Ken to get out unless he gets better. What can we do?"

"If the prisoner's family came to us and asked that we not let him out because they are afraid, it would have a big impact on what we do."

My voice breaking, I took a deep breath and went on. "How do we object?"

"You can either testify before the parole board when your brother's case is reviewed, or you can write a letter stating your concerns. Everyone who shares these concerns could sign it."

"Would my brother have access to that information?" Anxiety rose in me.

"By law it is his right."

"You mean he could see the names of everyone who signed the letter or who testified against him?"

"Yes."

"Oh, Lord. It looks like we are stuck, one way or the other. It is a matter if he gets out of who is going to be killed."

"I understand," he looked at me compassionately.

I left Mr. Hutter's office with a new set of worries. While he had convinced me that Ken would not get out in the next five years, my mind still could not rest. What would happen after that? Mr. Hutter was only one man. Even if he had been totally honest with me, parole board members and judicial orientations change over time.

I also knew that none of my family wanted their names listed in Ken's file opposing his release. If he got out it was too likely to produce dangerous consequences. There seemed to be no answer. Yet I knew I would have to go to any future hearing whenever it was and oppose Ken's release. Our lives depended on it.

While I struggled with these problems far from me another of the people, touched by Ken's crime faced struggles of a different kind.

A few dead leaves clutched at the maple tree in the center of a college campus.

Wind from the Sound blew through the quilted fabric of Cal's jacket. Pulling it more closely about him, he pulled up the zipper and walked beneath the tree branches.

He tugged open the door to the dining hall, served

himself some overcooked spaghetti and salad, and headed for a table. The room, normally noisy and crowded, was now mostly vacant.

"Say, Cal, where you going for Christmas?" Ted, a member of his debate class, patted him on the shoulder and sat on the edge of the table.

"Uh, . . . I'm not sure yet." A dumb stare accompanied Cal's words. Tears slid from his eyes, tears that Fred could not help but see. Didn't Ted remember? How could he ask such a question?

Ted rushed on, "My folks and I are headed to see my grandparents in Colorado this afternoon. It should be great."

"Well, got to go now. Mom and Dad are picking me up in a couple of hours. Got to get my skiing equipment together. Here, you can have my Danish. See you after the holidays."

Leaving his food on the table, Cal crept from the room. Outside he headed away from the campus. What was wrong with people? What was wrong with Ted?

He wished there was someone to talk to. Tears kept coming to his eyes, yet everyone he passed pretended not to notice.

Trudging along the sidewalk toward the water, he felt the anger wrenching through him. Near the Sound he found the railroad trestle and walked upon it, balancing himself on the smooth iron. Tears dribbled from his eyes; he began to talk aloud.

"What's the matter with these people? This is a church college. These people are supposed to care more than anybody else. They are supposed to be supportive. Why has all this happened to me, God? I can't stand this alone. I need someone to talk to. I need someone to love me.

"Tell me what I'm supposed to do?" He looked up into the heavens. "Are the people here shallow too, like the rest of the people in the world? Do they just pretend that love is important?"

An impersonal wind blasted him, and he nearly lost his balance. In the distant sky clouds readied for a downpour, the kind the northwest was famous for.

"It's just not fair. I hate this. This can't be right." Feelings and words jumbled together until only his confusion remained.

Along the tracks he walked and walked, struggling to make sense of the things that had happened to him, beginning with the killings.

It was almost Christmas, and there was no place he wanted to go, except home to be with his folks. And they were dead. There would be no tree covered with wooden ornaments that Dad had made, no turkey overflowing with dressing or Mom's special biscuits.

Christmas triggered more pain.

"Why, God, why?"

The inarticulate sky provided no answers. Finally he wearily went back to his room.

Picking up his guitar he searched for a tune and the words to express the things he felt. He needed a release.

He began strumming a melody. But the ache remained full in his heart.

Suddenly, his mother's face came to him. He thought of their conversation the day before she died, that day he had stayed home from school. They had discussed his future . . .

Waffles and hot blackberry syrup steamed up from the plate, caressing Calvin's nose. His mother poured him a glass of milk and joined him at the dining room table. Her face, real and warm, held a serious look.

"You don't seem to be too sick. What is it? Are you okay?"

"I don't know, Mom, I just needed to stay

home. I wanted to be close to you today. I've
been thinking of what to do after I graduate
high school. I can't decide."

"Have you considered Bible college?" She
had been hesitant to suggest it, not wanting to
overly influence his decisions.

"Bible college? Gee, I don't know," he
said between bits of waffles.

"I've always felt close to you, Calvin. Ever
since you were little, you've considered the
needs of others before your own. You make me
think of Jesus, and the kindness he must have
showed to the people around him."

"Ah, Mom." Calvin blushed and fidgeted a
little, pleased with his mother's praise.

"You're special, son. God has blessed me
with you."

Calvin looked at her lovingly, knowing
how deeply she meant the things she said. He
had always felt close to her, more so than the
other kids did.

"A year would give you a good foundation.
Since you don't know what you want to do, you
could spend the time discovering your op-
tions."

"A year might not be too bad—"

"There's one in the Seattle area that has a
bachelor's program and regular academic
classes, as well as religious studies."

"That might work. Since I've been working at the Christian radio station I've met some
neat people. All of them think I have a good
speaking voice," he said.

"You do, but it's more than your voice. It's
a quality you hold inside.

Outside, the snow had begun to fall. Inside

his room he felt the warmth once more of his mother's love.

Growing up he had thought of his parents as ordinary people, living out the lives they had chosen. Now they seemed beyond special. He missed them terribly but he rejoiced that their love had been his.

He picked up the folk guitar; this time the words to the first verse came clear.

There is joy amidst sadness
Even though it seems that everything has gone wrong
And there is weeping amidst gladness
And in sorrow, there is still a song.

The ocean gusts of April littered the beach with saltwater and seaweed. Momma and I buttoned our coats and climbed over the mounded sand. A dead gull with missing feathers and sunken eyes lay scrunched against an upturned stump near the edge of the dry sand. Driftwood lay in piles along the grass-covered ridge.

"Yesterday all he did was yell at me, so I hung up on him," Momma said sadly. "A few days before that I got a letter from Aunt Rose saying that Ken wanted me to know he had written me off."

"There wasn't anything else you could do," I murmured.

"I was upset, not as much for me as for him. For whatever reason, he is the way he is. If he gets an idea in his head about what someone else is thinking or doing to him, he has no way of figuring out what's real and what isn't. He just sits there in that cell day after day thinking about it. So he thinks we've all turned against him."

"He's isolated himself," I said. "He's removed most of us from his visitors list, even Aunt Rose."

"I know, but we don't know how it is to be like he is. All I know to do is pray. One of the ladies at the church

said as long as there is life there is hope. Maybe someday
the Lord will touch his life. That's what I pray for."

"Guess that's all we can do," I observed.

Momma sighed, every time he calls he's different. I
never know what to expect. "When he called last week,
he asked me not to write. He was so nice the time before,
and the one before that he yelled. He said that when he
gets letters from me and they don't contain completed
visitor's applications from Russ and Loni, it gets him really upset. It makes him shake inside, his heart starts
throbbing, and a pain runs down his left arm. Then he
can't sleep all night. So he asked me not to write until I
send a completed application from one of his kids. Who
knows when the kids will go see him."

I shook my head. "It never ends."

"Yeah, I know, but I don't think we should ever give
up on him," Momma said. "I mean, if you love someone
you never give up on them, no matter what they've done.
God doesn't.

"I still wonder about those little kids, you know, the
Bennett children. It's been nearly five years and I can
still see their little faces right after Ken did it. They just
stood there on the porch, the poor little boys. Sometimes
I still cry about it," Momma said.

"I checked around to try and find out," I said.
"Their aunt and uncle adopted them. I heard the couple
already had two boys. Nobody seems to know what happened to the family. One rumor says they moved to Af-
rica as missionaries. Another says the kids had all kinds
of problems."

"If only there was some way I could help them,"
Momma said softly. "It haunts me."

Chapter Twenty-nine

From her grandmother's cedar chest Christy removed the notebook of Xeroxed letters. They had been sent from her mother to Aunt Hazel while Hazel was in Thailand. Taking her treasure to the rocker in the corner of the bedroom, Christy balanced it on her lap. More than anything she wanted to know her mother as a person, especially now that Christy was married and planning to have a family.

Propping her feet on a stool she opened the plastic binder, remembering when Aunt Hazel had given her the letters. She had been unable to read them then. They had made her cry.

Now she was ready.

In each letter there was news about Christy and her three brothers. Her mother described her as "an active child who is into everything" and "a little girl who likes to be cuddled a lot." Cuddling was what she needed now. She ached for it at times.

Eager to read the other things her mother said, she continued reading. She read letter after letter, stopping to cry now and again, until she had finished them all.

Patting her stomach she thought of the baby that would grow there some day. What kinds of things would

she say about her child? What would she and her child
talk about? What was it like to give birth? Had her
mother been scared the first time?

Christy rubbed her forehead. If only she could talk
to her mother. If only she could see her, even for a few
hours.

Opening the chest once again, she inhaled the cedar
fragrance that wafted up to her. She pulled out the photo
album and studied picture of her parents and herself.
Then she saw one of Ken. An image of the past of them
all together flashed through her mind.

Days of early autumn spun golden leaves
around the houses where Christy, her brothers,
Loni, and Russ lived. Still, the days grew
warmer, and river levels remained low.

Running up to the neighbors' door Loni
banged on the screen.

"Christy . . . are you home?" Panting
and excited, she waited, catching her breath.

Wearing cutoffs and a tee shirt Christy
hurried to the door. Seeing her friend she
grinned.

"Daddy's going to take us up the river. He
wants you to come along. Hurry and ask your
mom before he changes his mind," Loni said,
fidgeting.

"Mom, where are you?" Christy found her
mother in the kitchen, making potato salad for
the potluck at church the next day. "Can I go
swimming with Russ and Loni up the river?"

"Ken going to take you?"

"Yes."

"Yeah, okay. Take a change of clothes and
the big green towel in the end closet. Have a
good time, honey."

Wind blew into the back window, caressing Christy's face and the face of her friend. On the front seat beside his father, Russ smiled to himself. After several miles the car left the pavement and moved along a logging road further into the mountains.

"You kids like the spot we went last time?" Ken asked, smiling. "I'm feeling so good I want you to have as good a time with me as I'm having with you."

"Yeah," said three young voices. Christy and Russ were close to the same age, ten and eleven respectively, Loni seven.

"I really love kids," Ken murmured half under his breath. "Kids never stab a person in the back the way adults do. Kids are rarely hypocrites."

Pulling off the road into the shade Ken parked the car and climbed out. A summer smell hung in the air.

Racing toward the water Russ stumbled and fell, scrapping his nose on a rock. Touching it with calloused fingers he discovered a little blood. Still, it did not hurt much. Besides, he had learned not to cry.

A rope hung in an alder next to a large pool. Beyond the pool the river eased into a set of shallow rapids. The buzzing of insects saturated the air.

"Wait until I get there to get in," Ken hollered. He opened the trunk, took out the wet suit and cooler, and followed the kids to the water.

"Christy, I think you're big enough for this now. Would you like to try it on?" Ken said, handing her the suit.

"Could I?" Grinning up at the big man, she looked beyond his beard and curly hair, trying to catch a glimpse of his eyes before he looked away. They were nice, almost the color of fudge.

"Here, put it on like this," he said and showed her what to do.

Delighted, she paddled out into the water. Beside her Loni splashed in an inner tube, twirling 'round and 'round, her hair dangling in the water.

Climbing the bank Ken reached the rope, grasped it, and handed it to Russ. With a lurch Russ swung way out until he reached the deepest part. A whoop and a yell proceeded from him as he dropped into the water. It whished up his body. Reaching the bottom he opened his eyes.

For once he could tell his dad was happy.

Pushing himself off the bottom he headed for the girls. A set of toes dangled below the inner tube. Swimming toward them he pulled and grabbed.

Squealing, Loni grabbed a patch of her brother's hair and tugged his head out of the water. "Russ's being a brat. Help me, Christy. Let's get him."

The two girls chased after him until they dowsed him good. After his getting away, his eyes started twinkling and his mind ground out the details of the next attack. They would not get away with it. He would fix them.

"There's pop in the cooler," Ken called, "and an ice cream bar for each of you. Be sure and eat them before they melt."

Sand toasted Christy's toes as she climbed out and headed for the cooler. Ken could be so nice at times. She was glad she had come.

Everything Christy saw became obscured by tears. She bent over the album, and putting her head on her arms she cried. When the pent-up tears were all released, she rinsed her face in cold water and waited. In an hour Candy and Harold would be there. They were old friends who would interview her about her feelings since the murders for a magazine.

The time passed slowly.

Finally they arrived. Opening the door, Christy led both of them into the dining room.

"You've been crying," Candy whispered as she hugged her friend.

Christy nodded. "I've been reading some letters Mom wrote and looking at family pictures."

"I was amazed to find you at church. It's been such a long time," Candy said. "My family had moved away and I never talked to you after what happened to your parents. Are you okay?"

"Sometimes."

"Does it bother you to talk about it?" Harold asked.

"Not really. It's a part of me, whether I talk about it or not."

"On the phone the other night you said it was a good time to talk because your husband was watching a cop show. and you couldn't stand to watch it," Candy said.

"I hate violent shows," Christy said. "I don't know why people enjoy watching other people get hurt. I try to get him to watch other things, but if he still wants to watch them, I leave the room." Her blue eyes glistened, smudges of mascara still around the edges.

"I hate violence too. Just thinking about it makes me sick," Candy said, "especially after what happened to your mom and dad. How do you stand living out here? It would scare me to death."

"I never planned to live in the country again. I'm

afraid of dark, uncurtained windows like these. He shot them through the window . . ."

Harold broke in sympathetically "It must have been horrible."

"After I moved from Jered and Patty's I lived by myself for six months, but that didn't work. I was scared all the time. I got a roommate, and then Denny and I got married."

"It must be pretty special to be married to the youth minister," Candy said. "Denny is so good looking and has such confidence."

Christy sighed heavily. "I needed someone so badly when I met Denny. When we got married I hoped to find what Mom and Dad had. They were always hugging each other and being playful. They cuddled me a lot too. They used to kid me about sitting on their laps when I was forty. But Denny isn't like them." She paused.

"What is he like?"

"His family didn't touch each other much when he was growing up. Sometimes I just want him to hold me, but he doesn't know how. I'm proud to be his wife. I want other people to know how much we love each other.

"I love when we sit near each other in church. It makes me feel we're a family. Sex isn't enough. I need him to hold me."

Harold looking uncomfortable and changed the subject. "The article you sent us provided the details of what happened that night. How do you feel now about the man who did it?" he asked.

"There are so many things involved in that question—"

"How do you make it through, day to day?" Candy asked.

Christy took a deep breath. "God holds me up. There's a verse in the Bible that helps. It's Psalms

116:15, 'Precious in the sight of the Lord is the death of His Godly ones.' "

In another place another victim awoke. Still groggy, Greg saw a person bending over him, the familiar face of someone he loved. Mom . . . no, it was a male face. Dad . . . no, the features seemed too round. Dad's face had been angular, like his.

"You awake?" Cal asked. He pulled the chair closer and took his brother's hand.

"Um . . ." Unable to move his mouth, Greg remembered. Of course, there had been surgery, his third one. He hoped it would finally stop the headaches and tension in his jaw.

"Don't talk. They wired you shut. The doctor was in a few minutes ago. He said it went well. You hungry?"

The thought of food surged through Greg's brain and into his stomach, churning the contents. Feeling as though he were going to vomit, he concentrated hard to keep it from happening.

"They said you might not want to eat, with the anesthesia and all."

"How long I been out?" Greg spoke through closed teeth, his words difficult to distinguish.

"They brought you back to your room a couple of hours ago. You've been drifting in and out."

"Thank you . . . for being here." The effort to talk exhausted him. "It's hard without Mom and Dad."

"I'm glad I could come. Do you want to watch television?"

"No . . . I'm tired." He closed his eyes and drifted in a maze of lights. They pulsed around him, drawing him up into a cosmic dream. Visions of his parents came close, then faded only to come again. Childhood memories mixed with grief played onward in his mind. Shuddering, he awoke.

"I'm here. It's alright," Cal reassured him.

Nausea surged up from his stomach. This time he could not contain it.

"Here," Cal said, "I've got the tub. I'll hold it for you." He wiped his brother's mouth and chest when he was through.

Folding back into the pillow Greg let the stupor capture him again. This time he slept for several more hours.

"You're still here," Greg said when he awakened and saw his brother.

"You can't get rid of me. I've been watching television and writing in my journal."

"Mom wrote things too."

"Yeah, she did," Cal nodded. "Jered and Patty called. They should be here to pick you up tomorrow morning about eleven. How long do you think you are going to stay with them?"

"I don't know. I hope Jered and I get along."

"Me too."

In central Oregon Jered tried to make his own life meaningful, tried to make it better for his wife and daughter. As a chemical engineer for the paper company he worked hard. Most times it was a good and satisfying job, but lately he felt burned out.

Morning had nearly escaped when Jered looked up from the stack of work on his desk, wondering if it was time for a break.

"Say, Jered, you want to have lunch?" Hans, his curly blond co-worker, stuck his head in the doorway and grinned his big German grin. "I think the company can spare us a little time."

"Give me a few more minutes. Let's go to that place off of Main Street. You know, where we went last month."

The Lunch Bucket was unusually quiet for a Friday when Jered and Hans found a seat in the corner next to the window. Ferns and spider plants almost covered the window space. Booths of varathaned wood added a rustic quality to the room. The aroma of freshly brewed coffee tantalized the nostrils.

After ordering, Jered sipped a cup of coffee and sat back on the seat.

"So it's going good, yes?" Hans said.

He nodded. "Yeah, the project Bob has had me working on for three months is almost done. It's been a lot of hard work."

"You know, Jered, you never did tell me where you grew up. Every time we have lunch I think about asking you and we get distracted talking about one of your projects."

Jered felt his throat tighten.

"On the coast."

"Where at?"

"Dayton."

"I worked in the Dayton plant for five years with Maurice McCall. He was killed just before I left. . . . You wouldn't be related to him, would you?"

Shock jolted through Jered's stomach, turning everything to acid. "He was my father."

"Oh, Lord, I'm sorry. It just never occurred to me—"

"I guess one never gets over it."

Jered nodded, unable to speak.

Hans, his face red, grasped for the right words. "How's your family? It must be rough on your family, especially now around the holiday."

"Us kids have tried to get by, you know, start our own traditions at Christmas and holidays."

"How about the rest of the family, aunts, uncles, and such?"

"My Uncle Joel is having a family reunion at his house next month. The whole family hopes to be there."

* * *

Venison roast provided by the hunters in the family, one
huge turkey and a good-sized ham, potato salad, and all
kinds of sweet things were heaped on the table. Three
generations of Joel's family lined up to eat, filling their
plates, eating, and then filling up again until only small
portions of food remained.

Outside, the February sky was partly covered with
clouds; inside, many of the clouds felt were hidden behind wan smiles. Joel's two older brothers and his sister
Hazel joined him next to the sliding glass door by the
deck.

One gap was apparent. Kathy and Maurice were
missing. Kathy, the baby of the family, had been the first
to die.

"Say, Joel, remember when we used to take Maurice out into the woods and try to get him lost?" John,
the oldest brother, asked.

"Those were crazy times," said Peter, the second
brother. "None of us had a lick of sense. Dad would cata-
pult out of his grave if he knew half of the stunts we
pulled."

"I'll never forget the time Maurice talked me into
smelt fishing near Fisher's Cove," Joel said. "He was just
a kid then, crazier than most. It was before he and Kathy
got married. He showed up in that old Plymouth he was
so proud of, shiny from all that wax. I didn't have any
hip boots, a net, or anything. But he said not to worry.
He had two nets, and the ocean wasn't too cold. Gees, I
about froze my future family right off my body. We got
way too many smelt. Every dip into the surf brought a
full net. It was cold . . . and windy. But you know Maurice, when he was a kid nothing fazed him.

"When we got back to the house, he put a dead fish
under Kathy's bed. It took a day to start stinking; but
then the smell was Godawful! Not to be outdone, Kathy
began looking for ways to get even."

"They were both nutty in those days," John laughed.

"Peter and I had already left home by then. You had too, hadn't you Hazel?"

"I think so," Hazel said.

"Kathy and Maurice had a special kind of relationship that few people are able to find," Peter observed.

"Kathy had a lot of spunk. She always stood up for what she thought was right. I wonder what she would think now, about what we've done with our lives since she's been gone?" John said.

"She and Maurice would probably understand everything a lot better than we do," Joel noted.

Hot chocolate and popcorn, cider and apple pie, the afternoon became congested with food and memories. Toddlers charged about the floor, and their young parents took them into the yard to play. Finally many in the family said goodbye and traveled back to their own homes.

Joel and Ima, his bride of one month, retreated to the bedroom that edged the deck. Frogs and river-rush drowned the silence. The half moon shone through the leaves on the massive trees edging the Umpqua River.

After the death of his first wife, Bitsy, Joel felt anguished. Five of the people he loved most were dead, his father, mother, Kathy, Maurice, and Bitsy. Bitsy had been killed when a truck veered into their lane on the way back from Dayton. The accident left Joel bruised and with a broken leg.

Though he loved Ima, he still ached inside. He was trying to find the courage to love again, but it was so hard. And all the while fear that someone else would be taken filled his mind.

Outside on the deck his children and grandchildren nestled together in sleeping bags. With them were Kathy and Maurice's children, Jered, his wife and baby, Christy and her husband, and Calvin. Greg, sick again with TMJ, could not make it.

Joel thought of each one now here. He would try

harder. Ima was a dear woman, losing her husband close to the time he had lost his wife. They could comfort each other. . . . And the others there needed him too.

"Uncle Joel, Uncle Joel . . ." Christy's voice came to him through the sliding door. "Tell us a scary story." There was giggling and the sound of squeaky children.

"Yeah, Uncle Joel . . . you don't have anything better to do," Calvin said. The kids began to clap, just as in the old days, when Kathy, Maurice, and the kids came to visit. Tiny voices said, "Yeah, Grandpa. Tell us a story."

Losses cascaded through him again. All the ones who were gone should be there. They were not.

"Come on outside and tell us a story, Uncle Joel," Christy said, "or we'll put oatmeal in your shoes like we did that time."

"Yeah, Uncle Joel," Jered said as he hugged his daughter closer.

Burying his sadness, Joel dressed in his robe. He and Ima stepped slippered feet onto the patio. Down the river and back in the hills coyotes howled. Shadows slid over the ground.

With a voice low and dramatic, Joel began the Hamburger story, a story of slimy caves and ravenous hamburgers.

For the children—he thought—*for my children and Kathy's.*

Chapter Thirty

Leaflets of·sunlight sprinkled through the alders and onto strands of fern a hundred yards up from the Clackamas River. Vining maple spread their limbs over a humid patch of earth surrounded by dense vegetation. Another year had passed. Beyond the edge of the quilted blanket a partly finished bottle of Almaden was propped against the root of one of the trees. The cork was halfway in.

Aaron lay beside me, his eyes a dreamy green, matching the summer grass. I rested my hand lightly on his hip. My head nestled his side.

"We can't catch many fish here," I whispered.

"I've caught what I want," he said. Slightly calloused, his hands pulled me closer. "You're all I could ever want in a woman. I'd like to spend the rest of my life loving you. I've never met anyone so gentle, so good, except for my mother. These days I've spent with you— there haven't been enough of them. I'd like to change that."

I turned onto my back and stared up at the blue above the trees.

"Let's not even think of anything beyond today," I

said. "Everything in life is so uncertain, so easily snatched away."

"Little one, you can't just live for the moment."

He gathered me to him. I could hear his strong heartbeat, and the love call of a nearby bird, calling for a mate.

Five days later we traveled away from the city again, this time to the entrance to a closed campground. The edges were growing over with weeds and tall grass. A chipmunk scurried about the site, and hidden birds sang from alder tops.

Aaron closed the trunk to the car and put on his fisherman's vest over his tank top. His muscles, deeply brown from the sun, shone with perspiration. Faded jeans covered his swimming trunks. A bare toe poked through the top of one tennis shoe.

"You got the poles?" he said as he grabbed the fishing reel and the cooler.

"Yep, you trained me good," I said, and patted his backside. "Hope we catch something for once."

"What do you mean?" he shot back at me as the two of us climbed down the bank along the edge of the abandoned camp site.

"Well, the last few times we've both gotten skunked." I grinned and my eyes twinkled.

We cut around the boulders beside the bridge and scooted down the loose gravel, sliding to a stop at the base of the metal structure. Beneath it was a large concrete platform that protruded into the water. Remnants of other fishing trips and other anglers were caught on the branches of trees and brush just a few feet away.

Aaron sat down on the concrete and began rigging the poles. I dangled my feet over the edge. The water spun and twisted ten feet below.

"If you're hot, there's a Diet Coke in the cooler. I also brought you some string cheese," he said.

"Would you like one?" I asked, popping the tab on the cold can.

"I'm not afraid of your germs, I'll share yours."

When the poles were rigged, he cast my line into a quiet pool close to the other bank. He stood next to the edge and cast and recast his lure into the rapids.

"I'm glad you could get away again. It was kind of short notice. I finished working on that grant a day early, so I decided I deserved this."

"Dave's been gone a lot lately doing stuff with the fire department. He's also volunteering for the ambulance service. Today he said he had to go in and help this other paramedic restock the ambulance."

"That wouldn't be the lady you told me about?" he said.

"The same."

"You still think they're having an affair?"

"Yep. I saw the look in her eyes when we met. Instant guilt.

"You've been hoping he'd find someone."

I nodded. "Maybe some other woman can please him," I said softly.

I handed the can of pop to Aaron and rested my head on his back.

"Damn," he said suddenly and jerked the pole.

"What?"

"You got me to thinking of other things and I got my lure stuck. Just can't keep my mind on it with you around." He smiled and jerked the line free.

"Is that a complaint?"

"No. As a matter of fact it's nice to let my mind wander with you." The two of us sat on the edge of the platform, his arm around me. "We've had a lot of nice times on this river the last few years. We've done some pretty crazy things. Left poor Henry in the boat getting drunk that one time. Remember . . . he had finished off all the beer and the fifth of whiskey by the time we got back."

He swigged some coke and looked up at the muggy sky.

"I've always loved being with you," I said.

"Think there will be a storm?" he asked.

"The air's got the feel of it. I love storms. They give me energy."

"Maybe we can put a little of that energy to work," he said and kissed me. "It's never changed. I like being with you more than anyone else I've ever know."

"Did you ever go fishing with your wife?"

"A little at first. She'd rather go shopping or spend time talking to her sisters than being with me."

"Are you ever afraid that she'll discover you're having an affair?"

"Yeah. Sometimes."

He tried a different spinner on the end of the line and cast it upstream. The bronze-colored blade disappeared into the surging white water.

"Ever wondered what your family would think if they knew about me?" he asked.

"Sometimes," I echoed him. "A lot of them would condemn me, think I was going to hell for sure. I don't believe in that kind of a God anymore. I think He brought me to you. None of my family was there for me when I needed them, except Aunt Rose, and now you have been. That means a lot to me."

I leaned into him and watched the afternoon go by. We stayed until the sun went down.

My nervous energy grew as I drove toward the city a week later. For an hour I struggled with words, the same words I had considered since our last trip to the river.

On the southwest side of town about a mile down the hill from the community college where Aaron taught a pizza parlor sat next to Highway 99, the major high-

way through the city before the construction of the freeway.

His car was already in the parking lot, nosed up to
the side of the building. When I entered the room, Aaron
joined me at the counter.

"A carafe of wine?" he asked.

"Please."

After ordering the pizza we returned to his table in
the back corner. There were no other customers. It was
still a little before the lunch rush. This time we sat across
the table from each other. He poured the wine.

"Aaron . . . I must know what you've been thinking. I—" My throat felt choked.

He looked back at me, puzzled. "What's wrong, Violet?"

"You've taught me so much about love and understanding," I said softly. "I've hoped we could spend the
rest of our lives together." I took a deep breath and
rushed on. "Have you ever thought of leaving your
wife?"

He nodded. "Many times since I met you. She
hasn't been loving to me for years," he said. "I always
wished somehow I could wake up with you in the morning and go to sleep at night with the scent of your skin,"
he smiled.

"We've known each other a long time now," I said.
"I remember when I met you I was afraid of caring too
much."

He nodded, "I remember."

"That was part of the reason I stayed away, along
with not wanting to cheat," I said.

"Do you still feel guilty," he asked softly.

I nodded. "There's always guilt when you break
rules you've grown up with, believe in; but mostly when I
think of you there's gratitude." I reached out and covered his large hand with my small one. "You've helped

me to put myself back together again. You've been there for me when no one else was."

His face was filled with sorrow.

"I can't leave my wife, little one. For years I've known I should. There's nothing left but the kids, and they're mostly grown now; but in my religion, there's no divorce. Even though I love you, I just can't leave."

"It's alright, Aaron. My decision is mine alone. My marriage was disintegrating long before we were together and now I need to take the next step," I paused, "as soon as the time is right."

My throat constricted and I said hoarsely, "The way things are, I can't continue to make love with you, Aaron. I would just keep hoping for a future that cannot be. I can't do that to myself anymore."

He nodded.

"I need to find what is right for me and make peace with myself." My heart clenched and then eased. "After that maybe I can find someone who is as gentle and giving as you are and willing to spend his life with me." I tried to smile.

He gripped the wine goblet and stared directly into my soul.

"I love you," I said.

"Friends always," he said and raised his glass in a toast. A single tear ran down his cheek.

Chapter Thirty-one

Cobweb-coated memories of times past accompanied me to my mother's house. Behind the house next to the free-standing stanchions my brother's ghost milked the cow and squirted me with a stream of warm milk. Up on the hill in the old barn that had long since fallen, he and I climbed to the loft and listened to the pigeons cooing along the edge of the eaves. Down on the dike by the slough, he cast the hook into the water and after a couple of hours tugged in a wide-mouthed bass almost as big as me.

Home, the place where love had dwelt—home. Something I had found no other place, ever. A wedding brought me back this time, the wedding of my brother's son to the daughter of Ken's former boss, a man Ken thought was his enemy.

A white gull flew over the chapel and the wooden area near the bay. A rainbow shone as if a heavenly presence had blessed the day. A choir sang the wedding march. The marble staircase was lined with golden roses.

People of the white elephant, the name we had given this huge church building so long ago, refugees of that murder-filled time came now in love to celebrate a time of joy, a time for hope to be reborn. A time for Kenny's son to be married.

Powder-pink carnations filled tall wicker baskets inside the chapel doors. Bridesmaids in floating rose chiffon hid around the corner and giggles bubbled down the hallway. Faces shone and friends squeezed into the vestibule awaiting the service.

Two women stood together and alone, without their mates, father and son. I watched them.

"Momma, did you see Russ wandering around in his white tuxedo?" I asked.

"Yes," she said. "He looks so handsome, even if he is my grandson, so much like his father . . ." Mists of cherished remembrances gathered in the eyes of a grandmother.

"You're looking pretty today, Teresa," I said. "New dress?"

"Yeah," Teresa replied. She grinned a genuine southern-style grin. It transformed her face and made her pretty and young again, as when we had first met. "I thought my momma wouldn't mind. I bought it with money from the sale of her house. That's what paid for the car too. Wouldn't have been able to make it up here otherwise."

"I'm sure she would be happy at how you've spent it," I said.

Teresa smiled again.

"Violet, there you are," Dave said. "I'm ready to go in. You can visit with all these people later. My word, I never saw anyone who could talk so much. Yackity, yackity, yack." I turned away.

"There's Terrence and Nola. I haven't seen them for years. And Robin and Edward. Good grief, I didn't know all these people knew Russ," I said.

"Come on," Dave insisted. "Let's get going. You can talk to them at the reception. It's about time for the wedding to start."

Dave and I followed the groomsman to a pew of stained fir.

"Violet, hi," Sandy, an old friend, whispered. She turned around from the row in front of us.

"I didn't know I'd see you today," I said.

"I used to sing in the choir with Russ before he, his mother, and sister moved to California. I always liked him. He came to church with Kathy and Maurice Mc-Call, you know."

I tried to concentrate on what Sandy was saying. "He always seemed full of mischief," Sandy went on. "I like that in a person. That way you know they're alive . . ."

My mind spun backwards.

Russ, that little rat. He was always full of it. There was that time at the beach. I wanted to strangle him then . . .

Spare car parts and old grease rags were stacked in the back of my parents' station-wagon along with the extra tire and a disas-sembled jack. On the front seat Aunt Rose rode beside my mother as she headed the car down the two-lane highway toward the beach.

Covering the blond upholstery a red and black blanket was spread beneath my jeans and Russ's bouncing feet. My seven-year-old nephew stood on the floor, then on the seat. He jumped into the back and forward again, smil-ing at me, daring me to do something about it.

"Russ, sit still. We're almost there," I said, but the boy paid little heed.

Momma parked the car in the lot next to the cove and the four of us walked across the sand toward the water, where seals came to play. Russ charged over the sand and into the water up to his thighs, splashing, jumping, and falling.

Aunt Rose and Momma meandered toward the boat launch at the far end of the cove. I kneeled on the wet sand and began scooping, patting, and shaping it, watching Russ from the side of my eye, making sure he did not go in too deep.

The body of a well-built woman began to emerge from the wet granules. Her form was a credit to the Giver of talents. When she was almost finished I stepped away to view the proportions.

Stampeding out to the water came Russ. He landed rear first in the middle of the sand woman and gleamed up at me.

I grabbed the boy, held him down, and stuffed wet sand under his tee shirt until it would hold no more. Startled he looked up at me, the smile leaving his face.

He never bothered me after that. Full of mischief he always was, but friendly and loving too.

". . . so when we got the announcement at the church that he was getting married, well, I knew I had to come," Sandy had been talking all the time my memories cut in and out. "He's such a good boy. Leads the youth group at his church, doesn't he?"

"Last I knew," I said.

Alone just inside the main door to the chapel Teresa waited for the rest of the guests to be seated. The music had nearly started when through the doorway came a young blond woman. I watched as a moment's recognition was born on the faces of the two, Teresa and Christy . . . and they held each other.

Christy McCall, that once-bereft little girl, had

grown into a beautiful woman in the two years since Daddy died. The fact that she did not hate us for what Ken did to her mother and father still baffled me. "God must have given her that kind of love," I murmured to Dave, surprised at my own words.

Music reverberated through the church. The groom and his attendants took their places on the stage. Girls adorned with pastel ribbons and rose chiffon waited on the edge of the room, then moved slowly down the aisle toward the place of union.

Looking toward the front of the church again, I studied those who stood with Russ. My eyes widened. Next to him a young blond-haired man, lean and sensitive, patted Russ's arm and smiled.

Amazed, I leaned forward and touched Sandy's shoulder. "Is that Calvin McCall standing next to Russ?"

"Yes," she whispered. "You know what good friends they were as children. Russ wondered how Cal felt about him after all these years and with everything that happened. But Cal was delighted when Russ asked him to be his best man."

Inside me canyons of grief yielded up that which for so long was hidden. Pain mingled with awe in my heart and soul.

The son of those murdered stood with the son of the murderer.

Epilogue

Recently I had the opportunity to talk individually with the McCall children. Each of them assured me that they held nothing against me or my family. They said their lives were going well now. A lot of the pain was behind them.

Christy McCall was first trained as a nurse. Currently she works as an orthodontic assistant. She loves her job and excels in that field. She is married and living in Willamette Valley in Oregon. She is planning to have her own family. Her first child is due before the printing of this book.

Cal McCall became a minister and is pastoring a church in Washington. In his current position he makes use of the growth and compassion brought on by tragedy. He is a writer, a composer, a counselor, and a friend to those in need. Three years ago he was married.

Jered and Patty McCall live in the Willamette Valley not far from Christy. They are the parents of three daughters. Jered still works as a chemical engineer for the paper company.

Greg McCall works as an engineer repairing computer systems. He and his wife of three years live in California. He hopes to have a family soon. For many years he has striven as a student and businessman and has become quite successful. He hopes in time to move closer to his siblings.

Uncle Joel is about to retire as a psychologist. By the printing of this book he will be pastoring a church in central Oregon. He's a sensitive man with a realistic approach to spirituality.

Aunt Hazel works as a public health nurse in Dayton, where she still lives with her husband. Her compassion and understanding are ongoing.

The McCall family has handled tragedy with faith and love.

The present condition of the Bennett children is unknown.

Russ Andre lives in California and is in the process of reevaluating his career. He does not see or write to his father, but occasionally they talk on the phone. Although at times he is still upset with his father, he has come to understand that Ken is mentally ill.

Loni Andre was married in the summer of 1990. She, her six-year-old daughter, and her husband live in California with her mother, Teresa. At this point in her life she is quite happy. Loni wants to be an actress. She occasionally writes to her father, but she has not seen him since the killings.

Teresa Andre developed rheumatoid arthritis and lives in great physical discomfort. She has achieved a sense of spirituality and this comforts her. She finally was able to understand Ken's disturbed mental state and has forgiven him.

Betty Andre continues to live on the farm. She raises a few calves each year and loves to work in her garden. She still writes to Ken and does whatever she can to help him.

Denise and Ted have adjusted to the problems caused by the killings. They find value in each other's company and enjoy their children and grandchildren.

Ken Andre remains the same, incarcerated in the state penitentiary, living in a world created by the schizophrenic mind.

The rest of my family have adjusted as best they could to the killings, some of them facing it, some of them hiding from the pain.

In the summer of 1986, Dave and I separated, then divorced. Aaron is still a friend. I married a lovely, sensitive man in December of 1990.

From all that has happened I have gained an intimate knowledge of pain. I have also learned that catastrophic experiences can be a catalyst for growth. The missing ingredient is love. My goal is to promote this kind of love whenever and wherever I can.

This book is a testament to that quest.